★ ★

PRAIRIE FORGE

The Extraordinary Story of the Nebraska
Scrap Metal Drive of World War II

★ ★

JAMES J. KIMBLE

UNIVERSITY OF NEBRASKA PRESS
LINCOLN AND LONDON

Publication of this volume was assisted by a
grant from the Friends of the University of
Nebraska Press.

Library of Congress
Cataloging-in-Publication Data
Kimble, James J., 1966–
Prairie forge: the extraordinary story
of the Nebraska scrap metal drive of
World War II / James J. Kimble.
pages   cm
Includes bibliographical references and index.
ISBN 978-0-8032-4878-6 (pbk.: alk. paper)—
ISBN 978-0-8032-5416-9 (epub)—
ISBN 978-0-8032-5417-6 (mobi) —
ISBN 978-0-8032-5415-2 (pdf).
1. Salvage (Waste, etc.)—United States—
History—20th century. 2. World War,
1939–1945—Nebraska. 3. World War,
1939–1945—Economic aspects—United
States. 4. Scrap metals—Recycling—
Nebraska—History—20th century. 5. Salvage
(Waste, etc.)—Nebraska—History—20th
century. 6. Nebraska—History—20th century.
I. Title. II. Title: Extraordinary story of the
Nebraska scrap metal drive of World War II.
HD9975.U52 K57 2014
940.53'1—dc23
2013044119

Set in Ehrhardt by Lindsey Auten.
Designed by N. Putens.

For my parents, Lowell and Diane Kimble

Contents

Illustrations

Preface

There was no way that I could have known what was in store for me nearly ten years ago when I opened an ordinary-looking folder in the advertising archives at Duke University. The label affixed to the folder simply described its contents as involving a scrap metal drive of some sort. Since I was looking for material on World War II advertising, I almost skipped it altogether. I recall thinking: *What do I care about scrap metal?* Had I embraced that fleeting thought, I would have missed a flurry of consequences in the subsequent years, all of them good.

Inside that folder, it turned out, was a document that would alter much of my research agenda. It eventually led to a journal article in *Great Plains Quarterly*, a feature story in *Nebraska Life* magazine, a documentary movie (co-produced with my colleague, Tom Rondinella), and now to this book. The critical document at the heart of these productions was a booklet that had been produced by the *Omaha World-Herald* in 1942 (and as far as I have been able to tell, Duke's copy is the only remaining one in existence). I recognized the newspaper's name immediately, as I'd grown up reading it, especially on fall Sundays when the sports section was filled with exhaustive analysis of and commentary on the Cornhusker football team's latest exploits. But what did the *World-Herald* have to do with scrap metal in World War II? I soon found out. The booklet drew me in, and I have hardly stopped ever since to look back at the decisive moment that started it all.

The scrappers, too, rarely looked back at the decisive moment that shaped their efforts. Most of them would not even have known where to look. New Englanders competing for bragging rights with their neighbors in the great national scrap metal drive in the fall of 1942, for example, could not have been expected to know that they were following an ambitious plan that had been drawn up in Nebraska. For their part, many Cornhuskers would have known that when they were feverishly collecting radiators, fenders, kitchen utensils, and tractor parts on behalf of their local county's scrap team, it had something to do with the *World-Herald*. Far fewer, however, would have known the identity of a certain Henry Doorly, let alone his role in devising the plan. Even many Omaha residents would not have understood that the genesis of their gigantic scrap mountain lay in the awkward moment when Margaret Hitchcock Doorly challenged her husband to stop grousing about the scrap disaster and do something about it. It was a private exchange, to be sure, but it was also decisive, and there can be little doubt that its echoes resounded across the vast home front and even into the world's various battlefronts.

My aim in this book is to examine what led up to that decisive moment and how the plan that emerged from it energized a state and then shocked a nation at war. The articles and the documentary mentioned earlier presented certain aspects of the story, but only a book can provide the rich historical context underlying such a momentous series of events. Only a book, moreover, can foster a narrative history that accurately leads interested readers back to its original sources: the primary accounts of the participants and witnesses who lived through these events back in 1942. Finally, a book is the best sort of venue for exploring the rhetorical and persuasive underpinnings of a massive, localized movement. After all, finding and hauling scrap metal was no walk in the park. Doorly and those leaders who helped him transform Nebraska into a veritable steel forge on the prairie had to figure out how to convince civilians not only that scrap metal was important but that every single person should pitch in. How they did so forms a strong undercurrent in this account.

It is worth mentioning that my interest in the scrap drive is also personal. As a Nebraskan by birth, this story drew me in from the moment

I understood its significance. Here was an inspiring tale that involved my own grandparents and their neighbors and friends, all doing their bit to change the course of the greatest war in history. Throughout the course of their efforts, the unadorned, down-to-earth, selfless stereotypes of life in the heartland constantly rang true. Even so, the state's scrap planners seemed to know that the surest route to success was to appeal to its residents' considerable pride, and so it is little wonder that I often felt a sense of pride as well, even if only secondhand and several decades later. To be sure, what came to be known as the Nebraska Plan was not without its flaws, and an important part of this story involves the shortcomings of the effort. But the most basic themes in my treatment frankly involve admiration and wonder. What would the nation have done, I keep asking myself, without these stalwart scrappers and their timely delivery of much-needed metal for the steel factories in the latter half of 1942? To borrow Governor Dwight Griswold's favorite metaphor for the scrap drive, one could say that their feat was akin to a last-minute, game-winning drive engineered by the state's beloved Huskers.

The world has changed a lot since those times, and for that reason some of the language choices in this recounting of the scrap story and its scrappers require explanation. Most critically, perhaps, the undesirable terms *Jap* and *Indian* appear only within direct quotations or proper names, with the understanding that standards of acceptability for such terms have changed dramatically since the war years — and for good reason. Similarly, the formal convention of the 1940s was for public accounts to refer to married women by their husband's full names (they simply added *Mrs.* in front). Except in direct quotations, I have generally adopted the more modern convention of using the given names of women who appear in the narrative. In the cases where I was not able to find given names, I have retained the original version.

A few other matters of language are important to point out. First, writers in the 1940s variably described scrap metal in terms of pounds, tons, or gross tons. Where possible, I have converted measurements to tons (i.e., 2,000 pounds) for consistency. The major exception in the book is for per capita averages (as in "50 pounds per person in the county").

On a similar note, the book uses the terms *scrap* and *scrap metal* (and, less often, *scrap iron* or *scrap steel*) synonymously, as was the common practice on the home front. I have tried to make it clear when I am referring to *scrap* in the more general sense, which would include other sorts of salvage activities, such as fats, paper, and so on.

Digging up the various pieces of the scrap drive's story took me to numerous archives over the last ten years and encouraged me to study reel after reel of microfilm newspaper. The occasional drudgery of that kind of work was balanced by the many people who pitched in to help along the way; not unlike the scrappers, they were willing to contribute and thus made this book possible. Among them, I would like to acknowledge Tina Potuto Kimble, who persevered through my research trips and writing binges; Tom Rondinella, who encouraged this book even as we shot a documentary; Karen B. Gevirtz, Anthony C. Sciglitano, and Greg Tobin, my writing partners; and Meghan Winchell, Gary R. Rosenberg, and Cherie Kimble, who all read portions of the manuscript. Special thanks are due to the folks at the *Omaha World-Herald*, who were beyond helpful in providing permissions (and who have proven to be justifiably proud of their institutional legacy).

Many, many others helped out in important ways, of course, including Mike, Christy, Emily, Ryan, and Kate Altman; Ron Altman; Chris Amundson; Maureen Kennedy Barney; Danielle and Aaron Blake; Laura Bonella; David, Hsiuchen, Ryan, and Ian Chan; Melba and Eugene Glock; Vauri Henre; Jim Hewitt; Todd Holm and Jennifer Baader Holm; Rodney Jewell; Cameron, Cherie, Kellie, Lindsey, Paul, Shelby, Troy and Tyler Kimble; Paul Libassi; Terrence J. Lindell; Bill Nicholas; Mary and Jack Ostergard; Kelli Pennington; Christopher Petruzzi; Jo Potuto; Susan Reisinger; Merle Rix; Lois Schaffer; Michael A. Soupios; Judy and Jim Wigton; and my colleagues in the Department of Communication and the Arts at Seton Hall University. I also acknowledge the financial and moral support of SHU, which provided a sabbatical leave during which much of the draft manuscript emerged.

Folks at numerous archives and institutes were also tremendously helpful, and I thank Kent Kiser and Tom Crane at the Institute of Scrap

Recycling Industries; Cindy Drake, Linda Hein, and Andrea Faling at the Nebraska State Historical Society; Lynn Eaton at Duke University's Hartman Center for Sales, Advertising & Marketing History; Lucas R. Clawson, Linda P. Gross, Roger Horowitz, Carol Ressler Lockman, Max Moeller, and Jon M. Williams at the Hagley Museum and Library; and Libby Krecek (and her colleague, Gary Rosenberg, also mentioned above) at the Douglas County Historical Society. The staff members at the University of Nebraska Press were also uniformly helpful and enthusiastic, especially Ann Baker, Bridget Barry, Martyn Beeny, Sabrina Ehmke Sergeant, and Rosemary Vestal. Special thanks are due to Elaine Durham Otto, whose copy editing skills worked wonders. All of these folks did their best to help me craft a compelling and accurate narrative; any inaccuracies that might remain are my own responsibility.

Finally, I dedicate this book to my parents, Lowell and Diane Kimble, who helped with several local research questions, read portions of the manuscript, helped identify scrap items in old photographs, and were always encouraging along the way. Ironically, perhaps, it turns out that they just happen to have known a certain Bill Nicholas, whose seemingly mischievous 1942 escapade involving a windmill near the small prairie city of Norfolk raises the curtain on the extraordinary story of the Nebraska scrap metal drive.

PRAIRIE FORGE

Introduction

Home Front, Battlefront

What have wars, thousands of miles away, to do with this peaceful, eternal business of living on the soil, by the soil, for the soil?
—A. G. Macdonell, *A Visit to America (1935)*

Bill Nicholas was on a quest. The high school senior's adventure had started on what seemed to be a typical youngster's prank. Still too young to fight the Germans, Italians, or Japanese, he and his school chums had chosen to spend a sunny day in the summer of 1942 driving around the rural countryside near Norfolk, Nebraska. The drive took a dramatic turn when the group spied a lonely windmill near a ramshackle barn. The idea hit them instantly: working together, they could climb the old metal structure and take it apart, piece by piece. After grabbing what tools they could find in their borrowed truck, they began to climb the rickety windmill. The dismantling was just getting started when Nicholas saw a farmer approaching in a hurry. "This windmill," he shouted, "waters my crops, so you boys better leave it alone and *get out of sight!*"[1]

The daring young Nebraskans were clearly in a tight spot, but their problems paled in comparison to the quandary facing the United States that hot summer. Seven months after the attack on Pearl Harbor, the country seemed to be facing ruin. Although the U.S. Navy had scored a surprise victory in June against a sizeable Japanese battle force at Midway Island, the remaining war news was generally uncertain or dire. GIs continued to train and mobilize for war, most of their battles still in the unknown future. German U-boats were sinking U.S. ships at an alarming rate. Japanese soldiers had already given the U.S. military one of the worst defeats in its history at Bataan. And everywhere there were rumors of Axis spies, agents, and saboteurs waiting for the right moment to wreak havoc on the home front. It was early in the war, wrote one correspondent, but already "the home team [was] trailing by two touchdowns."[2]

Perhaps the most dismaying news for the U.S. war effort in the spring and early summer of 1942 was that domestic steel mills were slowing production and, in many cases, halting operations altogether. The steel industry was a fundamental part of the nation's rapid attempt to construct war planes, battleships, tanks, and other armaments. Yet the vital process was lagging because the mills increasingly lacked an essential ingredient in steel processing: scrap metal. Ample amounts of scrap, as many observers pointed out, were available across the country in back lots, alleys, farmyards, abandoned factories, and attics. However, the more the government hectored citizens to find and turn in all of that valuable scrap metal, the less effective the appeals seemed to be. Not even the approximately 13,000 local and regional scrap committees across the country had had much success in persuading the home front to gather used metal for the war effort. The American Industries Salvage Committee confirmed that the production of steel in 1942 would likely end up 5 million tons below the industry's capacity, effectively eliminating the equivalent of 10,000 tanks and 1,300 cargo ships from the nation's arsenal. "We can never regain this lost time," lamented the committee, encouraging every citizen to gather scrap as quickly as possible in order to prevent more letdowns in war production.[3]

The unreliable supply of scrap metal in the country's industrial system presented a grave problem for the nation's armed forces, which needed the steel of modern war in mass quantities. Privately, officials in the Roosevelt administration worried that many steel mills had only enough scrap on hand to last a few weeks—a situation with the potential for disastrous effects on the war effort. Of course, announcements meant for public consumption tended to avoid such ominous undertones while still com-municating the government's sense of urgency. Lessing Rosenwald, head of the Conservation Division of the administration's War Production Board (WPB), told reporters that "any diminution" in the flow of scrap to factories "is an immediate threat to war production." WPB chairman Donald M. Nelson offered a more dramatic view, advising the home front that without a significant increase in the domestic supply of scrap mate-rial, "our boys may not get all the fighting weapons they need in time."[4]

WPB's ominous warnings had a special meaning for Nicholas and his high school friends as they fled the solitary windmill and the wrath of the farmer. As it turned out, this rowdy group of Nebraskans saw themselves not as pranksters but as soldiers. The windmill, in their eyes, had been not a rusty farming implement but a bonanza of scrap metal. Had they been successful in dismantling the metal structure, the group would have sent its various pieces on a multistage journey to be melted into muni-tions for the nation's GIs and sailors. Still too young to fight, in other words, these enterprising friends were far from the irresponsible youth they appeared to be. Instead, they thought of themselves as a squadron of scrap commandos.

The Nicholas windmill squadron was just one small part of an uncon-ventional statewide army. For three weeks, residents young and old found themselves involved in a complex, all-encompassing contest that histo-rian William L. O'Neill has called "the great Nebraska scrap drive of 1942."[5] The fierce competition that July and August pitted county against county, business against business, service club against service club, and, in schools across the state, class against class. Each civilian in the contest was responding faithfully to a widespread call for volunteers to enlist in grueling scrap metal duty. In this case, however, the call came not from Washington DC but from nearby Omaha, and the commander who captured the people's attention was not President Roosevelt but 61-year-old Henry Doorly, a naturalized immigrant who had risen to become publisher of Omaha's *World-Herald*, the state's largest newspaper.

Doorly's creative idea for a scrap contest seemed to have captured the imagination of the entire state that summer. The primary front of the competition—the race to see which of Nebraska's ninety-three counties could gather the most scrap per capita—inspired Cornhuskers of every stripe to sign up. They were successful beyond the organizers' greatest hopes. In the three weeks of competition, these scrappers found, hauled, and turned in over 67,000 tons of scrap material. No old tractor was safe, and no courthouse cannon was sacred. Nearly anything that might contain metal was subject to seizure. Scrap piles in practically every neighborhood and town square grew at a remarkable pace, offering visible evidence of community patriotism. Published county scrap standings riveted judges and contestants alike. Scrap leaders and even Governor Dwight Griswold himself encouraged Nebraskans to see their competition as a sports contest, with the state university's dauntless football team serving as an inspirational model. By the end of the affair, the *World-Herald*'s staffers wrote with some understatement that "the entire campaign had gotten out of hand." Indeed, editorialized the newspaper, the nation was watching Nebraskans in amazement, as "the latent patriotism of the people" came "pouring out in an irresistible flood."[6]

Before long, the Roosevelt administration realized that Doorly's competitive template was urgently needed for the entire home front. The resulting "nationwide plan," reported *Life* magazine, "is based on the Nebraska plan and will be launched through thousands of local newspapers" in a three-week blitz beginning in late September 1942. That phrase—*the Nebraska Plan*—soon became an indelible part of the national conversation. The country's newspapers immediately embraced Doorly's competitive model for scrap metal collection, devoting over 250,000 columns of display advertising and editorial appeals (some 31,250 full pages in all) to encourage citizens to compete against their neighboring schools, communities, and states. Edgar Bergen (and his ventriloquist dummy, Charlie McCarthy) joined James Cagney and Deanna Durbin in promoting the effort. Gallup polls revealed that an astonishing 94 percent of all Americans were familiar with the drive. All forty-eight states competed vigorously for bragging rights in the massive scrap metal contest, producing what *Newsweek* magazine called a "dizzy three weeks of stunts, gags, and cheesecake art." By the time the competition was over, the nation's various scrap commandos, scrap scouts, and scrap armies had gathered over *5 million tons* of scrap material to be used in making ships, planes, tanks, and munitions for the Allies. This improbable outcome, said the American Newspaper Publishers Association, was without a doubt "the nation's No. 1 success story" to that point in the conflict; after all, it had enabled "the furnaces where Victory is being forged to glow again with the white heat of peak production." But the "granddaddy of the national campaign," the Association hastened to add, was "the Omaha *World-Herald* drive."[7] The Nebraska Plan, it seemed evident, had significantly affected the war experience, if not the war itself.

Despite the historical significance of Henry Doorly's scrap campaign, its story has largely been forgotten. Historians have not found the scrap metal campaign as vivid as, say, Pearl Harbor or the D-Day invasions or the atomic bombs that ended the war. There is no scrap drive museum, and there has been no commemorative stamp to celebrate the drive's accomplishments. The occasional references to World War II and scrap in our cultural memory tend to conflate the scrap metal efforts with other salvage drives from the war era, such as campaigns to collect rags, to save kitchen fats, or to recycle paper. Amazingly, even the *World-Herald*'s own centennial history volume mentions Doorly's drive as an afterthought, despite the fact that the newspaper's scrap metal campaign won the 1943 Pulitzer Prize for public service.[8]

Still, one should not take the relative silence of historians and others to mean that the scrap metal campaign was without significance in relation to other events during the war. D-Day was a compelling historical moment, but if Allied soldiers had not taken with them the metal-based engines of warfare, they would have failed in their famous task. Hiroshima was certainly a crucial point in the conflict, but without the *Enola Gay* and its bomb, the mission would have been impossible. The Allies won the war, in other words, on the back of the vast system of American munitions production, itself a superhuman feat which would not have been possible without a well-supplied steel industry. And absent an ample supply of scrap metal in 1942, that industry would have found it difficult to provide the overwhelming striking power that the struggling Allied war machine needed so desperately. For this reason, as I have argued elsewhere, the Nebraska Plan was "a feat that could, with only some hyperbole, be described as the horseshoe nail without which the war would have been lost."[9] In spite of the scrappers' relative historical obscurity, then, their vital part in the war is a story well worth telling.

This book tells that story. It not only commemorates the Nebraska Plan and the sacrifices of those who made it work, but also contends that the plan was a resounding success on two levels. First, the scrap drive motivated significant numbers of civilians to address one of the war's most critical shortages at a pivotal point in the war. Before Doorly's campaign, the collection of scrap metal in Nebraska was at an embarrassing low. The state salvage director reminded the publisher that Nebraskans had already gathered 15 pounds of scrap metal per person earlier in the year. Finding more, he added in confidence, was unlikely.[10] During the three-week summer campaign, to the contrary, the state's citizens turned in nearly *104 pounds* of scrap material per person.

The national drive a few months later produced a similar result, albeit on a wider scale. There was no doubt that the Roosevelt administration's pleas for scrap following Pearl Harbor had failed to attract sustained interest. Paul C. Cabot, who served as the deputy director of WPB's Conservation Division, agreed with this assessment, complaining that while the country had recruited some 125,000 volunteer scrappers, they were working without adequate "stimulation and leadership."[11] In the wake of the national competition, in contrast, millions of volunteer scrappers had toiled to locate and gather those 5 million tons of scrap material, knowing that their efforts were enabling the steel industry to avoid further slowdowns and the country's armed forces to take the fight to the enemy. Doorly's plan, in this sense, had influenced countless citizens across the nation to take action by serving their country as scrap volunteers.

Second, and just as vital, this book contends that the Nebraska Plan was successful because it brought the war home to civilians, enabling them to participate directly in the battle as something akin to combatants. Students, retirees, housewives, blue-collar laborers, and even children felt themselves becoming integral parts of the war, distant but vital military cogs whose devotion to exhaustive scrap collection proved to be a catalyst in how Americans viewed themselves on the home front. As *Life* magazine admitted, involvement in the scrap drive "was a lot more thrilling than a movie or a night club." The Nebraska Plan, it concluded, "was the U.S. really going to war."[12]

Most of these ordinary civilians had no real relationship with the military. True, some would ultimately enlist. Young Bill Nicholas, for example, signed up for the Marines after graduation, eventually seeing action at Iwo Jima. Moreover, almost everyone in the country had a relative or close friend in the armed forces. Yet the legions of children who canvassed neighborhoods, going door to door with their scrap-filled Radio Flyer wagons, were engaged in a very different activity than Marines involved in hand-to-hand combat. Housewives who scoured the kitchen and the attic for unused metal scraps were a far cry from GIs searching for a deadly sniper. And bankers who organized trips into the rural countryside to scout for abandoned caches of scrap material were not actually engaged in daring thrusts into Axis-held territory. Indeed, the American mainland was thousands of miles from the nearest battlefront; the closest most civilians would get to seeing and hearing the ongoing war was the generally censored depictions of battle found in the nation's periodicals, newsreels, radio reports, and movies.

However, through the persuasive magic of Doorly's Nebraska Plan, every civilian on the home front was able to become a *de facto* soldier. Newspaper and radio ads used vivid appeals to turn rusting farm equipment into airplane wings and old toasters into rifle parts. World War I and Civil War artillery guns on display in parks and at memorials became new munitions in the fight against the Axis. Even aluminum gum wrappers, collected by millions of children across the country, joined the parade of repurposed scrap entering the nation's arms factories. Is it any wonder, then, that the dauntless civilians who scouted, secured, and transported this scrap could come to see themselves as soldiers of one sort or another? After all, as one scrap advertisement told readers, "YOU can help win this war just as surely as our boys on the world-wide fronts are doing it."[13]

In fact, the 1942 scrap campaign highlights an important aspect of the civilian mentality during World War II, one that has largely been lost in the nation's cultural memory. George H. Roeder Jr. uses the phrase "home front analogy" to describe this mentality, which involved the widespread portrayal of civilians and civilian activities as thoroughly military in aim and appearance. Newspapers, movie newsreels, cartoons, and numerous other sources, writes Roeder, provided "reassuring visual comparisons of military and home front activities" that consistently "used images of civilians in military dress and poses to suggest that service station attendants, bus drivers, secretaries, and housewives had a role in the fight." William L. Bird Jr. and Harry R. Rubenstein suggest that posters were another critical source of this comparison, since they addressed "every citizen as a combatant in a war of production" in order "to sell the idea that the factory and the home were also arenas of war" and that "every citizen [was] a soldier."[14] Although few civilians took these visual comparisons to be literally true, the relentless use of such imagery in wartime media doubtless enabled many on the home front to imagine themselves as playing a militarized role in the battle.

The home front analogy eventually appeared in countless campaigns and publicity efforts. Each campaign offered ways to militarize civilians and their homes so that they could enlist, at least metaphorically, as soldiers in what was not so much a home*land* as a home *front*. Men and women who worked in munitions factories were, for example, "soldiers of production." Millions of housewives joined the Women in National Service, or wins, a quasi-military organization with official uniforms and simulated army ranks. The nation's casual gardeners found themselves part of the "land army" as they fired at the Axis with potatoes and beans from their Victory Garden posts. And the U.S. Treasury's gigantic war bond machine used the image of Daniel Chester French's *Minute Man* sculpture to evoke the symbolic transformation of citizens into militia.[15] By the latter half of the war, in other words, numerous local, regional, and national campaigns were portraying those at home as the functional equivalent of a battlefront soldier.

The *World-Herald*'s statewide scrap metal drive in July and August 1942 was one of the earliest and one of the most influential of these quasi-military campaigns. Despite the temporary explosion of patriotism following Pearl Harbor, the first six months of the war in the United States had been marked by a confused public and declining morale. War bond sales gradually became anemic. Illegal hoarding of scarce goods was not uncommon. And, incredibly, pollsters found that nearly one-third of Americans confessed that they did not understand why their nation was at war. Officials felt compelled to condemn the "public lethargy" and "indifference." "Never in our history," suggested the *New York Times*, "has the outlook been so grim and so dark."[16]

Doorly's Nebraska Plan thus entered the public's consciousness at a most opportune time. The initial contest in Nebraska became an excellent means of energizing a state population that had "been sitting idly on the sidelines" of the war effort. With the campaign's nationwide expansion in the fall of 1942, Americans from coast to coast also found themselves involved in that war effort in a most dramatic manner. As the *World-Herald* commented in the midst of the national drive, these "eager Americans" offered "a thrilling display . . . of what a people could do when unified for a single purpose."[17] Although Doorly's scrap raiders were far from the actual fighting, the militarized heartland forge that they helped construct demonstrated rather convincingly just how close home front and battlefront could become.

On both of these levels, then, the Nebraska Plan fostered remarkable successes. This is not to say that the effort had no imperfections. The *World-Herald*'s team, for example, would probably admit that it could have used much more time to plan and organize the summer campaign. After the drive started, some of the state's citizens proved reluctant to take part—at least until their friends or neighbors prodded them into participation. There were even times when Doorly's ambitious plan appeared to have faltered. Such shortcomings were probably inevitable. Nebraskans were already leading busy lives when the scrap campaign came along. Working, harvesting, baling, housekeeping, and the other tasks of daily life could become overwhelming amid the labor shortages of wartime. Moreover, many citizens in the western portion of the state were already donating significant time and resources to the famous North

Platte Canteen.[18] To expect that these citizens would forget everything else in their day to engage in the hard labor of gathering scrap metal would have been quite a bit to ask.

The fact that the campaign somehow found a way to succeed in spite of its shortcomings makes its dramatic story all the more remarkable and suggests that it deserves a more central place in our cultural memories of World War II. Indeed, for those who experienced it, the 1942 quest for scrap metal—what one observer called "the greatest treasure hunt in history"—arguably had all the drama of the Battle of the Bulge and all the historical necessity of the battle for Iwo Jima. Like those battles, the search for scrap metal was dirty, sweaty, and even dangerous.[19] Unlike those battles, however, the story of the scrappers has received little postwar attention. Perhaps these patriotic citizens would have wanted it that way, as their work was directed not at personal glory but at community competition and patriotism. Nonetheless, some seventy years after their labors, it is high time that later generations acknowledge and appreciate their accomplishments.

Fortunately, many aspects of the 1942 scrap metal story survive in primary accounts from the war era. The *World-Herald*'s firsthand coverage of the drive, in particular, offers invaluable perspective on the effort. Local newspapers in Nebraska also wrote about the statewide campaign, while stories on the nationwide drive were recounted by major magazines and newspapers. Original documents, preserved in archives, offer an additional means of understanding the Nebraska Plan, its strategy, and its national impact. Finally, the recollections of dozens of scrappers—preserved at the Douglas County Historical Society in Omaha—provide a vibrant, firsthand resource on the scrap metal effort and its historical significance.

The chapters that follow draw on these resources to recount the story of the scrappers and their intriguing wartime quest. Chapter 1 examines the chronic scrap metal deficit on the home front prior to the summer of 1942, explaining its potentially dangerous impact on the war effort. Chapter 2 reveals Henry Doorly's growing concern about the scrap shortage and how his wife prompted him to develop an innovative plan to address it. In chapter 3 I show how the city of Omaha responded to

Doorly's plan, while in chapter 4 I examine the organizational efforts of scrappers in greater Nebraska. Chapter 5 details the drive's remarkable success across Nebraska in August 1942, which reverberated all the way to the White House. Chapter 6 shifts to explore the national drive, how it relied on Doorly's initial blueprint, and how its success, in a surprisingly literal sense, salvaged the war effort. Finally, the epilogue revisits the impacts of the Nebraska Plan. It returns, in particular, to the plan's role in providing much-needed scrap metal to the war effort, as well as its ability to symbolically unite those on the home front—individuals like Bill Nicholas and his windmill-climbing friends—with those on the battlefront.

1

The Scrap Deficit,
or How Not to Win a War

In a long war the nation that will have the last ton of scrap steel will win.
—*American Metal Market*, undated clipping

Emory E. Smith knew enough about scrap metal and war production to
be extremely worried about the unstable international situation. It was
early in 1939, and the former commissioner of the War Industries Board
was becoming increasingly alarmed as Nazi Germany rattled its sabers in
Europe even as Japan continued its brutal conquest of China. The United
States was avowedly neutral at the time, although President Franklin D.
Roosevelt had already condemned what he termed "international lawless-
ness" on the part of some European nations, and public opinion could
hardly be said to favor the Japanese. But as Smith and other industrialists
well knew, vital aspects of U.S. trade policy explicitly favored Japan's
war ambitions. In his view, the key concern was the exportation of scrap
metal. Since 1934, the United States had eagerly sold 12 million tons of
scrap abroad—7.5 million of them to Japan alone. Smith believed that
this policy was not only enabling the Japanese imperial war machine but
also destabilizing Europe. As he told reporters, "Without America's scrap
iron . . . there would have been no Japanese–China war and no bellicosian
European situation."[1]

Yet the most dramatic part of Smith's concern involved the fate of the United States itself in any future war. The way he saw it, the nation's generous scrap metal exports were arming potential enemies and preemptively disarming the U.S. military. Fewer stores of scrap, he argued, automatically meant fewer available munitions should the United States ever become involved in another war. The potential consequences were dire. America's "chances in any possible new world outbreak," he told the *New York Times*, "were being virtually sabotaged by wholesale export of scrap iron." Even if it wanted to, Smith continued, the nation "could not enter into or maintain a major war for the lack of a sufficient supply of scrap iron."[2]

Smith's concern about the high rate of American scrap exports in the midst of an unstable world situation was probably not surprising to those who knew him. After all, he believed that the world war had ended in 1918 primarily because Germany and its allies had abruptly run out of scrap metal with which to manufacture munitions.[3] However, most of his overwhelmingly isolationist fellow citizens of the late 1930s were unlikely to have understood his warning. To the average American at the time, the word *steel* would likely have brought to mind images of industrial might, vast mill complexes, and even the legacy of the late Andrew Carnegie. The word *scrap*, in contrast, would likely have brought to mind only images of junk yards, rusting heaps, and the local junk peddler. For most people, in other words, Smith's warning would have made little sense because to them there was no apparent connection between scrap and steel, let alone scrap and war.

In many respects, though, Smith's concern that U.S. scrap exports were contributing to a dangerous international environment was on the mark. The process of making steel was no secret on the eve of World War II. Although manufacturers could, in theory, craft new steel solely from veins of iron ore mined directly from the earth, most countries had opted to build a less expensive infrastructure that used substantial portions of melted scrap metal to mix in with new iron ore. This industrial setup made scrap steel a highly sought after commodity as nation after nation began to arm itself in the face of increasing world tensions. Thus in 1939 the United States found itself at the center of a series of converging factors: a neutral country with few restrictions on the export of scrap, a number of steel-hungry nations arming for battle, and high-demand prices making scrap profitable to sell to the highest bidder.[4] The situation would be fine, perhaps, if the United States could somehow manage to stay out of any upcoming war. But Smith and a number of others were very concerned about that worst-case scenario.

Three years later, the United States did find itself at war, and the concern about domestic scrap metal supplies was only growing more acute. On January 6, 1942, President Roosevelt used his State of the Union address to announce that he had ordered the production of 60,000 planes, 45,000 tanks, 20,000 antiaircraft guns, and 6 million tons of shipping—a breathtaking production goal for 1942 that would immediately stress domestic steel mills. Yet just two days later, the president received an urgent personal letter from U.S. Representative Michael Kirwan. The Ohio Democrat related to FDR that during a recent tour of his district, he had found that "in Youngstown alone, nine open-hearth furnaces, which manufacture 2,200 tons of steel each day, have been closed down and are not operating due to the lack of scrap." Kirwan's implication was enormous. "Without steel and 100% steel production," he wrote, "we cannot complete and keep up with the huge war program which you have outlined and deem so necessary to win."[5]

Kirwan's letter was not made public, but it touched a nerve within the administration. A week later, Roosevelt established the War Production Board (WPB), which was to be the government's newest authority on the prioritization and allocation of every resource and material needed for war production. Donald M. Nelson, formerly an executive vice president at Sears Roebuck, headed up the new agency knowing full well that steel production would be one of his primary concerns. As it turned out, much of his attention, especially at first, focused on the even more fundamental need for scrap metal. To appreciate Nelson's struggles with the persistent scrap deficit, it is worthwhile to detail the relationship among scrap, steel, and munitions, then to examine the steel bottleneck leading up to Pearl

Harbor. The troubles with steel before the United States entered the war led directly to Nelson's scrap battle in early 1942, ultimately putting the all-out production of munitions on an uncertain footing. The worrisome scenario was, in fact, the very sort of situation that Smith had warned about some three years earlier.

Of Scrap Peddlers, Steelmakers, and Donald Duck

If Smith had found it overly difficult to explain to his fellow citizens just why seemingly useless scrap metal was so important to a war effort, perhaps it was because he never thought to ask an animated duck to help. It was Daffy Duck, after all, who sang to American theater audiences from atop his gigantic scrap pile that "we're in to win, so let's begin — to do the job with junk!" By then, however, it was August 1943 and the message from Warner Brothers was a bit behind the times; nearly everyone on the home front had already internalized by that point just how vital their scrap metal was to the military.[6]

The *real* expert on scrap and steel, in any case, turned out to be *Donald Duck*. Not until 1965 did Donald reveal, in the 29-minute informational film *Steel and America*, that he knew all about the process of making steel. At one point in the film Donald even appears as a medieval iron worker, figuring out how to transform iron ore into a useful substance. Curiously, Donald himself implies that some of the essential facts of steelmaking are boring, since he quickly starts to fall asleep as the narrator drones on about smelting. Still, because the process of steel manufacturing retained its most basic elements between 1939 and 1965, Donald's adventures as a steelmaker provide a useful starting point for understanding the prewar relationship of scrap to steel — and thence to war munitions.[7]

One of Donald's first discoveries was that iron ore had some amazing properties. Once dug up or mined from the earth, it could be put together with charcoal and limestone in a rudimentary blast furnace, heated for the occasion with a huge bellows by a furiously laboring Donald. After the charcoal became hot enough to begin the smelting process, the limestone would soak up the iron ore's impurities. The molten iron would then discharge from the furnace into a series of forms, where it would harden into ingot shapes. Since the forms were typically arranged in a pattern resembling feeding piglets, this initial product came to be known as pig iron.[8]

While pig iron itself was too brittle to have many uses (an experimenting Donald shatters some against a tree), it could be refined in further stages to produce steel. In North America, ironmasters were refining pig iron into recognizable steel as early as 1655, and an actual steel furnace was in operation in Massachusetts by 1750. These steelmaking ventures, as one might expect, were imperfect. Early steel typically had any number of impurities, it was difficult to make and was thus expensive, and once its final products were no longer useful (due, for instance, to rust, over-use, or age), they were cast aside onto scrap piles—hence the original use of the word to mean *worthless* or *discarded*. Ongoing innovations, such as the replacement of charcoal with coke and the 1855 invention of the mass-producing Bessemer converter, gradually solved some of these issues. As a result steelmaking sped up considerably, with one of its more notable contributions being the dramatic expansion of the U.S. railroad system.[9]

However, not until the introduction of the open-hearth furnace in the 1860s was it possible to address the growing problem of those useless piles of scrap metal. Like the earlier Bessemer process, open-hearth furnaces could make steel from pig iron. But because this new kind of furnace operated at temperatures upwards of 3,000 degrees Fahrenheit, it could also produce steel by melting material taken from the unsightly heaps of scrap iron. This innovation was important in a number of ways. First, steelmakers found that it was easier to work with scrap metal because all of its impurities had already been removed when it was first made into steel. In addition, scrap piles were generally less expensive to purchase than iron ore and required significantly less labor to transport. Finally, from an ecological standpoint, the increasing use of recycled scrap to make steel preserved significant amounts of iron ore and limestone.[10]

Over time, the industry settled on a relatively even balance between pig iron and scrap as the ideal ratio with which to charge open-hearth furnaces (see fig. 1). By 1908, the economy of the new process allowed

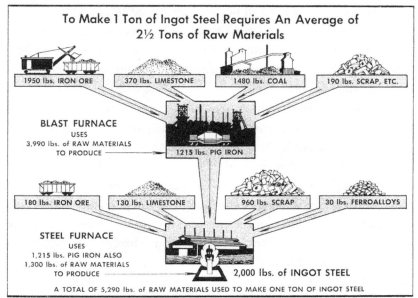

To Make 1 Ton of Ingot Steel Requires An Average of
2½ Tons of Raw Materials

| 1950 lbs. IRON ORE | 370 lbs. LIMESTONE | 1480 lbs. COAL | 190 lbs. SCRAP, ETC. |

BLAST FURNACE
USES
3,990 lbs. of RAW MATERIALS
TO PRODUCE ⟶ 1215 lbs. PIG IRON

| 180 lbs. IRON ORE | 130 lbs. LIMESTONE | 960 lbs. SCRAP | 30 lbs. FERROALLOYS |

STEEL FURNACE
USES
1,215 lbs. PIG IRON ALSO
1,300 lbs. of RAW MATERIALS
TO PRODUCE ⟶ 2,000 lbs. of INGOT STEEL

A TOTAL OF 5,290 lbs. of RAW MATERIALS USED TO MAKE ONE TON OF INGOT STEEL

BASED ON DATA COMPILED BY AMERICAN IRON AND STEEL INSTITUTE

1. In modern steelmaking, raw materials are processed in a blast furnace to produce pig iron, and then the iron is processed with more raw materials in an open-hearth furnace. Image courtesy of the Hagley Museum and Library, reprinted with permission from the American Iron and Steel Institute.

it to outstrip Bessemer facilities altogether. The open-hearth system soon overtook the growing U.S. steel industry in such a way that by the 1930s about 90 percent of the nation's steel emerged from open-hearth furnaces, with the remainder accounted for by Bessemer converters and specialized electric furnaces. Other countries, patterning their systems after the immense U.S. industry, generally opted to rely on open-hearth operations as well. Scrap metal thus became a coveted international commodity. It was particularly valuable to nations, such as Japan, that had little high-quality iron ore available to them.[11]

A vast, billion dollar industry eventually developed around the collection, processing, and shipment of scrap metal. Mills were themselves a major source of scrap, since excess material always remained after trimming, shearing, and shaping steel into its final form. This so-called *home scrap* accounted for about half of the scrap melted at most facilities. The remainder of a mill's supply was known as *purchased scrap*, some of which was obtained in bulk from other industries, such as railroad corporations. However, a substantial proportion of purchased scrap typically originated from the labor of some 150,000 junk peddlers, who solicited the country's households, farms, and businesses for scrap throwaways. This local scrap—ranging from discarded boilers to old golf clubs—made its way to scrap yards, which had the expert labor to sort it into any of seventy-five categories, as well as the equipment to break down larger pieces and to crush the lightest materials into compact bales for shipment to steel mills. As one might imagine, the availability of this purchased scrap could be rather unpredictable. One of the most important considerations, for example, was that nonindustrial scrap was much harder to obtain during the winter. Hence steel mills learned to stockpile scrap during the summer so that they would have sufficient stores to avoid shutdowns over the colder months.[12]

The scrap metal industry was a vital element in what the Institute of Scrap Iron and Steel described as a kind of modern-day "alchemy," a recurring process that gave steel its own series of life cycles. To illustrate this concept, the institute asked readers to imagine the adventures of a specific batch of steel, starting with its thirty years of service as a rail on the transcontinental railroad. Once the original track was taken up, a scrap dealer purchased the old rail, breaking it down into smaller segments and sending it to a steel mill, where it emerged as ship plates. After sailing the world as a tramp freighter, the batch of steel ended up rusting on a beach. It was then hauled to a scrap yard to be sorted, processed and transported again, whereupon another steel mill finally turned it into "the sheet from which the fender of your automobile was stamped."[13] The point, presumably, was clear: in a predominantly open-hearth system, steel and scrap are but mirror images of each other, meaning that the humble junk peddler and the scrap yard operator were indispensable players in the steelmaking process.

The institute's alchemic illustration was hypothetical, of course. But its rendering of the many life cycles of steel was indeed realistic. Scrap that was salvaged from scuttled German warships following World War I, for example, was eventually shipped to a Scottish steel mill, where it was melted down and refashioned into steel plates for the hulls of British warships. Those ships eventually would become part of the Allied war effort against the Axis. It was an ironic twist, since "the steel which the Germans fabricated for the fleet that was to give the Kaiser world domination literally rose to smite the next generation of Germans."[14] Here, in other words, was a dramatic, real-world instance in which scrap, steel, and war munitions had intersected.

Yet as Donald Duck was well aware, that kind of intersection was not at all unusual in the human experience. Indeed, every time medieval Donald produced a new kind of iron or steel, his first impulse was to cast a sword, which he immediately swung at nearby objects (often to comic effect). In a sense, Donald was merely following in the footsteps of countless would-be warriors. Even the prophet Joel advised the faithful to "beat your plowshares into swords and your pruning hooks into spears."[15] It was advice that untold millions of belligerents heeded over the centuries as they transformed scrap iron and steel into the weapons of war.

To be sure, by the twentieth century the admonition to beat plowshares into swords was no small matter. In an era of total industrial warfare, the violent purposes to which modern steel could be directed were tremendous. Aside from the obvious uses of steel in constructing warships, tanks, and other tracked vehicles, as well as airplane parts and guns of all sorts, the steel industry in a nation at war would be asked to expedite materials such as "armor-piercing shot steel, fragmentation bomb steel, or machine gun spring steel." By the 1930s, the products of the steel industry had become, in essence, "the sinews of war." As Winston Churchill himself bluntly put it, "Modern war is waged with steel."[16]

But the enormous amount of steel needed for munitions of various sorts in an era of total war was only one of numerous other wartime steel needs. "Before weapons can be made," wrote the American Iron and Steel Institute, "steel must build the machinery to make them, and the plants to house the machinery. . . . It must build shipyards and welding machines," and only then can it "build the ships themselves." In fact, even increasing national steel-building capacity required steel. The institute estimated that for every 10 million tons that war planners wanted to add to their maximum steel-producing capacity, at least 3 million tons of actual steel would be required in the construction of turbines, furnaces, blowers, and additional heavy equipment.[17] For this reason, nations planning for war required comprehensive industrial organization to ensure that scrap stores and steel products were consistently in the right place, at the right time, and with an adequate supply.

These were the sorts of logistical details that were unknown or that made little sense to the average U.S. civilian in 1939. Yet the interrelationship between steel, scrap, and war munitions, as Donald Duck himself had demonstrated, was by now an indelible aspect of world affairs. Still, even if the extent of Americans' knowledge of scrap metal at the time went little further than their local junk peddler, it was possible that the stunning 1940 German conquest of much of Western Europe on the back of a highly mechanized army offered them some enlightenment. By this point, Adolf Hitler had decreed death to hoarders of scrap metal, a clear indication that the Reich well understood the lesson that scrap was paramount in the prosecution of the war.[18] The question, for observers like Emory E. Smith, was whether or not that lesson would be ignored by the Roosevelt administration.

The Steel Bottleneck, 1940–1941

It was hard to upstage President Roosevelt, but on May 10, 1940, Hitler managed to do so. The president was scheduled to address more than 2,500 of the most eminent scientists from North and South America that evening. It was the eighth meeting of the Pan American Scientific Congress, and the president would be joining Secretary of State Cordell Hull and Dr. Albert Einstein in welcoming the scientists to the capital. Earlier in the day, however, Germany had suddenly undertaken a massive invasion of Belgium, France, Luxembourg, and the Netherlands, reigniting the European war that had been smoldering over the winter. Not surprisingly, Roosevelt's concern about the invasion was manifest in his address to the scientists, particularly in an accusatory passage which suggested that the world's aggressors would not rest until their domination extended to "every human being and every mile of the earth's surface."[19]

The president would only grow more concerned as the unsettling events of the spring and summer of 1940 unfolded. By June 25, Germany and its ally, Italy, occupied or controlled almost all of Western Europe. While more than 200,000 British troops had managed to escape the onslaught, their hasty and improvised retreat from the beaches at Dunkirk was a sign of how powerful the invaders had become. In mid-August, the Battle of Britain was under way, and in September, Japanese forces took advantage of France's utter disarray by invading French Indochina. When Italy, Germany, and Japan formally signed the Tripartite Pact on September 27, it was clear that the new Axis nations were sending a message to the United States. As Japan's prime minister, Fumimaro Konoe, told reporters a few days later, "If the United States . . . regards our pact as a provocative action directed against it, and if it constantly adopts a confrontational attitude, then the three countries will fight resolutely."[20]

In fact, Roosevelt could not risk appearing overly confrontational that summer. In November the president would face a reelection test, this time for an unprecedented third term. The worry in the White House was that forceful official reactions to Japan, Italy, and Germany might come across to voters as sheer belligerence, precisely when the majority of Americans wanted the nation to stay out of war. Indeed, anti-interventionist movements such as the Keep America Out of War Committee and the America First Committee became quite vocal in the fall, with the latter organization eventually attracting some 800,000 members in 450 local chapters to its cause.[21] In such an environment, Roosevelt could not afford to magnify the view of some Americans that he was anxious to go to war.

One significant action that the White House felt it *could* risk was to embargo scrap metal. On September 26—the day before Japan, Germany, and Italy signed their pact—Roosevelt used his authority under the Export Control Act to order an end to all scrap exports, with exceptions to be granted for the Western Hemisphere and for Great Britain. Japan was the most obvious target of this decision, since it had previously been the most significant buyer of American scrap. Paul V. McNutt, the head of the Federal Security Agency, justified the move by explaining that "during the last six years, Americans have sold to Japan eight and one-half million tons of scrap iron," enabling it to build "almost 500,000 tons of warships." Somewhat presciently, McNutt argued that this was "a very ugly picture" that could result in "powerful men-of-war steaming into Manila Harbor, into Guam, and the Hawaiian Islands." These enemy ships, he clarified, would be "flying a foreign flag," but they would be "made from American junk."[22] While Roosevelt's decision was largely overlooked due to the continuing debate over the September 16 Selective Service Act, McNutt's comments made it clear that the White House was carefully considering its prospects if the nation were to be drawn into war.

At the same time, the administration was scrambling to assess its scrap and steel resources within the context of a potential war footing. A number of internal reports in the fall of 1940, emerging from the National Defense Advisory Commission, the War Department, and the National Resources Planning Board, attempted to predict if the steel industry would be able to handle a dramatic upswing in munitions and simultaneously keep up with civilian steel requirements. However, the reports offered contradicting forecasts, in part because it proved to be extremely difficult to anticipate future demand in such a turbulent global environment. Making matters more complex, increasing civilian incomes were rapidly driving up domestic levels of steel consumption, leading the industry to raise its operating rate from 72 percent of capacity in May to 97.1 percent in January 1941.[23]

Roosevelt, now safely beyond the presidential election, provided a glimpse into the administration's steel deliberations early in 1941 by asking Gano Dunn, a veteran engineer and special consultant to the Office of Price Management (OPM), to conduct an impartial forecast of steel needs up through 1942. Dunn submitted his report to the president on February 22, concluding that if the industry's furnaces were able to run at a reliable rate, the nation would enjoy a surplus of over 10 million finished tons of steel in 1941 and would have an additional surplus of 2 million tons in 1942. The president was delighted at the findings and quickly shared them with reporters. "Beaming cheer," wrote *Time*, the president exulted "that the Dunn report showed ample facilities for all domestic defense and civilian needs." More important, perhaps, Roosevelt "added that no priorities need be established at present for steel."[24]

Unfortunately, the Dunn report faced immediate criticism. The War Department, for example, felt that the report significantly underestimated military requirements in the case of an all-out war. "Unless remedial steps are taken," the military responded in its own study, "requirements will pass production about September 30, 1941, and . . . steel consumption will have to be rationed or limited beginning that month." To make matters worse, Roosevelt signed into law the lend-lease program on March 11, suddenly increasing munitions exports to Great Britain. This move increased the strain on the steel industry, which would have to build most of those armaments. At the same time, it also resulted in a significant net loss of future scrap supplies, since those lend-lease exports would generally not be returning to the United States for another part of their life cycle. The implications for the accuracy of Dunn's optimistic forecast were evident.[25]

As a result of these developments, Roosevelt asked Dunn to revise his report. In late May, the revision was complete, and it was indeed much less optimistic. Increased estimates of lend-lease, civilian, and military steel requirements, noted the new report, now meant that the steel industry would likely fall some 1.4 million tons short of demand in 1941, and the following year the shortfall would grow to approximately 6.4 million tons. Dunn summarized that "a decision must be made whether to curtail the civilian consumption contributing to these deficits, or to expand the capacity of the industry to meet them." In other words, commented the *Wall Street Journal*, "mandatory steel priorities or rationing may be invoked shortly."[26]

In fact, voluntary industrial priorities for military needs had been in place since March, but since there was no legal force to back them up, they were often bypassed in favor of orders for civilian products. With demand for steel rising at every turn, the military thus found many of its projects foundering in a steadily developing bottleneck of steel. In May, for example, Major General Hap Arnold of the Army Air Corps complained to OPM of 200 separate incidents in which the unmet need for steel had hampered aircraft production. In July, Rear Admiral Howard L. Vickery of the Maritime Commission wrote to Harry Hopkins in the White House about numerous steel supply issues, warning that "I must have steel to produce ships." That same month, however, Roosevelt established a new Supply, Priorities, and Allocations Board, which would have the ability to assign preferential treatment to critical military orders for steel and other essential needs, as well as the statutory authority to enforce them. At the same time, OPM was working with producers of steel-heavy civilian goods, such as farm equipment and automobiles, to set quotas limiting production starting in August. On both fronts, the administration hoped to get ahead of the looming steel shortage before it could occur.[27]

But there was another way to address the potential shortfall in steel, and that was to build more furnaces and mills in order to raise the industry's overall capacity. Turning out even greater amounts of steel, the logic went, could presumably avert a materials crisis if the nation were to go to war. Soon after Dunn's revised report, the president asked OPM to consult with steel industry representatives to determine the feasibility of increasing the nation's annual steel capacity from 86 million tons to 96 million tons. OPM responded favorably, and organizational work began for a number of steel expansion programs. Yet planners soon came up against the very same steel limit that they were trying to address. Ironically, since creating new steel factories requires existing steel for the construction process itself, any rapid expansion in capacity would risk undesirable cuts in other areas of demand. The expansion, in other words, would have to proceed slowly.[28]

Meanwhile, the booming steel mills — now operating at near-full capacity — were becoming victims of their own success. The ever-faster production of steel in the first half of 1941 had begun to outstrip available supplies of raw materials, endangering the rate of output. By September, scrap was emerging as the most significant industry concern. The nation's open-hearth mills were now maintaining their accelerated operations by consuming available scrap stores at rates that were 40 percent higher than the previous year. As a result, the dwindling supply of scrap metal began to have significant impacts on the industry, with the threat of shutdowns becoming more and more realistic. Kansas City's Sheffield Steel Company, for instance, informed customers that it would be closing down on September 18 "due to the lack of scrap," a situation that the White House found was suddenly facing "many more steel mills . . . throughout the country." Across the industry, there was a 45 percent drop in available scrap metal stocks by the end of the year, a situation which meant that steelmakers "began to experience extreme difficulty in meeting even a substantial fraction of their commitments." As *Business Week* estimated, the growing shortage of scrap meant a shortfall of up to 8 million tons of finished steel. While this was somewhat under 10 percent of the nation's capacity, it was a shortfall that no nation arming for war could afford. Even worse, with winter approaching, the industry's scrap levels were unlikely to grow any time soon.[29]

As if to punctuate what was becoming a bona fide scrap crisis, Japan suddenly attacked the U.S. fleet at Pearl Harbor on the morning of Sunday, December 7. Amidst the loss of life, the outrage, and the subsequent declaration of war, it was easy to overlook the fact that the Japanese assault had been thoroughly grounded in the relationship between scrap, steel, and war. Since one-third of Japan's steel products were directly tied to previous U.S. scrap exports, here was a traumatic affirmation of Emory E. Smith's warning.[30] After all, the exported scrap had armed Japan even as it made it harder for the United States to arm itself—a situation that the steel mills could now fully appreciate. But here, at Pearl Harbor, that same scrap had gone one step further, returning in the form of enemy ships, planes, and bombs to further weaken the U.S. military's ability to wage war. The headlines of the day were understandably focused on the carnage of the attack as well as the shift to all-out war. Yet within the Roosevelt administration, another important lesson was not lost: if the nation were to continue as the fabled Arsenal of Democracy—not to mention to fight in its own right—it would need to hope that the soon-to-be-assembled WPB and its hard-charging chairman would be able to pick up the pieces of the perilous scrap mess.

The initial meeting of the War Production Board took place on January 20, 1942. Calling the attendees to order was the president's new point person on domestic resources and priorities. Donald M. Nelson was a tall, gregarious Missourian whose habitual pipe smoking could not hide a formidable personality. He was a chemical engineer by training, a speciality that had gradually helped make him an expert on manufacturing and industrial relations. When the president had plucked Nelson from upper management at Sears Roebuck two years earlier, few in Washington had ever heard of him. Yet anyone in the administration who pegged him as a civilian intellectual soon found out that he was "as tough as a Marine pleading for more Japs to consume." At that first WPB meeting, the tenacious chairman carefully observed the board's discussions about fats and oils, automobile production, and the rationing of household commodities. When it came time to focus the members' attention on the problem of scrap metal, however, Nelson himself led the discussion.[31]

The chairman was pessimistic. He told the board that national pig iron production and scrap supplies were uncertain enough that total steel output for 1942 could range anywhere from 86 million tons (which might be just enough for the year's estimated demand) to 79 million tons (which would fall significantly short of needs in the new war economy). Based on this uncertainty, he declared that there was a "serious shortage existing in this material." Not surprisingly, Nelson's pessimistic outlook soon found its way into media reports. Citing an internal government memorandum, the *Washington Post* warned readers that "unless scrap collection were stimulated, the 1942 production of steel—so urgently needed for munitions—would be smaller" than the year before. The looming scrap shortage, added the *New York Times*, was hard to dismiss, "especially when one of the largest armament programs in history is in the making."[32]

Yet both Nelson and the media were well aware that there were plentiful caches of scrap located throughout the country. As Representative Kirwan had written to FDR back on January 8, "There is no necessity for open-hearth furnaces being non-productive because of a scrap shortage, as there

are millions of tons of it lying around in yards, attics, and basements."
The problem, of course, was obtaining all that scrap metal. Kirwan was
convinced that civilians "would be more than willing to pile what they have
to their curbstones for collection if the proper appeal was made by their
President and through the Governor of each state." Apparently Nelson
was on to the same idea, as in that first WPB meeting he persuaded his
board to authorize "a vigorous nation-wide campaign . . . for the collection of scrap iron and steel from every possible source."[33]

Nelson directed WPB staffers to focus on several critical areas. The
organization had already inherited a "Salvage for Victory" campaign,
which was a low-key effort inaugurated by the now-defunct OPM in its
last days. However, while that program highlighted the importance of
scrap metal to the war effort, its emphasis was more on salvage of every
type, so other initiatives were in order. Perhaps the most publicized new
focus was on so-called automobile graveyards. Before the war, an average
of 2.5 million junked vehicles had been processed every year for return to
the steel industry as scrap metal, but Nelson was now intent on pressur-
ing the auto scrapping industry to increase that number to 4 million in
1942. WPB also elected to put significant energy into the establishment
of a nationwide scrap hierarchy, with thousands of volunteer salvage
committees from across the country signing up to lead neighborhoods
and regions in the search for scrap metal for the war effort. Moreover,
the agency enlisted the help of influential public leaders who did their
bit to try to bring the issue of scrap to the public's attention. As U.S.
Representative Charles I. Faddis of Pennsylvania remarked in a radio
address over the Columbia network on March 24, for example, "There
are today furnaces that are not operating because of a lack of scrap, and
it is essential that more be obtained. We need the scrap NOW."[34]

WPB's efforts, however, quickly ran into a series of obstacles. The
most obvious problem was that the structure of the massive committee
system made it difficult for local volunteers to communicate news of scrap
finds to anyone with the authority to collect the junk and haul it away.
Many workers became frustrated with the overly bureaucratic system,
and it soon became commonplace for neighborhood committees to exist

primarily on paper. At the same time, WPB officials learned that many citizens had wholly negative memories of a two-week aluminum salvage campaign that had taken place the previous summer. That drive had been promoted with urgent fanfare by the Office of Civilian Defense, only to result in apparently useless heaps of pots and pans that had remained in place for months. Now WPB was asking Americans to participate in what must have seemed to be a similar effort, but it was doing a poor job of explaining why the task this time was so much more important.[35]

By late February steel economists were pointing out that despite "the greatest demand in history," the appeal to Americans to gather and turn in scrap metal was falling flat. Indeed, with reduced civilian production already in place in some industries, not to mention the possibility of future rationing programs, many individuals and businesses were choosing to keep in use older equipment that would ordinarily have made its way to a scrap yard, for fear that no replacements would be available. Moreover, the scrap industry itself was beginning to face a labor shortage, with numerous scrap peddlers and yard workers joining the armed forces or, in some cases, shifting to better-paid munitions factory jobs. With a few exceptions, the resulting efforts to collect and process scrap were typically underwhelming at best. In April most steelmakers found themselves operating with only two weeks' supply of scrap metal on hand, and reports continued to surface that sporadic open-hearth furnaces were suspending operations. Within the Republic Steel Corporation alone, scrap stores were so meager during the first half of 1942 that the company's production fell behind by 173,000 tons — enough steel to construct three Iowa-class battleships.[36]

As one might expect, tempers soon began to flare over WPB's apparent failure to persuade the public to turn in scrap metal for the war effort, particularly after an April poll indicated that two-thirds of Americans had never even been approached by a scrap volunteer. At a May 5 committee hearing on Capitol Hill, Oklahoma senator Joshua B. Lee actually accused WPB's scrap officials of "discouraging State-wide campaigns to collect scrap metal." He wondered aloud if the bureau had "put any steam behind these State-wide scrap programs." When WPB's Paul C. Cabot replied, "All we can," Lee's retort was pointed: "Then you haven't much steam." The resounding criticism of the scrap effort was still ongoing in late June, when trade union president Philip Murray told the press that "the government's failure to gather scrap was 'almost criminal.'"[37]

WPB defended its efforts vigorously, pointing out in early June that mill shutdowns were becoming less common. In fact, an effort dating from early in the spring to run the country's blast furnaces at an all-out pace in order to produce record amounts of pig iron (which open-hearth furnaces could process into steel, though not as efficiently as with the normal percentages of scrap) was by now helping steelmakers to regain some of their lost ground. Unfortunately, the industry would not be able to maintain the rapid pace indefinitely, since iron ore could not be transported to blast furnaces over the frozen Great Lakes in the winter months. Moreover, while the government and industry were doing everything possible to increase overall steel capacity, additional blast furnaces (and the resulting long-term growth in pig iron stocks) now seemed unlikely to go online until the spring of 1943. Increasingly the steel bottleneck seemed to be headed for a crisis. As the Office of Emergency Management's George S. Pettee confirmed in July, "The steel shortage is real." Even worse, he noted, "the entire war program is in a straitjacket fixed by steel capacity."[38]

Widespread concerns thus began to emerge regarding the potential for a major steel slowdown during the coming winter and into 1943. With both iron ore and scrap supplies expected to slow to a seasonal trickle, the industry seemed likely to face its biggest challenge yet. "The specter of severe shortages next Winter," as the *New York Times* called it, had definitely captured the government's attention. As military and lend-lease demands continued to spiral, WPB predicted that the industry would need a stockpile of 10 million tons of scrap metal to make it through to the spring. Even the president was growing alarmed about the deficit, noting in a letter to U.S. Representative John J. Cochran that "we anticipate that the scrap shortage may become more acute during the winter of 1942–1943."[39]

It was increasingly clear that failing to find additional sources of scrap metal would have undesirable consequences. Even as WPB official Harold

J. Ruttenberg warned a House of Representatives committee that "steel operations may well drop to as low as 80 percent of capacity this coming winter unless the failure to accumulate adequate scrap iron and steel stock piles at the various steel mills is converted into a success," Nelson himself was pointing to the hazards of such a shortfall for the armed forces. As the WPB chief suggested, the looming steel crisis was threatening "to delay both the Navy and Maritime shipbuilding programs," not to mention other "vital construction programs" involved in arming the military.[40] In a nation girding itself for an offensive war on numerous fronts, such worries were troublesome indeed.

The situation must have seemed even more dire given the miserable progress of the war effort to that point. The government implied that production problems were to blame for the recent disasters at Bataan and Corregidor, arguing that the defenders "needed planes — more planes — and the planes did not come. We didn't have them to send." There was, to be sure, some obvious hyperbole in such statements, since arms alone could not win a battle, let alone a war. Moreover, a plentiful supply of scrap would not by itself be a magical solution to production worries. But there was no doubt that many people on the home front viewed the scrap deficit as a key variable in the continuing course of the war. After all, contended the Office of Price Administration's Donald H. Wallace, in this "war of metals . . . our boys can't fight with their hands."[41]

In many respects, then, the summer and fall of 1942 were turning out to be a critical crossroads in the scrap battle. The administration was now reflecting a great deal of pressure to go on the military offensive later in the year, meaning that the production of munitions was even more important than before. At the same time, the president's overall production goals for 1943 had already been set at rates significantly higher than those of 1942. The stress on the nation's steelmakers had never been more intense. *Collier's* observed, with some understatement, that "the steel industry has a tough job on its hands to make the steel" that will, in turn, "make the guns and tanks and ships" so necessary to take the fight to the enemy. "Millions and millions of tons," the magazine added, "must roar out of the furnaces every month."[42]

If the industry were to withstand this stress through the upcoming winter, it would need to avoid bottlenecks, ensure continued cooperation between labor and management, and have adequate stores of scrap metal on hand. Unfortunately, given WPB's overly bureaucratic approach to its public outreach, there was every reason to believe that the scrap impasse would continue—with sporadic slowdowns and shutdowns a continuing thorn in the side of the war effort. It was a situation that steel experts like Emory E. Smith could easily understand. But the question was how to reach out to the American public in such a way that they, too, could understand the vital nature of scrap metal in the war effort. Ironically, in order to accomplish that seemingly impossible goal, Donald Nelson would soon find himself turning to a most unexpected resource, one that was located not in Washington DC but in Omaha, Nebraska.

2

Henry Doorly and the Nebraska Plan

This is the story of an idea. It began with one man and one newspaper.
—Omaha World-Herald (1942)

Margaret Hitchcock Doorly might have seemed, at first glance, a rather unusual person to be playing an indispensable role in any event involving either scrap metal or warfare. Mrs. Henry Doorly, as the society columns of the day referred to her, was one of the leading ladies of Omaha and no stranger to cultured circles. Her maternal grandfather had been an early governor of Nebraska, and her father had been a two-term U.S. senator as well as the founder and publisher of the *Omaha World-Herald*. As would be expected for a woman in her social position, she was tirelessly active in midwestern high society and charity work. She was even a playwright. In short, she would most likely have been more comfortable at a high profile fund-raising event than in a scrap yard full of rusting metal parts.[1] Ironically, it was this feminine paragon of Omaha's elite society who served as the initial catalyst for the toil and sweat of the Nebraska Plan and all that would follow from it.

The inspiration took place on July 1, 1942. Margaret was going on a train journey, and she asked Henry to drive her from their elegant Fairacres home to Omaha's Union Station. During the drive, Henry began to complain to his wife about the dismal results of the national rubber salvage

2. Henry Doorly, publisher of the *Omaha World-Herald*. Doorly was an immigrant who rose to a powerful position in his adopted city. Image reprinted with permission from the *Omaha World-Herald*.

drive, which had just ended. President Roosevelt himself had expressed disappointment in the public turnout, extending the campaign for another ten days in hopes that the American public would finally respond. Henry grumbled on about the fiasco until Margaret asked a question that would resound in his mind for days: "What did you do about it?"[2]

On his way home from the train station, Doorly purchased a newspaper and learned that the War Production Board (WPB) would soon be unveiling a national ad campaign to appeal for scrap metal due to ongoing concerns that the steel mills might have to cut back on production, at the potential cost of soldiers' lives. As the publisher of the *Omaha World-Herald* (see fig. 2), Doorly would no doubt have been familiar with this chronic problem, which had been in and out of the national headlines since the spring. But recent news reports suggesting, for example, that "meager stock piles of scrap . . . were being whittled rapidly down to where in some cases they were becoming nonexistent" were especially worrisome.[3] After all, if the public had not responded well to the appeals for rubber salvage, what were the chances that citizens would respond to renewed pleas for scrap metal?

But there was, of course, a more fundamental question plaguing the publisher on the way home that night: what could Henry Doorly, an immigrant and resident of a medium-sized city in the middle of the country, actually do about any of these problems? As he sat at his home that evening, the list of reasons why he could probably do little or nothing about them must have seemed rather lengthy. He was, for example, 61 years old, well past the age when he could lead a group of muscle-bound laborers in hauling heavy pieces of scrap metal to a collection point. He was also no expert on wartime salvage campaigns, whether they involved metal, rubber, rags, paper, or grease. Finally, he was a provincial publisher, his newspaper a regional daily with relatively few influential connections in the federal government. In fact, since the *World-Herald* had backed Republican Alfred M. Landon over FDR in the 1936 presidential election, Doorly had become a strident opponent of the New Deal; in the process, he had burned a lot of bridges with the current administration. Put in the simplest terms, even if Doorly had a sudden, brilliant insight into the scrap problem, there was little chance that the president would take his call.[4] Certainly, there seemed to be many reasons why the publisher was powerless when it came to the national scrap mess.

Yet Doorly had been stung by his wife's gentle chide, and he was determined to do his best to rise to the challenge. Even if he were too old to heft metallic heaps, or too inexpert on salvage, or too disconnected from the government, perhaps there was still a way for him to make a precise, well-placed contribution to the war effort. So thinking, the publisher stayed up late that Wednesday night—1:30 a.m., as he recalled later—considering in detail what could be done within his own circle of influence and with his own particular gifts.[5]

The course of action that Doorly formulated during that long summer night and with his staff in the following days would soon become the talk of the town—and of the state. Yet the approach of the embryonic Nebraska Plan, as it developed over the next few weeks, was deceptively simple. To understand Doorly's thinking, it is useful to consider the paradoxical strengths inherent in his position, predecessor efforts that might have influenced his direction, and the strategic vision revealed within his plan. Ultimately, the preparations he oversaw as the curtain began to rise on the *World-Herald*'s grand scrap drive would, Henry hoped, be a truly emphatic response to Margaret's pointed but timely question.

Out of Weakness, Strength

Henry Doorly was born in 1879 on the Caribbean island of Barbados, one of England's many colonies at the time. He trained as a civil engineer and emigrated to the United States at age 19. Working as a construction laborer for the Union Pacific and then as a draftsman for the U.S. Army Corps of Engineers, he soon found himself in Omaha, meeting and courting Margaret Hitchcock, whom he married in 1904. Margaret was the daughter of Gilbert M. Hitchcock, the publisher of the *World-Herald*, and so even before the wedding Henry was invited to join the newspaper staff as a crime reporter, at the rate of $17.50 per week. Unfortunately, he was awful at the job. Even the police teased him, calling him "the Duke" due to his British accent and reserved manner. He kept the job, or so it was said, "mainly because he was the publisher's prospective son-in-law."[6]

But Hitchcock soon moved Doorly into the advertising department, where the younger man swiftly proved to be an able worker and, before long, the newspaper's business manager. In early 1907, Hitchcock left for Washington for service in Congress, forcing him to make a choice that would shape the *World-Herald* for a generation: he risked leaving oversight of the newspaper to his son-in-law. By the time the retiring senator returned in 1923, Doorly had somehow managed to turn the newspaper into a well-structured, competitive, and profitable operation. Eleven years later, Hitchcock passed away, leaving the newspaper itself to Margaret and Henry. Although Henry was finally the publisher in his own right, he had by that point been essentially running the *World-Herald* for twenty-two years. In that time, total circulation had increased from 30,000 to over 120,000.[7]

By 1942, few employees would have been able to remember reporting to a different boss. For over thirty-five years, Doorly had operated the *World-Herald* as a strict, no-nonsense disciplinarian. His manner was often remote, which led his enemies to view him as cold and some employees to view him as unfriendly. As one editor said, "I don't believe anyone was really close to the man—at least not during office hours." But others saw him as a "smiling, hustling" boss or even as "a man of action." Indeed, although Doorly was not at all the type of person to try to please everyone, he was quite willing to lend others a helping hand, such as when he personally approved generous loans to employees who found themselves in financial strain.[8]

Still, it is probably fair to say that Doorly would not have been the first civilian on the home front to come to mind when it came to finding someone to solve the scrap dilemma. Nor would the *Omaha World-Herald* have been at the front of the line if anyone in 1942 had been seeking a publication that could adequately address an issue of such overarching significance. From a national perspective, both Doorly and his newspaper were too unknown, too remote, and too disconnected to have made much of a difference. Or so it must have seemed. Yet as it turned out, both the disciplined publisher and his newspaper had some important, if subtle, strengths when it came to this particular issue, place, and moment.

For Doorly's part, it was evident that the scrap problem would require a creative mind, one able to generate unorthodox strategies that might not have occurred to anyone else. In this respect, the publisher had excellent experience. Because he had never been trained as a journalist, Doorly had had to come up with creative solutions. One example that was recalled fondly by employees involved the newspaper's onetime competitor in Omaha, the *Bee-News*. Early in the 1920s, Doorly had approved the purchase of a market wire service, which gave the *World-Herald* the area's only access to the daily array of New York stock listings. But when the *Bee-News* promptly began printing stock figures as well, Doorly deduced that the rival newspaper was simply parroting his own market listings, right from the page. To prove it, he decided to insert a fake stock listing in his financial section, using the symbol *SBTB*. When the other newspaper dutifully published the exact figures for the phantom stock, Doorly's paper immediately printed an exposé on the theft. The *World-Herald*'s story, aiming to embarrass its rival as much as possible, revealed to readers that *SBTB* actually stood for "Stolen by the *Bee*."[9] It took many years, but eventually Doorly's newspaper won the battle for Omaha when its rival folded in 1937, and such creative tactics were an important reason why.

The scrap impasse would also need an individual who was no stranger to public causes. Doorly fit the bill here, too. As editor Frederick Ware recalled, the publisher was prone to directing the newspaper in acts "of unselfish charity and kindness and humanity, which warmed all who read our paper, and made us who produced it mighty proud." One memorable instance took place in 1934 when the publisher heard about Helen Siefert, a 7-year-old from Bridgeport, Nebraska, who could neither see nor hear. Moved by her plight, Doorly marshaled the considerable statewide resources of the *World-Herald* to establish the Helen Siefert Fund. Despite the financial hardships of the ongoing Great Depression, the newspaper's dramatic effort raised enough money across the state for Siefert to be able to enroll at the Perkins School for the Blind in Massachusetts. It was only one of Doorly's many public campaigns over the years, but it proved that when he became impassioned for a cause, he could convince others to listen.[10]

A final characteristic that would be necessary to address the scrap problem was a sense of personal determination. Once again, Doorly's personality fit the bill. *Time* magazine noted, for example, that "if a close personal friend or a big advertiser got in the way of one of the paper's local crusades, Doorly had no compunction about running him over." A case in point was the lengthy controversy over the Nebraska Power Company, which, like the scrap problem, began in 1942. In a pitched battle that came to include the mayor, the city council, and even the state legislature, Doorly relentlessly advocated public ownership for Omaha's electric power. As the turmoil persisted throughout the war years, the publisher lost powerful friends and even found himself publicly labeled a communist for his position. But he stuck to his guns, and in 1945 his side won the cause. It was, in the end, a testament to his stubborn persistence in the face of adversity. "You might not have agreed with him," remembered Nebraska Supreme Court justice John W. Yeager, "but you had to give him credit for having the courage of his convictions."[11]

These personal strengths would bring a lot to the upcoming scrap effort, but they would surely have been of little use without the *World-Herald*'s paradoxical fit for this exact situation. Doorly was well aware that the reach of his newspaper was not broad enough to shape national opinion, let alone the scrapping behavior of millions of Americans. But it did boast some 320 employees in the city, as well as more than 1,000 special correspondents throughout the region. Moreover, no other publication in Nebraska could approach the *World-Herald*'s size or scope. As a result, Doorly's newspaper attracted readers from every corner of the state. It was, in fact, by far the most influential publication of any sort in Nebraska in 1942. That influence could function, Doorly realized, as a kind of fulcrum on which he could leverage a successful campaign in order to gain national attention. As the newspaper put it later, "Sitting at home that evening, Mr. Doorly decided that while he could not do the job for the nation, he could at least do it in Nebraska, thereby setting an example for the nation."[12]

As it turned out, then, the publisher's newspaper was the perfect vehicle for such a scrap campaign. Unlike, say, a daily in San Francisco or Dallas, the *World-Herald* could reasonably be expected to command the attention of not only its home city but almost an entire state. It was an ideal place for a grassroots movement to start, to grow, and—if it were successful—to capture widespread attention. WPB had repeatedly avoided such a localized, grassroots approach to scrap collection, preferring instead to value a confusing bureaucracy run primarily from Washington. But that strategy lacked immediacy and discouraged personal involvement. The *Saturday Evening Post*, later commenting on the genius of Doorly's contrasting approach, agreed that his "plan of action" was especially effective because it "was not burdened by co-ordinators who had to devote time to co-ordinating co-ordinators who were co-ordinating other co-ordinators."[13]

To be sure, it is unlikely that Doorly was consciously pitting his developing framework against the failed WPB scrap model. His interest was probably aimed more at taking advantage of his personal experience and of his newspaper's position within the city of Omaha and the state of Nebraska. In combination, these strengths would soon prove to be surprisingly effective. Despite the unexpected advantages, however, Doorly could not afford to ignore the efforts of citizens around the country who had also attempted to grapple with the scrap mess. Intriguingly, a careful perusal of predecessor drives from earlier in 1942 suggests that Doorly's Nebraska Plan might have found at least some of its inspiration in the ideas of other scrap innovators.

Inspiring Scrappers

What might well have been the first fatality from scrap metal collection occurred in Clarksville, Iowa, on May 21, 1942. Abe Markle, a laborer at the local McNeilus junk yard, was part of a crew that had been crushing scrap into compact bales for shipment to a steel mill. But when he attempted to replace a belt on the tractor that was powering the crusher, his overalls became caught up in machinery; he passed away later that day from the subsequent injuries. There was no question that Markle's death was a tragedy, and the *Waverly Democrat*'s story the next day was appropriately somber. Yet a nearby report in the same issue could not help but be positive, since Iowa's state salvage director had singled out Bremer County for praise. In a few months of work, it seemed, the county's farmers had been enthusiastically heeding WPB's pleas for scrap metal. By early April, the patriotic local effort had already sent 20 tons of material to war.[14]

In fact, several sporadic campaigns in far-flung locales had demonstrated throughout the first half of 1942 that with some organized local effort, citizens would often respond to scrap appeals. Just a few weeks after Pearl Harbor, for example, a farm campaign in Hoke County, North Carolina, brought in 150 tons. Later that month, a four-day drive in Birmingham, Alabama, used the donated time of garbage crews to collect 200 tons for the steel mills. Many of the participants in these drives donated their scrap metal for patriotic reasons, while others sought the cash that scrap yards were willing to pay. In most cases, however, the campaigns were either marginally successful or exceptions to a widespread rule of public indifference. Thus it was no surprise that the Department of Agriculture (USDA) noted of the Hoke County drive that it was the only "minutely organized plan of attack . . . to collect scrap" within North Carolina to that point in the war.[15]

It is likely impossible to know if Doorly was aware, in the weeks and months before his wife's challenge, of many of these local scrapping efforts. After all, there appear to be no remaining records of his original planning. However, Doorly had ready access to local, regional, and national news sources. Moreover, many of these efforts had been well publicized in national news outlets. Hence it is quite possible that he knew — or that he was able to find out — about at least some of them.

Amid the country's scattered instances of scrap collections, depots, drives, and sweeps in early 1942, three efforts stand out as the most likely influences on Doorly. The largest of the three began in February as a corporate initiative of International Harvester, an implement manufacturer. Harvester knew that farm scrap tended to be of the highest grades and thus was desirable to steel mills. It also had, through its

10,000 dealers, personal connections with hundreds of thousands of farmers. On instructions from corporate president Fowler McCormick, each dealer thus became a local promoter for the scrap metal cause, with the implement lots themselves available to host piles of old farm scrap. In an impressive show of organization, each dealer received from Harvester a detailed campaign manual, posters, and content to place in area news outlets. The local results were often notable, including the experience of a North Dakota dealer who collected three train car loads of scrap in a few days, and that of an Illinois dealer whose parking lot heap grew to 100 tons. By May the lengthy corporate drive had helped collect as much as 1 million tons of scrap metal in rural locations throughout the country.[16]

Meanwhile, a more compact campaign took shape in Coatesville, Pennsylvania, a town of 14,582 located on the Lincoln Highway about 45 miles west of Philadelphia. Coatesville was the hometown of the Lukens Steel Company, whose president, Robert W. Wolcott, had become a passionate supporter of scrap drive efforts after his steel mills experienced several scrap-related shutdowns earlier in the spring. With his encouragement, city leaders inaugurated a cleanup week from April 13 to 18. As with the Harvester campaign, the local press was actively involved in promoting the drive. But Coatesville's overt emphasis from the start was on using a variety of appeals to saturate the community in order to raise public consciousness. For example, a loudspeaker-equipped car roved the streets, alternately playing military music from a phonograph and projecting announcements about the drive. At the same time, organized teams approached every home, business, and industrial concern within city limits, asking citizens for scrap and awarding window stickers that proclaimed to one and all that a contribution had been made.[17]

Yet Coatesville's most intriguing innovation was a graphic scoreboard, which planners located on a corner of the city's Victory Scrap Yard. Drive officials would calculate when the scrap collection had accumulated enough material to create a light army tank, then would place a silhouette of that tank on the scoreboard for all to see. It was a compelling way to visualize the city's progress and to encourage scrappers to work harder. By the time the five-day campaign was done, thirty-six tank silhouettes had appeared on the board, representing 340 tons of material for the war effort. Remarkably, that total was an average of 46.68 pounds of scrap for every citizen in the town, a fact which became widely known when Lukens Steel quickly published a twenty-page booklet touting the city's accomplishments and encouraging other locales to do the same.[18]

The third prominent effort took place not long after the Coatesville drive, when a group of Nebraska farmers also found themselves garnering scrap accolades. A cooperative venture among the state salvage committee, USDA, and the Works Progress Administration (WPA) targeted eight counties in northeastern Nebraska as the location for a pilot scrap blitz, soon dubbed the "whip the Jap with scrap" drive. Salvage officials in the state capital first sent mailings to every farmer in the region, asking them to return a postcard indicating how much scrap metal and old rubber they had on hand. The results suggested that the average farm had at least one ton of scrap material that could be gathered. Beginning on April 28, WPA work crews and trucks began to call on Cuming County's farms, with other counties to follow in subsequent weeks (see fig. 3). As with the Coatesville drive, individuals who contributed were recognized, this time with a red, white, and blue symbol painted on a fence post or other visible place outside the home. Furthermore, like the International Harvester campaign, the early Nebraska effort demonstrated that targeting farm scrap was a useful long-term strategy. But what set this particular campaign apart was the unusual synergy among its various sponsors. By pooling their resources, the three government entities had been able to complement each other's strengths. Not only did they end up gathering some 850 tons of scrap material, but they also demonstrated that a cooperative venture was a feasible way to go about it.[19]

Doorly was certainly aware of this last campaign, since his newspaper reported on it several times, and his farm editor traveled to Cuming County to file an on-the-scene report. It is more difficult to establish with any certainty that the publisher was also familiar with the International Harvester and Coatesville campaigns. Still, elements of each of these drives appeared in Doorly's approach, so it is not unreasonable to

3. Cuming County, Nebraska, was the initial focus of an April 1942 scrap blitz. Volunteers are collecting this scrap metal at the farm of Arthur Nossberg near West Point. Image reprinted with permission from the *Omaha World-Herald*.

suggest that he was influenced by them, even if indirectly. For instance, the *World-Herald* campaign — although it was based in a medium-sized city — ended up focusing much of its attention on appeals to farmers and their rich caches of scrap. Doorly's staffers also planned to make their campaign materials available to the state's other newspapers and to radio stations, allowing them to promote the effort locally and to enable personalized connections. Furthermore, the effort would blanket the community with appeals (including the use of a loudspeaker-equipped car) and provide stickers to recognize notable scrap accomplishments. By pooling the resources of the *World-Herald*, local government entities, other media outlets, and countless service groups, the drive also aimed to build a vital spirit of synergy. Finally, like Coatesville, it would provide a kind of scoreboard for everyone to watch. Clearly, the publisher could not claim that these aspects of his plan were original. They were, on the contrary, most likely inspired by similarly minded civilians who were themselves interested in developing a scrap plan.

Nonetheless, there were several important differences between the predecessor drives and Doorly's approach. As the publisher sketched out his plan, and as it was refined in the following days in cooperation with his staffers, these new elements gradually became more apparent. Indeed, a close scrutiny of the campaign offers several telling insights into the Nebraska Plan's strategic vision.

Voice and Vision: Doorly's Scrap Strategy

Thursday, July 2, 1942, was no ordinary day in the *World-Herald* building. That morning, Doorly convened an impromptu meeting with his managing editor, George Grimes, and several other department heads. He shocked them by announcing that the newspaper was about to take on another public cause, one that would put them into the very center of the national scrap situation. They were going to develop a statewide competition, he explained, with the goal of involving every Nebraskan in the effort. To back up the campaign, the newspaper would be offering prize money as well as numerous pages of unpaid advertising. After presenting the outline of his plan, Doorly began making assignments for each department. It was clear that they would need to hurry; the publisher had given them only ten days to prepare for the official announcement.[20]

The urgency was not without reason. Doorly had in mind from the beginning that the Nebraska effort, if it were to meet his jaw-dropping goal of 100 pounds of scrap for every citizen, would become a likely model for other states to emulate. Even operating at top speed, it would take a lot of time to prepare for the statewide effort, to conduct the drive itself, and then to publicize the results. Any states that wanted to follow Nebraska's example would therefore be unable to start their own preparations until at least early September. If the *World-Herald* delayed too long, other states wanting to follow the same plan would risk running up against the colder weather of November, potentially hampering collection at the very time when the mills would most need the scrap metal.[21]

Working rapidly, the new scrap staff thus began to prepare announcement stories and ad copy. Others began the tremendous task of coordination with the business community, the police department, local unions, various state and federal representatives, and many more. In several cases, Doorly's determined nature was necessary right from the start. J. M. Harding, who shared management of the campaign with Grimes, recalled that "we ran into plenty of trouble right away. When we called a meeting of several leaders in Omaha, we discovered more darned reasons why this couldn't be done than even we had imagined." One of the more unexpected skeptics was Mark T. Caster, the state salvage director himself. In conversation with Doorly, Caster remarked that "Nebraska had turned in 15 pounds per capita" already in 1942, and so he doubted "we could get very much more."[22]

But the scrap team was undaunted by pessimistic predictions. As the staffers developed the plan further, their work began to focus on three primary fronts. The first involved the organization of Omaha itself. Such tasks as finding a centralized location for a scrap heap, lining up donated trucks, drivers, and loaders, and arranging for the support of both the mayor and the city council were time-consuming and yet paramount. On a second front, Doorly and his managers also had to focus on persuading key leaders from outside of Omaha to sign up for the drive. Doorly approached the governor's office in Lincoln, for instance, seeking endorsement materials that would encourage all state residents to participate. Simultaneously, the scrap planners contacted both daily and weekly newspapers in greater Nebraska, hoping to persuade them to pledge their assistance. For this purpose, the team prepared a host of promotional materials and made it available to those publishers who expressed initial interest in being part of the drive.[23]

Yet the final front was perhaps the most central, as it involved developing the strategic vision behind the plan itself. Here the scrap team drew on Doorly's creativity to establish the drive's philosophical direction. In order to elevate the campaign from what could easily become a superficial operation into a bona fide movement that would capture national attention, the *World-Herald* needed to consider several important questions:

Who would participate in the drive, and what would motivate them to do so? What would capture their attention, and what would keep them going after the novelty was gone? Perhaps most important, what could the campaign do to help create an enthusiastic population of willing scrappers, one whose citizens would not only heed the drive's call themselves but who would try to persuade their families and neighbors and friends to participate as well?

There were no precise responses to these sorts of questions—or, at least, none appear to have survived in the *World-Herald*'s internal records. In retrospect, however, the campaign's strategic vision is not difficult to discern. When considered together, the text of Doorly's July 12 radio address that introduced the drive to Nebraskans, later recollections from the publisher and others on the newspaper staff, and subsequent national press reports on the effort suggest that the plan's vision was anchored in what one might describe as three paired themes.

The first pair of themes, *competition* and *camaraderie*, represents what is probably the drive's most novel feature. Doorly obviously recognized that an effective means of motivating many Americans is to appeal to their competitive nature. While the Coatesville effort had featured a scoreboard, there was no head-to-head competition. Doorly's innovation was to transform the mundane labor of scrap collection into a contest, one that the most motivated, organized, or skilled team could win. The primary players were to be Nebraska's ninety-three counties, with each contestant's total divided by its official population from the 1940 census to create a level playing field. The *World-Herald* planned to collect reports from each county so that it could publish a daily scoreboard in the form of per capita scrap standings, in a manner similar to baseball standings on the sports page.[24]

Although simple pride and competitiveness might have been sufficient motivation for many counties to participate, Doorly heightened interest in the contest even more by creating a group of prizes. Of the $2,000 in war bonds that he pledged to the campaign, half would go to the county with the top scrap average at the end of the three weeks of competition and $500 would go to the second-place county. The remaining funds in the contest purse would encourage other levels of competition within the state, including prizes for the top business firm, the top individual, and the top junior organization. The *World-Herald* also encouraged Nebraskans to donate their own prize money, and numerous business and service groups soon complied. All of this competition, as Doorly said in his statewide radio address, would help show the nation what "an aggressive, fighting state" could accomplish if it were motivated enough.[25]

On the other hand, the campaign counterbalanced its appeals to competition by repeatedly stressing the value of patriotic camaraderie. The underlying goal of the campaign, after all, was not to recognize the battered survivors of a brutal and divisive contest but rather to bring Nebraskans together in a communal effort to help solve a persistent national problem. Appropriately, Doorly's radio address emphasized the "ruthless, murderous, and efficient" Axis enemy as a contrast to "every red-blooded American" in his audience who would be "willing to do his part in helping win this war." Similarly, the *World-Herald*'s initial advertisement in the campaign, published on a full page the day after the publisher's address, discussed competition and prizes, but at the same time appealed to unity by urging readers to "show the rest of America how Nebraska does the job!"[26] By thus allowing for *both* competition and camaraderie, Doorly's plan helped plant the seeds of a comprehensive effort that would not only captivate and motivate citizens but also bring them together in a common cause.

Meanwhile, a second pair of themes, what one might call *tractors* and *tricycles*, summarizes the breadth as well as the depth of Doorly's approach. As the International Harvester drive had convincingly demonstrated, farm scrap was a vital resource in time of war. Given the added factor of the *World-Herald*'s significant readership in rural areas of the state, it made sense for the campaign to include farmers and ranchers in its organization and appeals. It was probably no coincidence that the three contest judges included not only a state supreme court judge and a college president but also Max Junkin, "winner of master farmer and pasture-forage-livestock awards."[27] The newspaper, in other words, was doing everything it could think of to focus attention on the importance of old tractors, combines, plows, and the many other heavy implements and tools that could be found rusting away on most spreads.

But to focus solely on farm scrap would not only damage the campaign's unifying emphasis, it would also effectively turn away countless other forms of scrap metal. Tricycles, in this view, were just as important to the campaign as tractors. Although most such household items did not weigh very much individually, when collected in a massive sweep they could still be crushed into useful bundles. Moreover, emphasizing scrap of all sorts would include citizens of every stripe, helping to build cohesion in the drive. Even if, say, a child's roller skates were relatively unimportant by themselves, getting that child's enthusiasm involved on behalf of the drive had its own unique value. Simply put, citizens young and old were asked to search for everything with metal content that could be scrapped for the war effort. Doorly even included rubber items in his appeals, probably as a nod to the national rubber campaign that was wrapping up even as his own drive commenced.[28] Even so, the campaign's appeals kept circling back to the state's countless items made of metal, whether they were tractors, tricycles, or anything in between.

The final pair of themes that together capture an important aspect of Doorly's initial vision involve appeals to both *fact* and *fancy*. Marshaling facts was particularly important given the potential skepticism of the target audience. Most Nebraskans on the eve of the *World-Herald* campaign would likely have remembered the previous year's national aluminum drive fiasco, which motivated millions of citizens to act urgently in gathering old pots and pans in central depots, only to see the aluminum heaps remain in place while the government dithered over their fate. Some older citizens would also have been able to remember the aftermath of World War I, when government officials revealed that they had used propaganda techniques on civilians as a means of increasing home front morale.[29] In many respects, then, it would have been natural for the *World-Herald*'s readers to view the new effort with some doubts or even with outright suspicion.

Perhaps for this reason, the scrap planners seemed to sense that fact-based appeals were an indispensable tactical choice, especially at first.

Doorly's radio address, for example, spent roughly half of its broadcast time emphasizing the essential facts of the current wartime context. The enemy was tough, he proclaimed. The United States and its allies could realistically lose the war. The home front itself was a vital part of the effort. All of these observations were widely understood to be facts at the time. In using them, the publisher not only began to establish trust but also laid the groundwork for three further observations: the steel mills were slowing down, the primary trouble was a need for scrap metal, and plenty of scrap metal was available on the home front. These same observations appeared in the drive's initial ad, which treated them together as a single "fact [that] has been reported in recent press dispatches."[30] If some Nebraskans were going to hesitate to commit to the new campaign due to their prior experiences, such fact-based appeals were likely essential.

Yet the drive's emphasis on arguments rooted in fact did not at all eliminate more fanciful sorts of appeals. Most prominent among this type of appeal were consistent references to scrap as a weapon of war. Such colorful and dramatic claims — what Anne Marie Todd has referred to as the "weaponization of waste" — were, of course, exaggerated.[31] Not only did a piece of scrap metal generally bear little resemblance to a weapon, but it might just as easily become part of a new munitions factory's framework as it might become an actual ship or a plane or a tank. But the fanciful appeals would enable the scrappers to see their labor in a new way, in the process helping them to define and justify what they would do during the drive. Indeed, before long the drive's fanciful appeals would provide new ways for civilians to see themselves, too.

Both *fact* and *fancy*, then, were vital themes within Doorly's Nebraska Plan from the start. They joined *competition* and *camaraderie* as well as *tractors* and *tricycles* as paired themes that would consistently emerge within the campaign's appeals and reports. While the *World-Herald*'s effort in some ways followed the lead of predecessor drives, these new themes helped position the Nebraska Plan as an innovative approach to scrap collection. Combined with the newspaper's and Doorly's unexpected strengths in fostering the plan, the drive's novel features were a sign that something special might be developing in the state of Nebraska.

All of the potential in the world, to be sure, was no guarantee that the upcoming drive would succeed. The only factor that Doorly and his scrap team could control as they wrapped up their intense preparations was their own commitment to giving this new idea a fighting chance. No doubt, each member of the team realized that the idea had arisen from the vision of one man and one newspaper. A few might even have known that the actual inspiration emerged from Margaret Doorly's timely challenge. But by the time the publisher's determined voice went out across the vast state on the evening of July 11, 1942, everyone at the *World-Herald* must have known that it would now be up to the people of Nebraska to ensure that Henry's response would be good enough to make a difference.

3

Summertime Scrapping in the City

Omaha, rising far above the muddy waters of the Missouri River, is a scrapper come up the hard way.
—Debs Myers, "The Grain Belt's Golden Buckle," *Holiday*, October 1952

They said it was the smell of money. Visitors to wartime Omaha could hardly disagree, even if the air was disagreeable. After all, the city's stock-yards facility was among the largest in the world, processing millions of cattle, sheep, and pigs every year on its 200-acre site in South Omaha. Here, at the ornate Livestock Exchange Building, ambitious investors made their prairie fortunes even as sweaty laborers worked to slaughter enough livestock to feed a nation. No one who came to this restless city on the Great Plains could overlook its fusion of wealth, toil, and com-motion, particularly when the southerly summertime breezes spread the stockyard's unmistakable odor across the bustling metropolis.[1]

The Omaha stockyards and its teeming synthesis of humans, animals, labor, and ambition were an apt symbol for the conflicted identities of the river city on the eve of World War II. Indeed, the many guises of Omaha were evident to any observer. At the turn of the century, Rudyard Kipling had found it "but a halting-place on the road to Chicago . . . populated entirely by Germans, Poles, Slavs, Hungarians, Croats, Magyars, and all the scum of the Eastern European States." Two generations later, the novelist Carl Jonas pointed eloquently to the city's "bellowing steers being trucked in to the packing houses," its "men in Levis and spike-heeled boots . . . [the] barking dogs, farm wives hanging out wash, and wind, and the transcontinental buses, the great supermarkets, and man himself, perfectible, but imperfect."[2] In its short history, this remarkable settlement had been defined and redefined by the prairie, by its great river, by the explorers and pioneers and their strained relationship with local native tribes, by the railroads, by the cattle industry, and, most of all, by the area's dynamic and varied ethnicities and classes.

Henry Doorly's radio listeners on the evening of July 11, 1942, thus hailed from a variety of demographics, lifestyles, and outlooks. On one level, his message had to appeal to every age range. Many in the audience would have been among the ranks of Omaha's elderly, a multiethnic generation of "oldsters" born as far back as the Civil War and, shortly thereafter, Nebraska's origin as a state in 1867. Thousands of Omaha's middle-aged laborers, career men, and married folks—a generation that had primarily come of age during the Great Depression and its attendant struggles—were also listening to the Saturday night broadcast to hear what the publisher of the *World-Herald* thought was so important. And, of course, many members of the audience would have been local youth, including children from the Omaha Home for Boys and the famed Boys Town campus west of the city limits. In fact, Doorly's heartfelt remarks addressed "the young ladies and gentlemen especially," recognizing that youthful optimism and energy would be necessary if the upcoming drive were to be successful.[3]

On another level, Doorly's local listening audience was composed of a wide range of ethnicities, nationalities, and classes. Thousands of city residents young and old hailed from haphazardly mixed ethnic neighborhoods filled with crowded rooming houses and boxlike but colorful clapboard homes. South Omaha in particular featured a polyglot series of subcommunities, with Czech, Italian, Polish, Irish, and Danish immigrants frequently communicating in the vibrant languages of the old country, their families supported by breadwinners who worked long hours in the packing and railroad industries. The Near North Side, in contrast, was a segregated neighborhood, home to an active though overcrowded community of some 12,000 black citizens. Meanwhile, large numbers of middle-class residents (and more than a few wealthier families), most of them from relatively distant European heritages, clustered around neighborhoods to the west of the downtown area and in annexed areas around the city's periphery.[4]

The Omaha of 1942, then, was less a melting pot and more an under-cooked stew, what one might even call "a cauldron of discontent." Its various ages, neighborhoods, classes, and ethnicities at times got along famously, as when most everyone pitched in to help clean up after the widespread damage of the 1913 Easter tornado. At other times, though, there was friction and even outright violence. The legacy of lynchings and race riots hung over the city, including mob violence targeting the Greektown community in 1909 and the infamous Omaha Race Riot ten years later. At the same time, organized crime, gambling, prostitution, and other vices brought additional undertones to the city's life on the eve of war, even as Omaha's more self-consciously genteel population met at social balls and discussed fine arts and the events of the day.[5]

The *World-Herald* was perhaps the only voice in the early 1940s that could possibly have brought such fractious factions together in a common cause. True, Doorly's newspaper was not the only journalistic outlet in the area. The *Star* and the *Guide*, for example, served thousands of readers in the city's black neighborhoods, while several ethnic publications, such as the Danish-language *Den Danske Pioneer*, were successful ventures in areas to the south of downtown. Yet the *World-Herald* had absorbed its largest competitor, the *Bee-News*, five years before, and so its circulation (over 190,000 in a city with not much more than 220,000 residents) made it easily the most visible and influential newspaper both in the city and across the vast state.[6]

For their part, the city's few radio stations could also have potentially reached much of Omaha's diverse population. Doorly's newspaper, however, was more tangible than fleeting radio messages, a quality that made newsprint inherently more suitable for an ongoing, sustained public campaign. In print, the *World-Herald*'s appeals could be read and read again, could be saved for later reflection, could be passed from wife to husband to children, and could be shared among families in close-knit neighborhoods where only a few individuals subscribed to the publication. The newspaper's ability to print photographs, moreover, offered campaign planners a considerable rhetorical advantage over radio broadcasts, one that would enable Doorly's staffers to provide compelling visual appeals for readers. To be sure, radio's immediacy and inherent drama would prove to be an excellent supplement to the newspaper's scrap metal stories and pictures. But if the drive were to unite Omahans in a common scrap effort, the *World-Herald* would have to be its primary messenger.

Still, the obstacles facing Doorly's ambitious blueprint were formidable. To succeed within the city, the Nebraska Plan would need cooperation, inspiration, leadership, sacrifice, and determination. It would also need some old-fashioned competition. All of these factors played a significant role as Omaha's scrap metal effort proceeded from rallies to readiness, from ads to intrepid news reports, and from small local piles of scrap to the city's top tourist attraction of 1942: the downtown Scrap Mountain. Above it all—the countless scrap volunteers, the wandering trucks, the creative and occasionally bizarre items tossed into heaps of used metal—the stockyards' indelible aroma provided an intermittently pungent backdrop, serving as a frequent reminder of the city's blue-collar, hard-working ethos as well as the striking diversity of its denizens.

Rallying Omaha: The Road to Readiness

Henry Doorly's urgent Saturday evening radio message brought immediate results from some of its listeners. *Life* magazine, in its detailed coverage of the Nebraska Plan's effectiveness, recalled that the first phone call came in to the *World-Herald* building just three minutes after Doorly had signed off the air. The caller was Helen Dodendorf, a housewife in the Florence neighborhood. She told the newspaper's staffers that she had recently seen a sizeable cache of abandoned metal rails and auto parts in a field near the city waterworks. The metal, she lamented, was just "rusting in the mud."[7]

The following morning's *Sunday World-Herald* was quick to build on such initial enthusiasm by dramatizing and magnifying the drive's unveiling. "Nebraska is challenged," blared the front page, "to lead all other states' metal, rubber salvage." Another headline stressed the contest angle, emphasizing that the "*World-Herald* offers $2,000 to spur drive." Yet another proclaimed that "Gov. Griswold commends [the] scrap contest." In all, this Sunday edition provided nine separate stories and one full-page advertisement, all focusing on plans for the emerging scrap drive. It added seven photographs for good measure: portraits of the governor and the four contest judges, and—in a telling precursor of the fanciful appeals to come throughout the campaign—side-by-side images of a crowded scrap yard and a 57-ton tank. It was obvious that Doorly's staff had been working hard to prepare for the dramatic unveiling of the drive.[8]

But it would be another week before the contest actually got under way. Given the distractions of wartime, not to mention the stresses of everyday life, drive officials seemed to realize that there was a realistic chance that the scrap drive would become an afterthought even before it began. The newspaper's challenge in this intermediate week, then, was to build public interest instead of losing it, thereby readying Omaha's citizens for a truly massive undertaking. Put simply, in order for the *World-Herald*'s readers to become relentless scrap collectors, they needed not only to understand *why* they were being asked to act but to become *impassioned* about doing so.

An important aspect of the newspaper's attempt to ready the public involved adopting a reasoned, educational tone, one that was based in the twin themes of fact and fancy. Here the drive planners published a series of features and columns aimed at informing readers and answering their questions about the need for scrap steel. Among the first such articles was the matter-of-fact editorial "What You Can Do." The account patiently explained that the country's typical "open-hearth method" of steelmaking "requires the use of a considerable percentage of old metal—about half, according to the usual formula." Unfortunately, "last winter more than 30 steel mills were obliged to halt their operations for varying periods because they had run out of scrap," meaning that now "we haven't . . .

as many tanks and guns . . . as we might have had." A similar message emerged a few days later during a fifteen-minute radio sketch, which warned listeners that "mills would be slowing down without scrap" from "Mr. and Mrs. Nebraska." The conclusion to be drawn from these educational appeals, and many others from that week, was fairly obvious: the *World-Herald*'s readers simply *must* take the upcoming drive seriously, since there was in fact a shortage of scrap metal in the country, and its effect on the war effort was potentially disastrous.[9]

If the newspaper's educational tone was based on facts at times, at other times its tone relied on fanciful conceptions, which imagined for readers just where their scrap might end up. The July 14 issue, for instance, told readers that a single "garbage pail" could be turned into "one thousand .30 caliber cartridges," while "if you and nine neighbors each could round up an old kitchen stove you'd have sufficient steel to furnish the army with a scout car." The article even provided a useful pictogram to demonstrate visually these sorts of fanciful transformations. The diagram showed a steam iron next to a drawing of two combat helmets, an equals sign helpfully placed in between them. The same sort of visual equivalence matched up a set of golf clubs and a machine gun.[10]

The director of the *World-Herald*'s household arts department, Maude Coons, provided an even more fanciful equation for her readers, this one in the form of a scrap recipe. Among numerous other items, Coons suggested starting out with "one double-acting threshing machine," "one-half cup fancy chopped razor blades," and "three-fourths bushel assorted bolts." After sifting and measuring the concoction (and "garnish[ing] with pitchforks"), the resulting "devil's food recipe" would be served "at 1,500 degrees Fahrenheit, right down Hitler's throat."[11] Clearly such equivalents bordered on fantasy. Yet the fact that a significant proportion of the home front's scrap generally *would* become war munitions of some sort was always present in the background. Either way, the newspaper's scrap team seemed to be adopting an educational tone in order to convince readers that participating in the upcoming drive was vital.

While the *World-Herald*'s educational strategy appealed to readers' sense of reason, a second aspect of its approach in the week before the drive appealed to the city's passions. Financially motivated scrappers always had the option of accepting cash for their caches, but receiving payment from the local salvage yard was not always enough incentive to participate. The drive's planners thus elected, probably wisely, to give citizens patriotic reasons to participate as well. In this regard, the most obvious step was to hold a massive rally.

Ironically, the idea for the initial scrap rally came not from the *World-Herald*'s staffers but from the Omaha-based Union Pacific Railroad (UP) and its charismatic president, William Jeffers. Early in the planning process for the drive, Doorly had sought the support of Jeffers, who was a fellow resident of the city. At the time, the UP chief had been on an inspection tour of railroad facilities in western states. However, neither the distance nor the impersonal nature of frequent telegrams could disguise his enthusiasm for the scrap competition plans. Jeffers immediately seized on Doorly's idea, becoming an unexpectedly central figure in the Nebraska Plan.[12]

In retrospect, "Bull" Jeffers was a perfect champion to enlist. A native of North Platte, Nebraska, he had worked for the UP most of his life, starting out at the age of 14 as a lowly office boy, then steadily working his way up to become the railroad's chief executive. Along the way he had developed a reputation for toughness, due perhaps to his extreme intolerance for slackers and his history of knocking out insubordinate employees with one punch. In describing Jeffers's feistiness, one admiring profile even suggested that he "has been around locomotives so long that he vaguely resembles one."[13]

Yet the UP's leader was also known for his personal and detail-oriented leadership; in some accounts, he is alleged to have known over 10,000 of his employees by their first names. Indeed, he seemed to be less comfortable in his Omaha office than he was on the rails with his workers, occasionally jumping in to spell an engineer or to advise a luxury passenger car's hostess on proper etiquette. This direct, results-oriented nature made Jeffers not only respected but also revered by UP's employees. As one subordinate suggested, the UP president's "effectiveness lies in knowing what he wants and then getting just that."[14]

Jeffers had been grappling with the scrap problem even before Doorly. Heeding the government's pleas for scrap metal, the UP had begun a massive internal drive earlier in the summer. The organization's employees had gathered scrap at every rail yard and corporate location as well as along thousands of miles of railways, collecting over 3,000 tons for the steel mills in only a few weeks. Thus, when Doorly sought the UP chief's assistance, Jeffers was an instant convert. It soon became clear that the *World-Herald* could not have found a more influential and driven supporter. In the words of Omaha citizen V. A. Bradshaw, when "William Jeffers . . . gets back of Mr. Doorly in this salvage campaign it is a foregone conclusion it will be a complete success."[15]

In offering advice for Doorly's ambitious statewide plan, Jeffers recommended that a public rally take place after the newspaper's splash introduction of the drive but before the contest officially opened. The UP chief even insisted that the railroad itself sponsor the rally, with the public invited to participate. Intriguingly, Doorly and Jeffers agreed that rally attendees should have an unusual entrance fee: at least five pounds of scrap material. UP employees and members of the public would be asked to pile their admission fees on the street outside the meeting, not only creating visible and dramatic evidence of the city's desire to gather scrap for the war effort but also jump-starting the upcoming drive under the public's watchful eye.[16]

One of the *Sunday World-Herald*'s nine scrap stories on July 12, then, was the enthusiastic announcement of the UP rally. The event was to take place the following day, at 7:30 p.m. "Another 'shot heard 'round the world' will be fired Monday night," related the newspaper, "when the Union Pacific Railroad stages a giant rally at the city auditorium." The Monday morning edition of the *World-Herald* featured a full-page ad for the rally and also revealed that the auditorium's doors would open at 6 p.m., but that the public could start contributing to the "big junk pile" by early afternoon. Several hours before the rally, a noticeable heap of salvage material had indeed begun to appear. Even though less than forty-eight hours had elapsed since Doorly's radio address, it was apparent that scores of Omahans were already in the scrap.[17]

4. The Union Pacific scrap rally from behind the main floor audience. Image courtesy of the Douglas County Historical Society, reprinted with permission from the *Omaha World-Herald*.

At the rally itself, reported the UP's employee newsletter, "patriotic citizens jammed the auditorium to the rafters." The railroad's own drum and bugle corps provided inspiring music to set the mood, and crowd sing-alongs helped to create a sense of camaraderie (see fig. 4). Crucially, the enthusiastic audience featured a diverse mix of Omahans, including blue-collar members of the UP's rank-and-file, children, housewives, and representatives of the city's various ethnic neighborhoods. By all accounts, each of them applauded wildly when Jeffers's assistant, Paul Rigdon, announced that twenty-three UP employees—and twenty-one

UP spouses—were dropping their regular duties for the duration of the drive; they were about to become full-time scrappers in the *World-Herald*'s competition.[18]

Among the numerous speakers at the rally, Omaha mayor Dan Butler offered what was perhaps the most direct appeal to the enthused crowd (see fig. 5). "I call upon every resident of Omaha, young and old, to join us in this collection. . . . Search the attics, the basements, the yards, the vacant lots, and every place where metal may be found. Turn in every bit of it." Nebraska salvage committee head Mark T. Caster took a different approach, referencing civic responsibility in time of war: "Does any red-blooded American dare to face the future with the knowledge that he has in his possession materials . . . which Uncle Sam needs to make guns?" Such challenging rhetoric, commented the *World-Herald* with approval, quickly turned the rally into "a brass-tacks affair that bodes no good for Hitler and Hirohito."[19]

Meanwhile, another crowd had gathered outside the auditorium, relegated to listening in on the rally through a public address system. Although no doubt many in the group were disappointed not to have made it inside, the newspaper confided that most of them "were having too much fun watching the scrap heap grow" to be upset. In fact, there seemed to be dozens of fascinating stories in the pile. Various items included "the body of a car with a California license, the gleaming swords that had slapped the sides of many a smart young captain, a youngster's tricycle, [and] a battered alarm clock that had sent many a yawning man to his daily work." For a short time, there was even a set of $35 tools atop the pile, although the tools were quickly retrieved when their annoyed owner discovered them missing from his parked car.[20]

In all, reported the *World-Herald*, the rally's collective admission fees amounted to 53 tons of material, which were soon hauled to the local salvage yard in fifty truckloads to begin the sorting process. But most observers felt that this first collection arising from the Nebraska Plan was more than just a large pile of metal. "There was something as personal in that huge heap of odds and ends," wrote the newspaper, "as sending your own brother, son, or husband to the front lines. . . . It was metal

5. The stage lineup for the Union Pacific scrap rally in Omaha's Civic Auditorium, July 13, 1942. Image courtesy of the Douglas County Historical Society, reprinted with permission from the *Omaha World-Herald*.

torn from the heart of Midwestern homes and basements," as well as "a message in metal of the Nebraskan's defiance to the Axis, concrete evidence to the men over there that the home folks are doing something beside[s] reading the accounts of their daring."[21]

In many respects, then, Doorly's radio address, the *World-Herald*'s educational coverage, and the stirring UP rally seemed to have been successful at enthusing a significant number of Omahans about scrap collection. True, not everyone had received the message. Two days after the rally, for instance, a merchant near the intersection of 11th and Jackson witnessed a large truck dumping a load of junk metal in the center of the vacant block across the street. After several hours, the pile had not been disturbed, so the merchant called a local scrap dealer, who paid $1.50 for the load and hauled it away. Unfortunately, both men soon found themselves at police headquarters. There they learned that the empty block was about to become the primary site for the city's scrap pile and that they had effectively stolen the very first load. The *World-Herald*'s mirthful headline writers had some fun the next day at the defendants' expense: "Here Are 2 Men Who Now Know about Scrap Drive."[22]

For many other residents of Omaha, however, the pre-drive publicity blitz had been a bit more successful. Much of the city was frankly abuzz with anticipation as the drive's opening approached. Several neighborhood rallies and events that week, including a musical extravaganza hosted by the Negro Chamber of Commerce, confirmed that communities and neighborhoods were responding to the newspaper's dramatic pleas.[23] The evidence was accumulating that the diverse populace might just be able to work together. Omaha, it seemed, was nearly ready; it was time for the *World-Herald*'s scrap team to begin the drive in earnest.

The Scoop on the Scrap Story

"Men! Women! Children! This job is YOURS! It is urgent. It is vital. We MUST NOT fail our boys in the service." It was July 19, 1942, and the *Sunday World-Herald*'s full-page appeal was firing the opening salvo of an intense campaign barrage for all of Omaha to see. "Today, gather up all the scrap you can find," exhorted the ad. "Here is your chance to do one job that is vitally needed NOW.... We must not fail!"[24]

The newspaper's sense of urgency on the drive's first official day was clearly directed at its readers. It would be members of the public, after all, who would find, gather, and haul the bulk of the scrap material. Conversely, if the citizens of Doorly's own city failed to embrace the drive, the effort would inevitably turn into an embarrassing failure. The intense language of the opening day's ad confirmed this notion: "Only you know where your scrap is. Only you can find it and bring it out where it will be used. Success depends on you."[25]

Despite the drive's emphatic stress on the need for public participation, however, the level of participation *within* the *World-Herald* building was already at a fever pitch. "I wanted every department in the newspaper," Doorly said later, "to look upon it as its personal job." Not surprisingly, the staffers did exactly what the boss wanted: the newspaper's entire family, from Doorly's office to the typesetters to the secretarial pool to the various editors, all found ways to contribute. Even the young news carriers stationed throughout the city became a vital part of the effort.[26]

What made this extraordinary undertaking all the more stressful, of course, was that the avalanche of scrap drive stories and events and phone calls from the public did not change the fact that the staffers still had to produce two editions of the newspaper six days of the week, not to mention the big Sunday paper. Lawrence Youngman, the lead reporter on many of the scrap stories, wrote at the time that "I am handling one of the most important assignments—perhaps the most important—that I have ever had." The newspaper "has launched a state-wide scrap salvage campaign in which we hope to set a record for the whole nation to shoot at." The drive's urgency, in his view, was formidable: "I've never seen so much pressure put behind anything in this state before."[27]

Two principal figures on Doorly's staff helped apply the pressure by supervising the newspaper's multifaceted scrap effort with a passionate flair. J. M. Harding, known in some quarters as the "hardheaded assistant publisher," and George Grimes, the *World-Herald*'s managing editor, became Doorly's chiefs of scrap, opening an office dedicated to the campaign. From this operational base, they methodically organized regular planning sessions, fielded phone calls from readers with tips and suggestions for the drive, coordinated with city and state officials, and assigned reporting challenges. It was "an all-out effort" by the staff, recalled Harding. Despite the inevitable hardships, however, everyone within the building seemed to feel that they were working on a meaningful task. "It stirred them so deeply," Harding related, that "it got clear down to the bottom of their shoes."[28]

For their part, many of the newspaper's staff reporters quickly found themselves intimately involved in the drive's activities. A few days before the official start of the contest, for instance, Ernest Jones embarked on a quest to see "how much scrap iron could be collected . . . in an eight-hour day." Thinking strategically, he decided to track down obsolete safes in the downtown area. In that day's evening edition, he reported that by knocking on business doors and following numerous leads, he had found 18 tons of derelict safes and, somewhat unexpectedly, four tons of farm machinery. "I still have until 6 o'clock tonight to go on this drive," he wrote, "so if you've got one of these old clunkers . . . why don't you call me or leave word [that] the salvage committee can have it?" "If you haven't a safe," he added impulsively, "I'm not finicky; [an] old iron bridge, a bank vault, or a locomotive is just as good."[29]

Jones may have regretted adding that final line, as the *World-Herald*'s dedicated scrap hotline soon became inundated with calls for him. In addition to safes, callers dutifully provided tips on a few abandoned bridges and even an unused locomotive. The next day, the reporter tallied the long list of scrap metal items he had been offered and expressed his sheepish appreciation to readers; in his playful words, "You 'safed' my day yesterday." He then ruefully recounted the unexpected final destination of his quest, an exhausting incident in which he found himself in a field on the grounds of Omaha's Immanuel Deaconness Institute, helping several citizens dig up a heavy safe that had been buried there years earlier. As Jones had apparently discovered, there was no way to remain at a distance from the public's growing awareness of the need for scrap.[30]

Reporter Bill Billotte also found a way to experience the scrap drive in a personal way. On Monday, July 20, the first day that a fleet of volunteer trucks combed specific Omaha neighborhoods, Billotte was assigned to grab a camera, jump into the passenger seat of driver Robert Burk's truck, and report what he saw. With the reporter gamely taking detailed notes and snapping pictures, the 3-ton truck stopped at scores of houses along its twelve-square-block route in the Florence neighborhood. At nearly every home, noted Billotte, residents either had created a pile for the truck to collect or came to the curb themselves, carrying what they could.

As the morning progressed, Billotte soon found himself leaving his notebook and camera in the truck so that he could jump out to load scrap at every opportunity. He then helped Burk unload the truck downtown at the city's official scrap lot. Like Jones before him, Billotte was drawn into his own story. Fortunately, the reporter seemed to be in good humor despite the unplanned labor. As the *World-Herald*'s description put it to readers, here was one reporter who "held up his end — and liked it."[31]

Billotte pursued his scrapping tour of duty the rest of the day, continuing to note his experience for readers. Significantly, his most indelible impression of the day's events had little to do with the daunting amounts of scrap metal that he and Burk had gathered, nor did it focus on the unusual items in the residential heaps. Instead, Billotte's attention fixated on the nature of the scrappers themselves. The opening lines of his story put it this way: "I saw an inspiring spectacle today. From the pitching deck of a scrap metal truck, I saw the housewives of Omaha go to war . . . just as surely as if they were embarking for the front lines with a tommygun under each arm."[32]

Billotte's colorful account punctuated this remark by prominently featuring his photograph of Mrs. J. J. Stewart, a housewife whose home was one of many that had given up a large collection of scrap material that day (see fig. 6). The captivating image, which ran on the front page of the next two issues (as well as in a full-page advertisement on July 26), was noteworthy for two reasons. First, in what might have been a shock for many readers, it joined Billotte's accompanying story in focusing not on the masculine aspects of the drive but on the primary role of women in the exhausting effort. "Omaha housewives," confirmed the newspaper's caption, "are scrap-ironing the Axis."[33] This perspective was surely both surprising and persuasive. If the reading public's impression of scrap metal and munitions had previously provided room only for muscle-bound laborers and courageous male warriors, the Stewart photograph was a powerful corrective, not to mention an efficient means of encouraging Omaha's women to participate in an activity that may not have felt very welcoming to them at first.

Stewart's picture was also noteworthy because it subtly proposed a visual extension of the drive's fanciful transformation of metal into munitions. Readers could easily see that the homemaker was holding a tail pipe, not a rifle. Yet the way she *held* the pipe was reminiscent of a soldier's port arms position. In fact, the image went further. Not only did it portray scrap as a kind of armament; it also planted the suggestion that the civilians wielding those armaments—a group that obviously included far more than just Omaha's adult males—were actually *soldiers* engaged in

6. Mrs. J. J. Stewart holding a martial pose with her scrap. Image courtesy of the Douglas County Historical Society, reprinted with permission from the *Omaha World-Herald*.

battle against the enemy.[34] Here was a tremendous rhetorical appeal, one that would reappear in numerous formats and contexts as the campaign reached its climax.

In hindsight, however, the Stewart image is useful in another way, serving as a telling reminder of the unusually collaborative behind-the-scenes effort Doorly's scrap team had put together. Ordinarily, a picture and story originating from an assignment reporter would have no effect whatsoever on the activities of the advertising department. Yet in this case, the scrap campaign had relaxed such artificial barriers, allowing the development of a fluid and creative spirit within the newspaper building. Harding later recalled thinking that the *World-Herald* team "would either have to make this an all-out effort or it would be unsuccessful."[35] Consequently, even as he and Grimes orchestrated the drive's metaphorical battle lines, they were also careful to foster an internal synergy, a mood that encouraged every staffer to work together toward their common goal.

After a week or so of experimentation and improvisation, the newspaper's unorthodox team began to mature into an efficient and motivated publicity machine. Hence it was no real surprise that Bud Abbott and Lou Costello, arriving in Omaha on July 30 for a previously scheduled war bond sales show, instantly found themselves drafted by reporters into scrap duty. Donning borrowed overalls, the comedy duo, with journalists in tow, got onto a scrap truck that was making rounds near 24th and Dodge Street. After scrapping in their own peculiar way ("Hey! You got any old stoves, bathtubs, or washing machines up there?"), the two good-naturedly bickered for the record on the return trip:

"What have we been doing this morning," asked Costello. "Wasting our time?"

"No," retorted Abbott, "we have been collecting scrap."

"Scrap what? We haven't been fighting!"

"I don't mean that," Abbott replied after a thoughtful pause. "We have been collecting scrap metal. Scrap. Like scrap meat."

After playing around with the idea of *scrap* for a while, however, the two became serious. Said Costello: "We know we have both been broadcasting on the most important program on Earth this morning—congratulations, Nebraska."[36] It was the first celebrity endorsement of the Nebraska Plan, but for the increasingly confident scrap team, it was just one more scoop among many as the effort gathered speed.

As it turned out, *World-Herald* staffers may have gotten more than they bargained for when they agreed to support Doorly's initiative. But amidst the planning, the late nights, and the pressure, the team also found that it was promoting an unprecedented social and civic event, one that was having a direct (and often entertaining) impact on the city's citizens. Even more impressive, this emerging group of scrappers was building a tangible and dramatic arsenal of scrap metal that would soon be the envy of the nation. For this reason, the *World-Herald* team's attention, and that of the entire city, gradually found itself focusing more and more on the tremendous events taking place on that formerly empty city block at 11th and Jackson.

Making a Mountain from Molehills

On Tuesday, July 28, an official from the U.S. Office of Price Administration (OPA) came across a stunning sight. He had arrived at Omaha's passenger station on a business trip, and his taxi took the most direct route to his hotel. It so happened that the route took him due north on 10th Street, directly past an enormous, blockwide mass of scrap metal, its flanks teeming with noise and activity (see fig. 7). The official, shocked almost beyond words, dropped off his luggage at the hotel and "immediately . . . hotfooted it back to the lot to talk to the men who were in charge." He had himself been in the salvage business for fifteen years, and so he was well aware of the government's desperate pleas for scrap metal. Yet he readily acknowledged that he had never seen anything like Omaha's Scrap Mountain. As he told campaign officials, "I'm not ashamed to tell you that it brings tears to my eyes. It is one of the most inspiring sights I have seen in the country."[37]

The *World-Herald*'s drive had been ongoing for ten days when the OPA's representative took note of Omaha's efforts. That Tuesday, in fact, had been the most frenetic day yet, with no less than forty-two volunteer scrap trucks and numerous private vehicles adding some 275 tons of scrap material—over half a million pounds—to a heap already bursting with 1,375 tons of previous contributions. It was a new daily record, achieved even though the trucks had filled up so quickly that they had had time to cover only half of their assigned routes for the day.[38]

All of this commotion meant that the government official was not alone in his revelatory experience nor in his astounded reaction to coming upon the huge pile of metal. By this point in the drive, in fact, the heap had grown to dimensions so tremendous that it began to attract awestruck observers by the dozens. Many of these "railbirds," to use

7. Omaha's Scrap Mountain in late July 1942. Image reprinted with permission from the *Omaha World-Herald*.

Bill Billotte's term for them, were locals. Yet *Life* magazine later pointed out that more than a few of them were out-of-town visitors who were brought downtown by their hosts to witness for themselves the "scrap pile [that] made history."[39]

In many respects, then, there was reason to be optimistic as the *World-Herald*'s scrap campaign steamed past its halfway point. While the city's per capita totals thus far were lagging significantly behind Doorly's initial goal of 100 pounds per citizen, no one could deny that the Scrap Mountain had become a visible testament to both determination and civic pride. And if visitors, especially representatives of the Roosevelt administration, happened to be impressed with the gigantic heap of used metal, so much the better. After all, the campaign's original purpose had been to impress others by setting an extremely high standard for scrap metal collection, one that would motivate other U.S. citizens to do the same.[40]

For his part, the OPA official asked numerous questions of the drive's organizers during his visit, as it was his intent to inform his superiors of the city's achievement. The most crucial question, of course, was also the most essential: *How had they done it?* This question is still worth considering, as the road from small neighborhood scrap piles to Scrap Mountain provides many insights into the initial success of the Nebraska Plan, not to mention the later national drive that was modeled on it.

No doubt, the official received plentiful responses, since the many facets of the campaign each had something to contribute to its success. One response, for instance, would likely have focused on the drive's consistent use of inspirational stories to motivate the populace. Whether it was the series of features on Mrs. C. T. Brewer (a resident who had used her own car to canvass a 10-square-mile area, producing more than 20 tons of scrap metal), or the profile of R. C. Wellshear (an insurance supervisor who gave up his summer vacation so that he and his children could work full time hauling scrap), the newspaper's coverage of the drive was filled with overtly inspiring narratives. The *World-Herald*, of course, did not hesitate to point to these narratives as examples to be emulated by readers.[41]

Another possible response to the OPA official's question could have focused on the role of competition in motivating residents to gather scrap metal. To be sure, most everyone realized that metropolitan Douglas County had little chance in the county vs. county race; the farming and ranching areas of the state were far too rich in the heaviest grades of scrap for the city to compete on a per capita basis. Yet there was still a healthy amount of competition among various groups and residents within Omaha. For example, many service clubs, church organizations, sewing circles, and veterans groups challenged their counterparts to spirited scrap races, each one carefully weighing their respective piles of used metal before sending them on their journey downtown. In some cases, in fact, civic organizations and businesses donated prize money above and beyond the *World-Herald*'s original awards in order to motivate such local competition and to keep the city's heaps growing.[42]

Still another response from those trying to explain how the modest piles on the city's countless curbside collections had somehow turned into this gigantic downtown collection of metal could have pointed to the logistics of the campaign's constant scrap reminders. As it turned out, the fact that almost every household was prepared when a scrap truck arrived on the scheduled day was no accident. In order to facilitate the process, Red Cross block chairs asked households to prepare their scrap metal several days in advance of a neighborhood pickup. The day before the truck was to arrive, local Boy Scout troops circulated through the neighborhood, reminding residents to begin transporting their personal household scrap to the curb. That evening, a loudspeaker-equipped car, donated by the Metropolitan Utilities District, announced "Put out your scrap" over and over again as it traveled through the streets (see fig. 8). The following morning, Girl Scouts walked ahead of the trucks, knocking on residents' doors if no scrap was already at the curb. Finally, Camp Fire Girls and local church organizations made house calls on subsequent days to ensure that everything had been collected at every household in the area.[43] Such thorough organization was, of course, a testament to the newspaper's scrap planners. More to the point, however, it undoubtedly played a vital role in ensuring the Scrap Mountain's steady growth.

Each of these responses to the OPA official's question would have been useful for his report. Yet a careful examination of the *World-Herald*'s scrap coverage in the first half of the campaign suggests yet another possible response, albeit one that requires a bit more detail. This last explanation locates an important source of the city's ability to gather so much scrap in a strategy that modern-day campaign managers might call *segmentation*.

With Omaha's population topping 200,000 by the early 1940s, it would probably have been impossible for the *World-Herald* to describe an average resident in any generalizable way. Indeed, the city may have been as culturally and socially diverse as any similarly sized population center in the United States at the time. Appealing in a uniform manner to such a wide-ranging group of backgrounds, interests, ages, financial situations, and the like would have been a challenge under almost any circumstance. But when the appeal requested significant changes in both attitude and behavior—not to mention some form of physical labor—its chances of success diminished rapidly.[44]

The *World-Herald*'s scrap planners apparently recognized the inherent difficulties in appealing to diverse elements of the city with an

8. Omaha's Metropolitan Utilities District donated the use of this loudspeaker-equipped vehicle to alert residents of an upcoming scrap pickup. Image reprinted with permission from the *Omaha World-Herald*.

undifferentiated approach. To overcome this problem, they first provided comprehensive scrap coverage—incredibly, up to ten columns a day—with a variety of stories, features, and columns, all in an attempt to appeal to an array of constituencies. Second, the campaign encouraged and at times even fostered the establishment of what one might call drives within the drive. Specifically, the *World-Herald* strategically targeted the drive's community outreach efforts so that subcultures and social groups of various stripes could experience the campaign from their own perspective.[45]

To illustrate, consider the scrap drive's approach to citywide sports activities. Since the campaign took place in the heat of summer, numerous athletic events were scheduled over the same time period. Rather than try to abbreviate or cancel these activities, the newspaper built the campaign *around* them. Before long, baseball and softball games were requiring scrap material from spectators, and one softball outfit even promised to bench its own players if they themselves failed to bring scrap to a game. Golf courses inaugurated a heated competition with each other, their employees and members pitching in to comb clubhouses, fairways, and maintenance facilities for elusive metal treasure. Local tennis pros insisted that their students provide scrap in exchange for lessons, while Omaha's trap shooting club sponsored a popular "bullets for buzzards" competition. In this way, the scrap campaign allowed sports-crazed segments of the city to embrace both their passion and the drive. In fact, as the *World-Herald* pointed out, by July 29 Omaha's sports community had gathered 47 tons of scrap material for Uncle Sam.[46]

Another segment of Omaha's populace that embraced a drive-within-the-drive mentality was the business and industrial community. The *World-Herald*'s drive organizers were well aware that inside city limits the heaviest caches of scrap were likely to be found in warehouses, factories, mechanical sites, and storefronts. Gaining access to these venues was the specialty of Allen A. Tukey, a World War I hero and head of a chamber of commerce scrap team. Tukey and his corps of 140 volunteers—the commandos unit, as they were called—took their task seriously. They organized Omaha's business culture into districts, and then smaller squadrons arranged tours of their assigned premises with the owners or managers as personal guides. Realizing that lower-level employees were unlikely to release a business's potential scrap to the drive, the unit adopted the slogan "It takes the boss to get rid of scrap!" Omaha's Harding Creamery was one host of such a personalized tour, resulting in the designation of 20 tons of scrap material after only one hour with the organization's president. Even the *World-Herald* subjected itself to one of Tukey's tours, a visit which furnished the drive with 9 tons of antique press machines that had been in permanent storage.[47] As with Omaha's sports community, then, the business and industrial interests in the city found themselves immersed in a specialized component of the overall campaign, an effort that added vast amounts of scrap material to the city's growing collection.

Not to be left out, the city's youngsters also found that aspects of the scrap drive were adaptable to their own interests and abilities. For instance, organizers encouraged Camp Fire Girls, Boy Scouts, and Girl Scouts to compete with their peer groups — even as they participated in organized truck routes in their neighborhoods. Schools, too, engaged in hearty scrap races; the competition was so keen that many students went to great lengths to get ahead of their peers. Scrapper Melba Glock, for example, recalls that her cousin "had somehow got a large magnet." After tying it to a string, she adds, "We kids went up and down the alleys collecting whatever would stick to that magnet." But if plain old competition was not enough to motivate such youngsters, even more incentive was available in the *World-Herald*'s coveted "Scrap Scout" badge, awarded only to those children who had gathered at least 25 pounds of scrap. "These badges," advised the newspaper, "will be handed out by the truck drivers, who will have explicit instructions to see that they are given only when earned." No wonder, the account reflected with pride, that kids were contributing to the drive "from early morning until late in the afternoon," hauling their scrap "on bicycles with handlebar baskets loaded, pulling coaster wagons and in one instance pushing a hand truck." While such young scrappers probably produced lower volumes of scrap than other subgroups in the city, there was no matching their enthusiasm.[48]

Of course, it was true that the *World-Herald*'s segmentation strategy could not address every constituency and community within the city limits, at least not consistently. Anyone discussing the scrap campaign's approach with the curious OPA official would have had to acknowledge that the space in the newspaper was finite, as was the time the staffers could devote to developing outreach plans that were adapted to specific groups. Yet the tremendous level of participation in scrap collection by Omaha's residents in its many neighborhoods suggests that the newspaper was successful in reaching most of its diverse audience.

Even some of the city's racial and ethnic divides, perhaps the most difficult fissures to reach across in the prejudiced world of the 1940s, seemed to have narrowed somewhat during the campaign. Judging from reports in the *Omaha Star*, for instance, the Near North Side's largely

9. Many of Omaha's communities held local scrap rallies during the *World-Herald*'s drive. Here S. Edward Gilbert weighs new contributions after a Near North Side rally as the Rev. L. A. Story (background) and Richard Stanley (right) observe. Image reprinted with permission from the *Omaha World-Herald*.

segregated black community embraced scrap collection with enthusiasm, sponsoring neighborhood scrap rallies and providing special prizes for top area scrappers (see fig. 9). The various ethnic communities on the city's South Side also gathered scrap at an impressive rate. As one drive official testified, "It's the communities which have a large percentage of people of foreign nationality that are responsible" for the rapid collection pace in South Omaha. Francis P. Kawa, president of the city's Polish American federation, was not surprised, reminding readers that "we must all work together . . . to bring victory for our country."[49]

No matter their ethnicity, social group, age, sex, or political affiliation, then, it was evident in that final week of July that the city's diverse residents had tacitly agreed to set aside their many differences for the sake of the scrap campaign. The boundless *World-Herald* coverage had educated and impassioned them even as it provided them with stories of inspiration and sacrifice. Numerous local efforts had augmented the campaign and brought the need for scrap home to ever-smaller portions of the populace. From it all, this midwestern city's tremendously divergent components had banded together, creating a veritable mountain out of sundry molehills of scrap. Indeed, it was likely that Omaha's fabled Scrap Mountain had already become the largest municipal scrap heap in the country's history.[50]

To be sure, Omaha's residents were well aware that much more work remained. Not only was their own Douglas County lagging behind in its quest to hit 100 pounds per person, but it was trailing the county vs. county competition quite badly. In fact, the *World-Herald* employees whose task it was to provide coverage on the campaign in other areas of Nebraska knew that Henry Doorly's scrap contest had produced several impressive and dramatic scrapping efforts outside the city. Omaha's scrappers, the staffers realized, could learn a lot from some of these rural cousins.

As the final, climactic week of the campaign neared, however, all eyes in Omaha kept returning irresistibly to the monumental operation at 11th and Jackson. The site was active from dawn to dusk and then guarded at night from potential thefts. But even the quieter moments at Scrap Mountain occasionally featured the infectious spirit of the campaign. Several dozen pianos had been donated to the drive, and a few were still in working order even as they awaited processing amidst the maze of old metal. The pianos, as one might expect, proved irresistible to the watchmen who could pick out a tune, and at times those on duty would gather to sing quiet melodies. Thus it was not unusual for evenings at the scrap heap to be filled with drifting songs of patriotism and of nostalgia and of war. And on those hot July nights when the pungent southerly breezes happened to enhance the peaceful summer tableau with the distinct scent of money, so to speak, it was just one more reminder that this was Omaha in wartime, and just about anything was possible.[51]

4

Mobilizing Greater Nebraska

It's every county for itself and the larger the county the harder it will fall before us.
—"Dundy Holding Third in State Salvage Drive,"
Benkelman Post and News-Chronicle (1942)

The region of the Great Plains that the Otoe tribe once called *Nibrathka* has long embodied a sort of wilderness in the imagination of its visitors. Lieutenant Zebulon Pike's 1806 description of this area of the country as being akin to an African desert set the tone for later impressions. In 1820, Major Stephen H. Long and Dr. Edwin James journeyed west from what would one day become Council Bluffs, Iowa. James, notes the historian Ralph C. Morris, "described the country as having grown less pleasant, less abundantly supplied with game, and less fertile with every mile." For his part, Major Long published a detailed map of the region and famously affixed the label "Great Desert" on what would eventually become the border between Kansas and Nebraska. Long's map was highly influential, shaping perceptions of the territory for generations. By 1904, then, it was no surprise to find that a British writer, R. B. Townsend, was casually using the phrase "great empty Plains" to describe the area.[1]

While the gradual flowering of much of Nebraska under plow and harrow effectively refuted claims that the area was in fact a desert, Townsend's description was arguably a reasonable fit for much of the state, even as late as 1942. He was certainly correct in describing Nebraska's vast reaches as *great*. Pioneers traveling west by caravan on the Great Platte River Road had understood this notion well, since their daily pace typically kept them within the future state's borders for over a month. By the war years, of course, one could drive that same route, if one could somehow get around the gas rationing. But the slow highway speeds required by the war emergency—not to mention the frequently poor condition of rural roads—made such a long trip inadvisable at best. In some respects, passenger trains would have been a more efficient means of moving around the state's great spaces during the war. But since trains carrying either troops or military equipment had the right of way on the rails, even regular passenger service was often disrupted, inefficient, and uncomfortable. Remarkably, Nebraska's great distances seemed to have become even greater under the stresses of war.[2]

Townsend's use of the word *empty* also still had merit, at least in a relative sense. Nebraska's population density in 1940 hovered at just over 17 people per square mile, a rate that put it at thirty-seventh among the forty-eight states. Yet one in every five of those Nebraskans hailed from Omaha's Douglas County, an area whose 340 square miles made up only a tiny fraction of the state's territory. West of Omaha, the concentration of citizens dwindled considerably. In fact, Lincoln's 82,000 people represented the only other grouping of more than 25,000 residents. In the western half of the state, reported the Federal Writers' Project in 1939, the "fields give way to the great cattle ranches of the sandhill area . . . [and] the Old West still survives." In this pastoral region, the writers concluded in apparent awe, "one can travel for hours without finding a sign of human habitation." By 1942 it had been more than eighty years since the *New York Times* had printed the ugly phrase "half-peopled wilds of Nebraska." Yet for anyone who wanted to sponsor a successful statewide campaign, Nebraska's vast spaces remained an obvious concern.[3]

Remarkably, however, Henry Doorly's prospects of motivating anyone outside of Douglas County to embrace scrap metal collection faced an even more formidable obstacle as he began to publicize his campaign: the sporadic history of mistrust and outright antagonism between big-city

Omaha and the rest of the state. Dating back to bitter struggles over the location of the territorial capital, this tension was still noticeable in the city folks' casual (and sometimes contemptuous) use of the term *outstate* as a blanket designation for the rural and presumably backward reaches of Nebraska. The hostility was generally mutual. *Vanity Fair*, writing in the midst of the Great Depression, summarized the relationship like this: "Omaha, with its back to Nebraska and its face turned east across the Big Muddy, is either a pariah or a rose in a cabbage patch, depending on whether the commentator lives outstate or in the city itself."[4]

It was therefore understandable that many rural Nebraskans were initially wary of the *World-Herald*'s big idea. Areas outside of Omaha had their own newspapers and perspectives and opinions, so for any big-city publisher to attempt to unite the state under a central plan naturally invited healthy skepticism. Edgar Howard, the editor of the *Columbus Telegram*, frankly acknowledged some of this mistrust. Howard had been a six-term Democratic congressman, a position that had put him into direct conflict with Doorly on more than one occasion. As Howard pointedly noted in an editorial for Columbus readers, one of his first reactions upon hearing about the scrap drive was to recall that "not always has Henry Doorly held me very close in the embrace of friendship." Although Howard did go on to recommend that Columbus citizens join the scrap fray, his wary undertone was evident.[5]

So how was it that the *World-Herald*'s drive was able to sell the remote Sandhills ranchers, the storekeepers and grain elevator owners of the small towns, the panhandle sugar beet workers, the university community in Lincoln, and farm families across the state on the idea of a statewide effort? After all, as the newspaper later noted with pride, during the campaign "Nebraska had but one thought — to get in the scrap."[6] Ironically, it turned out that the road to initial cooperation was paved with determined internal competition. Given Nebraska's far-reaching distances, it was a competition that primarily played out in the pages of the state's newspapers, prompting each county to compare its efforts to those of its rivals. In the case of about two dozen particularly ambitious counties, that peer comparison proved to be an intensely motivating factor. Thus as the diverse regions put aside their initial mistrust of Henry Doorly and his big-city plan, they soon found themselves responding to the seductive call to hard-fought competition, mobilizing their county teams, and then vying against each other in what would gradually become a riveting scrap wrangle.

From Gridiron to Scrap Iron: The Call to Competition

Although greater Nebraska is notable for its variety of landscapes and terrains, by the 1940s most residents would have readily acknowledged that the state had come to foster two primary kinds of agricultural pursuits. The eastern and southern portions of the state, when irrigated generously, transformed into excellent crop land. Such areas typically boasted countless acres of wheat and corn fields, most of them tended by traditional farm families. Much of the north central and western areas of the state, in contrast, seemed to early pioneers to be a barren wasteland, "a vast, mysterious land of rolling hills, very like the restless waves of the mighty Pacific, but frozen forever into immobility." Yet what is known today as the Sandhills region and its 20,000 square miles of grass-covered dunes soon proved to be first-class grazing land. Over several generations, the area came to foster a vast system of ranching operations, where cowboys still rode the endless ranges and the cattle outnumbered the people in county after county.[7]

But not every resident of greater Nebraska was a rancher or a farmer. Nestled sporadically among the state's farms and ranches were hundreds of villages, towns, and small cities. Dubbed "central places" by geographer Brian J. L. Berry, the primary function of these locales was to furnish a concentrated agricultural infrastructure. Depending on their location and size, such centers typically provided one or more grain elevators, warehouse facilities, a business district, an implement dealer, at least one church, and a school system. Perhaps most important, rural towns nearly always offered access to a regional highway and a railroad line or spur, which enabled transport of the area's agricultural products to market. The residents of these towns, in most cases, were not ranchers or farmers in their own right. Yet neither were they urbanized in the same way that Omahans were.[8]

For its part, the city of Lincoln was in some ways the exceptional case. Although residents liked to say that they lived in the "Athens of the West," the city served nearby farms in much the same manner that small towns like Beatrice, Fremont, or Kearney did. For example, in 1942 Lincoln boasted fourteen feed dealers as well as a grain elevator and a bank specializing in farm loans. At another level, however, the city was host to Nebraska Wesleyan University, Union College, and the University of Nebraska, with their large communities of students, faculty, and support staff.[9] Moreover, Lincoln had been the Nebraska capital for over seventy years and had come to serve as a focal point for state politics. The striking capitol building's various meeting spaces provided a suitably neutral space for urban and rural lawmakers to mingle, clash, and cooperate.

One of the most vital clues in explaining why Nebraskans from these tremendously divergent regions agreed to sign up for the *World-Herald's* scrap metal competition lay just a few blocks north of the new capitol complex. It was the university's Memorial Stadium, an imposing shrine to the state's obsession with college football and the natural place for urban and rural citizens alike to find common cause. "Football," wrote Robert Burlingame in 1932, "has given this school a hold over its entire constituency such as no other state university approaches." Only through such an intense love for competition, he concluded, "can Ogallala and Wahoo and Broken Bow be made comprehensible," since nothing else could "hold this hodgepodge state together."[10]

Part of the genius of Doorly's scrap invitation thus emerged in its seductive call for an intense statewide competition among otherwise diverse regions. Just as the state's football fans avidly cheered on their Cornhuskers in passionate rivalries against neighboring Iowa and Kansas, so too did Nebraska's various regions and communities have their own rivals within the state. James W. Hewitt, who competed as part of the Adams County scrap team, believes that the campaign's planners were wise "to draw on the community pride that existed in Nebraska." The state's communities, he adds, "were proud of their towns. If Gothenberg had the opportunity to beat Lexington or beat Cozad . . . they were going to do it if they possibly could. The rivalries between those towns were very strong."[11] By encouraging such communities to measure their scrap totals against those of traditional in-state rivals, the scrap contest was tapping into a preexisting competitiveness among many of the state's citizens.

In fact, the contentiousness underlying the county vs. county contest was an extension of the simmering tensions already inherent in Nebraska's license plate numbering system. Since 1922, every license plate in the state had identified the driver's home county by using a numbered prefix. These official county numbers were originally assigned according to total automobile registrations, meaning that vehicles from Omaha's Douglas County used *1* as their prefix while those hailing from sparsely populated Hooker County used *93*. By the 1940s the tradition had become a sort of tribal marker system in which, according to Jon Farrar, "most rural Nebraskans, with varying degrees of competence, memorized county license plate numbers" as a means of "categorizing the occupants" of other cars. As a result, says Robert Nelson, the system continuously reinforced a host of county-based "prides and prejudices." It was not unusual for local residents to look askance (or with outright suspicion) at drivers with different county numbers. This ingrained practice naturally intensified regional rivalries within the state by making it easy not only to identify those from outside the county but to view them as interlopers with allegiance to another place.[12]

At the most basic level, then, the call to scrap competition was a persuasive appeal to transform existing tensions and rivalries within a highly competitive population into a specific, formalized contest. The *World-Herald* itself was an important source of this persuasive appeal, even for readers outside Omaha (see fig. 10). The rural-urban split within the state did not stop many far-flung Nebraskans from subscribing to the state's largest newspaper. As with their city cousins, such readers were thus able to read in one of Doorly's initial scrap stories that "the contest proposes to add a note of interest and rivalry to dramatize a job which . . . is about as serious as anything can be." The *World-Herald* even highlighted the drive's competitive aspects by asking Frederick Ware to supervise the "outstate circus" of scrap events. As it turned out, Ware knew a great deal about the value of competition, since in 1942 he was serving as the newspaper's sports editor.[13]

10. Fred Rehmeier, of Weeping Water, calls a friend about the scrap drive. He is holding the *Sunday World-Herald*, which introduced the campaign's details to readers. Image reprinted with permission from the *Omaha World-Herald*.

But there were also influential voices from outside Omaha encouraging Nebraskans to join the upcoming drive. Some of the most prominent of these voices belonged to the leadership of the Chicago, Burlington & Quincy Railroad (known locally as the Burlington). Unlike the rival Union Pacific, which was based in and associated with Omaha, the Burlington had operations throughout most of the state. Indeed, the railroad had once founded many of Nebraska's small towns as a support system for its growing local lines. With the UP's scrap drive support emerging primarily in Omaha (and, to a lesser extent, in North Platte, the site of a massive switching yard), the Burlington responded by exploiting its connections in the rest of Nebraska to position itself as a passionate non-Omaha supporter of Doorly's idea.[14]

The Burlington's acute interest in the drive appeared to have begun with the UP's successful rally in Omaha, after which an anonymous UP official reportedly telephoned a Burlington counterpart with a taunting message: "Let this be a fair warning, chum, we are out to show you up." The Burlington official was quick to reply that his railroad would "take that challenge. And let the devil take the hindmost!" Soon thereafter, Edward "Red" Flynn, the Burlington's executive vice president, stormed into the *World-Herald*'s scrap drive headquarters. "We are ready. We have come here to go to work," he exclaimed to J. M. Harding. "We are going to show the Union Pacific that we know how to get scrap." Flynn meant what he said. On July 17 the first of several scrap rallies across the state took place, each one pointedly advertised for and funded by the Burlington. A week later, several of the organization's officials upped the ante by taking a personal tour across the state in support of scrap efforts in company territory. As Harding recalled later, the railroads' passionate rivalry was quite influential in motivating citizens across the state to support the drive. It was, he said, "responsible in a rather large way for the success" of the entire effort.[15]

Yet as influential as the Burlington's scrap enthusiasm was in greater Nebraska, another voice may have been even more powerful in the call to competition. For political observers from outside the state, Dwight Griswold had built a respectable reputation as "one of the best governors in the nation." Within Nebraska, citizens were just as familiar with his proud rural background, since he had grown up on the northwestern edge of the Sandhills, in Sheridan County. They were also, no doubt, well aware of his extremely competitive nature. *Life* magazine agreed with this assessment, noting that Griswold's early election losses, including three failed attempts to win the governorship, had shaped him into "a hard campaigner for whom no political chore is too small."[16]

Not surprisingly, when Griswold learned of Doorly's scrap plan, he was particularly enthused by the contest angle. "I like the competitive spirit," he wrote to Doorly, exhibited "through the giving of substantial prizes in war bonds to winning counties." He was confident that the competitors "will not quit until the job is done." Tellingly, Griswold's office sent a more personalized missive to numerous smaller newspapers. Many of them published the governor's explicit endorsement of the competition. Speaking to rural folks directly, Griswold's letter challenged them to forget about the state's earlier attempts to gather scrap. As he wrote, "I urge you to redouble your efforts." The scrap competition "is getting under way," he concluded, "but there is yet much to be done."[17]

Despite the state's rural-urban animosities, then, Doorly's ambitious scrap plan appeared to have captured the attention of influential people outside of Omaha. Nebraskans already possessed a contentious culture, only truly becoming united in their mutual desire for the state's football team to beat nearby rivals. A scrap collection plan that rallied communities against one another—while at the same time pledging that their combined scrap totals would shock other states—was thus an ideal means of appealing to Nebraska's diverse wartime citizens. Still, to echo Griswold's letter to rural readers, there was a lot of work ahead. Although the *World-Herald* later emphasized that "the contest idea aroused early and sustaining interest," county scrap teams now needed to become serious about girding themselves for the competition.[18] It was time to respond to the drumbeat of anticipation by getting the would-be scrappers to mobilize.

A Heap of Work: Mobilizing the County Scrap Team

Dundy County, population 5,122, was out to win it all. Located on the extreme southwestern corner of Nebraska—over 300 miles from Omaha's scrap headquarters—Dundy residents swiftly responded to Doorly's contest challenge. The county seat's *Benkelman Post and News-Chronicle* exuded confidence: "We have read about your state-wide Salvage Contest[,] Mr. Omaha World-Herald[,] and we like it." Amid enthusiastic headlines, such as "DUNDY COUNTY GLADLY ACCEPTS THE CHALLENGE" and "Dundy County Wants to Win," the account taunted potential county challengers, advising them to "look at your state map now and watch for the record of Dundy County." As the newspaper promised, with obvious relish, "You'll be hearing a lot about Dundy County before August 8th."[19]

Dundy's enthusiasm was matched by numerous other counties in the days following the *World-Herald*'s scrap announcement. Residents from several places across the state apparently had reason to believe that their team would have the inside track to the top prize. Several historic county rivalries reemerged, this time resounding with a metallic clash. Washington County, for example, confidently asserted that it was sure to be the overall winner, in the process leaving neighboring Burt County behind in the dust. And Lancaster County leaders, informed that Lincoln County's scrap team "believes the county first prize . . . is 'in the bag' for the North Platte area," stated that, to the contrary, its scrappers would "better the record in the contest that may be made by our friends in Lincoln county."[20] There could be no doubt that, for many Nebraskans, the scrapping gauntlet had been thrown down.

Fortunately, one could argue that a good proportion of the would-be contestants were hardy enough to undertake such a grueling competition. Many hailed from families with vital experience in the hardships of Great Plains life. Settlers on the great expanse west of the Missouri River had long dealt with any number of hardships, such as the general lack of trees for lumber and fuel, temperature swings, drought, aggressive insects, crop failures, prairie fires, wildlife, and, for the earliest settlers, strained relationships with Native tribes. The settlers who could not handle these challenges gave up and left or even perished. Those who remained were survivors of the toughest kind, and they taught their descendants the value of tenacity, cooperation, and thrift. For many rural Nebraskans in 1942, these survivors were their own parents and grandparents, and the life lessons the older generations imparted were close at hand.[21]

But mental and physical toughness was not enough to ensure the success of the campaign. If it were, these same rural Nebraskans would have broken scrap collection records back when the federal government initially began asking the public to collect salvaged metal. In retrospect, those earlier efforts lacked the comprehensive competition element that was such a central aspect of Doorly's plan. Crucially, however, the earlier efforts also lacked two other mobilizing elements: a relatively informal organization and what contemporaries might have good-naturedly called "ballyhoo."

To begin with, the Nebraska Plan's logistical structure was admirable in its simple yet comprehensive reach. In order to avoid duplicating the existing scrap apparatus (and to avoid crossing lines of authority), Doorly persuaded each county's salvage chairman to serve as the local scrap contest official. These ninety-three chairmen were already acting as countywide representatives in the War Production Board's federal salvage effort. For this reason, they were familiar with the importance of scrap as well as the local landscape. One of their primary functions, according to the contest rules, was to serve as their county's scorekeeper, which entailed accurately weighing and tracking scrap contributions at any of a number of sites. At the same time, they were responsible for communicating the daily and cumulative county totals to the local *World-Herald* correspondent, who would wire the results to Omaha.[22]

Because almost all of the county chairs were male, the *World-Herald*'s plan also factored in a separate women's division that would extend the contest into areas left untouched by the men. Eva Grimes, who happened to be married to Doorly's managing editor, enthusiastically agreed to serve as state chairwoman of the division. Pointing out that "certain phases of the salvage program could be accomplished better by the women than by men," Grimes began by appointing a scrap chairwoman for every county. Their assignment, she stipulated, was to organize local competitions among women's groups, church auxiliaries, home extension groups, and girls' clubs. In a statewide radio address, she soon complimented the chairwomen on how quickly they had gone to work. "In spite of the heat and the threshing and the canning and the thousand and one other chores that men like to call women's work," Grimes commented, the county chairwomen had swiftly "got their war paint on."[23]

Beyond the assignment of specific county chairmen and chairwomen, however, Doorly's plan did not specify how each county should pursue its contest strategy. This freedom allowed individual areas to adapt to their regional circumstances, as when Box Butte County set its sights on the plentiful scrap available in numerous abandoned potash plants to the east of Alliance, or when Cheyenne County sought permission to comb the thirty square miles of the local Sioux Ordnance Depot. The lack of an unwieldy structure also encouraged counties to dream up unique ways of promoting the contest to area scrappers. Washington County, for example, planned to organize a troop of Minute Men to visit every home in Blair, seeking household scrap. Chase County decided to spread the word by using the local telephone system's "general line call" function, which used an emergency ring to communicate to everyone on a party line. Dawes County, for its part, recruited seven pilots to bomb the city of Chadron with cardboard flyers touting the drive. Burwell, meanwhile, adjusted plans for its huge annual rodeo by turning it into a bewildering "triple salvage–war bond–rodeo rally," to which one could gain free admission by turning in a ton of scrap metal to the Garfield County drive.[24]

Some contestants developed fantastically detailed plans right from the start. Scotts Bluff County, on the western edge of the Nebraska panhandle, announced to competitors that it had "declared war on the Axis" and thus had "drafted every man, woman, and child for an all-out drive." The county's strategy did in fact appear to involve nearly every citizen and organization, including local newspapers and radio stations, 531 Boy Scouts, 150 Camp Fire Girls, 115 so-called Victory Leaders, 4-H clubs, and drivers of both municipal and county trucks. The city of Scottsbluff was plotted into districts for canvassing, lumber yards and filling stations volunteered as collection points, and officials asked every citizen to reserve July 31 for a dedicated scrap day, an event proclaimed in advance by every mayor in the county. Not to be outdone, Phelps County complemented its detailed collection plans with the formation of its own scrap corporation, the Non-Profit Junk Co. To encourage the county's citizens to participate in the drive, the entity offered to pay for their scrap at $10 per ton—a price that was $1.50 higher than the market rate at the time. Fortunately, a prominent town bank, clearly a strong believer in the importance of the scrap competition, backed the new corporation's resulting expenses through a series of loans.[25] Both Phelps and Scotts Bluff Counties, it was apparent, were taking full advantage of the scrap contest's flexible organization as they prepared for competition.

The drive's other important mobilizing element took shape in various forms of ballyhoo. This intriguing word was useful in a number of contexts on the home front. It had emerged at the turn of the century from the mischievous language of circus sideshows and was thus invaluable in referring to dramatic, colorful, and occasionally bizarre publicity. Since the competing counties in the *World-Herald*'s scrap campaign wanted to inform and motivate their numerous residents in as many ways as possible, the drive soon became a perfect environment for ballyhoo to thrive.

The initial source of ballyhoo was, of course, the *World-Herald* itself. Doorly knew very well that a halfhearted approach to publicizing the drive would risk losing the state's sustained attention, particularly in rural areas. Using several full-page ads, he quickly demonstrated that he was willing to use dramatic measures to promote the effort. In a July 19 ad, for instance, the newspaper presented a forceful appeal to the entire state. "Let's Go, Nebraska," the ad blared in a bold font. "Let's Top the Nation!" Below, the pressure mounted: "Men! Women! Children! This Job Is YOURS. It Is Urgent. It Is Vital. We MUST NOT Fail Our Boys in the Service." And, as if there were any doubt, the ad reiterated, "That call means us, Nebraskans! Let's go! Today!"[26] Even for casual readers, it was clear that Doorly's newspaper was eager, from the start, to promote the drive throughout the state.

Local newspapers were also a prominent source of ballyhoo on behalf of the emerging campaign. Here Griswold's avid support for the drive was particularly important. Most of the state's newspaper staffs were well aware that before moving into the governor's mansion, Griswold had been the publisher of the modest *Gordon Journal*. His enthusiasm for the competition, not to mention his letter to rural readers, surely spoke volumes to his former colleagues. It was no surprise, then, that a significant number of small dailies and weeklies quickly found themselves offering passionate support for the new campaign. It was a source of enthusiasm that local communities would have found difficult to ignore.

One particularly enthused publication was the weekly *Hooker County Tribune*, which informed readers that "Hooker County declared war this week on the Axis! WE ARE AFTER IT ALL. LET'S GO FOLKS—OVER THE TOP." The *Sidney Telegraph* was also excited, using ad space to shout, "Let's Go, Cheyenne County! Let's Top the Entire State!" *The Frontier*, published in O'Neill, elected to take a sterner approach, arguing in front-page coverage that "every patriotic person and organization must feel it their duty to put forth their best effort to move every piece of scrap in this county." Those who were "too busy" to turn in their scrap for the contest would be "guilty of an act of sabotage equal to destroying war production plants." Meanwhile, several other newspapers—among them the *McCook Daily Gazette*, the *Grant County Tribune*, and the *Thomas County Herald Clipper*—borrowed liberally from the text of the *World-Herald*'s "Let's Go, Nebraska" ad to create their own appeals to help mobilize area residents.[27]

Local merchants also became prominent sources of ballyhoo on behalf of the drive. Although Doorly had pledged not to accept sponsored scrap advertising (he feared losing support for the drive if smaller newspapers saw that the *World-Herald* was profiting from the campaign), local publications were under no such restriction. As a result, scores of businesses from across the state jumped onto the scrap bandwagon, using ads to promote not only area collection efforts but also their own names and products in the process. The North Platte Loan and Finance Company, for instance, sponsored an especially passionate scrap ad in the local *Daily Telegraph*. "*It's not* JUNK," suggested the text, "*it's a* GUN. . . *it's a* PLANE. . . *it's a* SHIP. . . *it's a* TANK." Sketches of junk and war implements were combined with vibrant font styles and sizes to emphasize the ad's fanciful contention that readers' roller skates and old doorknobs were the equivalent of military weapons. Turning in such scrap material, suggested the ad, would benefit not only the country's GIs but also the county's competitive chances in the contest. "Help put Lincoln County over the top," concluded the appeal. "Every bit helps."[28] Through the widespread publication of ads like this one, the campaign's fervor reached yet another level of intensity.

In the end, however, both the drive's simple structure and at least some of the localized ballyhoo supporting the effort inevitably revolved around the county chairmen and chairwomen. These indispensable leaders organized county scrap committees, area contests, local press relations, and countless other aspects of the campaign. At the same time, they also functioned as cheerleaders, using their own authority and enthusiasm in support of the drive. In this manner, Dakota County chairman Henry C. Hodges confirmed to area residents in "a barrage of publicity that should awaken every man, woman, and child" that "this job is yours, it is vital, we must not fail our boys in the service." Cuming County chairwoman Patty Sweeney offered a similar perspective, suggesting that all of her county's developing efforts would be directed toward helping to "salvage scrap to whip a Jap in the Axis lap."[29] In terms of structure and ballyhoo, then, it began to appear that a sufficient number of the scrap leaders and their county teams were both motivated and mobilized. It was time to test their preparations in the actual competition.

The Jingle-Jangle Wrangle

On July 21, the third day of competition, the *Omaha World-Herald* noted that "it was jingle, jangle, jingle all over the state Monday as Nebraskans tossed their spurs and practically everything else onto salvage contest scrap heaps that were growing by the ton." The report's unusual wording was no accident. It so happened that one of the most infectious songs to emerge in that summer of 1942 was Kay Kyser's peppy "Jingle, Jangle, Jingle," the fable of a restless cowboy who cannot seem to stay in one place for long. The lighthearted tune must have seemed almost like a tribute to the drive, since it had both a western flavor and, in the recurring word *jangle*, a suitable allusion to jostling metals. At the same time, it was not popular just in Nebraska; it was a bona fide national sensation. If Kyser's hit was, in effect, the unofficial song of the Nebraska Plan that summer, it was also a subtle reminder of the larger implications at stake in the contest. As Doorly's newspaper put it a week later, "The eyes of the nation are watching Nebraska."[30]

Indeed, anyone observing the opening days of the scrap contest likely would have been struck by the exuberance of the effort in a number of areas across the state. Governor Griswold himself kicked off the competition with a statewide radio address on Sunday, July 19. Calling the emerging Nebraska effort "the grand drive of them all," the governor emphasized that "we need guns and munitions. Our factories need your scrap metal . . . they need it badly, right now." His final appeal was disarmingly simple: "Turn it in, Nebraska, will you?" The immediate response to the governor's plea, by all accounts, was enthusiastic. The *McCook Daily Gazette*, for instance, was clearly impressed with the campaign's opening day, writing that "every city, town, village, and home in Nebraska is rolling up its sleeves . . . in the statewide $2,000 scrap metal collection campaign."[31]

But there were also signs of potential trouble in the earliest days of the campaign. On July 22, the *World-Herald* felt that it had received enough reports to be able to put together the first unofficial standings for the contest. Undoubtedly, these initial county-by-county results were disappointing at best. The newspaper put a positive spin on the story, describing Burt County as having "jumped far into the lead." It was true that Burt was off to an impressive start, with a per capita total of nearly 12 pounds after only four days. Yet no other county had reached an average of 2 pounds. Even worse, seventy-four counties had not yet even tendered a report. The state's overall total so far, the *World-Herald* noted pointedly, was up to 296 tons—but 107 of those tons had been gathered in Omaha itself. The rural portion of the drive apparently needed a bit more time before the race would become interesting.[32]

Washington County, with a per capita average of .32 pounds in the initial standings, was particularly upset. The county had grown used to being a state leader in home front activities, such as war bond sales. But now, as was apparent to anyone viewing the standings, Washington found that its scrap totals were dramatically behind those of Burt County, its neighbor and rival. The local *Pilot-Tribune* deplored the efforts of area scrappers, writing that "there will be no bragging done this week about how well Washington County is doing in the big statewide scrap salvage contest. . . . The fact is, this county is not doing so well." A few days later, the newspaper's cartoonist presented a dramatic scene in which several GIs had run out of ammunition in the midst of a firefight. "Kinda looks," intoned the commanding officer, "as tho' our friends back in Washington

County are 'too busy' to send us more stuff." Local officials received the message. E. Clark Lippincott, the Washington County scrap chairman, insisted that the county "can and will do better than that before the drive ends August 8." As was the case with several other counties in the early going, then, Washington residents appeared to have found the initial scrap standings a source not only of embarrassment but also of renewed motivation.[33]

One reason for at least some of the counties' meager results in the first part of the contest was that many local efforts were having trouble finding ways to gather the irreplaceable scrap that was located on farms and ranches. Earlier in the summer, national scrap officials had ascertained that the average midwestern spread possessed a ton or more of the highest grades of scrap metal. Unlike some other areas of the country, most of Nebraska's farmers and ranchers had mechanized their operations by 1942. Consequently, their obsolete equipment (some of which had been horse-drawn) had typically ended up in a nearby pile of scrap, which served as a useful resource for creative repairs and quick fixes. All told, estimated Lincoln's *Evening State Journal*, rural Nebraskans held enough scrap metal in such piles to construct 155 merchant ships weighing 10,000 tons apiece.[34]

Unfortunately, the scrap drive was taking place at a time when nearly all of the region's farmers and ranchers were actively involved in their operations. Many farmsteads were finishing up the greatest harvest in years, with bumper crops of wheat, barley, and oats all but forcing farmers into the fields. At the same time, Sandhills ranchers and their crews were busy harvesting hay, work that was urgent if they wanted to feed their cattle over the winter. To make matters worse, the average spread was shorthanded to begin with. The Nebraska countryside had seen a net decline in population during the 1930s, and many of the young workers who had remained at the time of Pearl Harbor were now in the armed forces. The timing of the drive, for a good number of farms and ranches, was thus more than inconvenient.[35]

Despite these sorts of challenging problems, however, the scrap drive in greater Nebraska did manage to gain some momentum after the initial standings were published. Cass County, for instance, reported that workers were starting to raze Plattsmouth's sixty-seven-year-old Central school, providing the area's drive with plentiful scrap in the form of boilers, radiators, plumbing, and even student desks. Burt County officials set their sights on an abandoned brick and tile factory, which would produce some 400 tons of scrap metal and pad the county's early lead. In Lincoln, the Burlington reported that it had cleaned out 850 tons of scrap from its Havelock Yards (see fig. 11), even as University of Nebraska staff members began combing scores of buildings and nearly 400 acres of campus grounds. On the state's northern border, Cherry County scrappers reported that they had added just over 6 tons to their total by taking down the courthouse's cannon (which had, appropriately, been seized from the German army after World War I). Further west, the Dawes County salvage committee organized one of the largest rallies in county history to celebrate the reenlistment of "the old Howitzer," a venerable courthouse artillery piece, with the crowd lugging it and additional loads of scrap down to Chadron's railhead in an impromptu parade. Finally, in Antelope County, shoppers in downtown Neligh could barely use the sidewalks, which is where the city had elected to locate its local scrap collection, ensuring that the heaps could not be missed by citizens and visitors alike.[36]

The county vs. county race soon began to attract more activity as well. The second standings report, published on July 23, revealed that seven additional counties now had a total in the contest. Early leader Burt County, according to the standings, had been demoted to second place behind Dawes County, whose defunct Howitzer had helped produce a per capita average of nearly 20 pounds. Ambitious Dundy County, in third place for the day, noted that the competition was "increasing daily as other counties move to eliminate [the] leaders." On the 25th, Hooker County seized the unofficial lead, with Saunders, Cheyenne, and Dawes Counties not far behind. By the 29th, the standings had shuffled again, with Red Willow and Thayer Counties chasing new leader Grant County and its stunning initial report of 111 pounds per capita. Counties located on the western side of the state, lamented the *Norfolk Daily*

11. The Burlington Railroad shipped over 850 tons of scrap from its Havelock Yards near Lincoln. Several of the items in this carload are chalked with the letter V, for victory. Image reprinted with permission from the *Omaha World-Herald*.

News, were now outpacing eastern counties at the top by a 3 to 1 margin. The *World-Herald*, by now awash in scrap coverage from every corner of the state, proudly noted that Nebraskans' "competitive spirit [was] waxing warmer."[37] Indeed, counties that were ahead at first redoubled their efforts in order to keep the lead, while those that were initially left behind found additional motivation to raise their scrap totals ever faster.

But even though the rural scrappers viewed the drive through highly partisan eyes, there appeared to be plenty of room left over for creativity as well as a scrap-based sense of humor. Larger items in scrap piles often featured witty chalk inscriptions, such as numerous variations on the notation "C.O.D., Adolf Hitler" or, on an older mower, "To Help Mow 'em Down" (see fig. 12). Colorful children's scrap groups began to emerge, such as Cuming County's 4-H-based Snappy Wappy Club, Dodge County's Scrap Happy Singers, and Adams County's Ben's Boys

Club. In dozens of other counties, area youth adopted the simpler name Junior Commandos in homage to a fictional children's group led by Little Orphan Annie on the funnies page. Even some adult scrapping groups adopted creative names. In Holdrege, for example, a collection of business owners inaugurated the Scrap Snoopers. Admission to this organization required three grueling nights of scrap collection. Those who made it through eight nights of such volunteer labor were then invited to join the group's inner circle, appropriately dubbed the Super-Duper Scrap Snoopers.[38]

As the contest moved forward, these sorts of groups energetically joined their scrapping brethren in scouting and gathering nearly anything that appeared to be metallic. Doorly's principle that tractors and tricycles were equally important in the contest was validated over and over again, even in the competition's earliest days. Numerous tottering tractors, for example, did in fact find their way to scrap heaps—some of them, at least at first, driven or hauled in by townspeople who were scouting area farms. After careful deliberation on the part of many children, hundreds of tricycles were donated, too.

Of course, among the tractors and tricycles there awaited a tremendous variety of material, such as scrap that offered a revealing glimpse into forgotten struggles with scofflaws. In the town of Stanton, officials elected to tear apart an old jail cell block, which produced 6 tons for the Stanton County drive. Garden County officials donated old whiskey stills that were found in long-term storage at Wilbur, apparently remnants of a long-ago raid. And Columbus city administrators, not to be outdone, proudly presented the Platte County scrap effort with several ball-and-chain sets, which the police department had used before 1910 as a means of preventing the escape of convicts sentenced to work on the city's rock pile.[39]

At times, the bizarre items in the growing scrap heaps even included material of dubious provenance. Johnny Carson, then a rising senior at Norfolk High School, later confessed that "in our zeal to help the war effort, we sometimes appropriated metal and brass from people who did not know they were parting with it." World War I veterans, in contrast,

12. This wrecked Ford Model T was donated to the Hall County scrap committee for the contest. The chalk inscription refers to the model's popular nickname, the Tin Lizzie. Image reprinted with permission from the *Omaha World-Herald*.

were generally well aware of the often-illicit nature of their own donations, which included war trophies such as bayonets, ornamental swords, firearms, and even live ammunition that they had seized from the enemy a generation earlier. Geo. Strassler vividly remembers seeing a well-preserved Prussian officer's helmet in a Lancaster County scrap pile. "Even as nine-year-old kids," he recalls, "we saw the irony of the German officer's helmet being destined to create some piece of armament that would help destroy the hated Axis."[40]

By most accounts, then, almost nothing could be considered too obscure or too small to be included in the effort. Children, in particular, did not discriminate in their search, many following the lead of young scrapper John P. Shaw in gathering anything metal that he and his friends could lift into his red Radio Flyer wagon. Before long, he recounts, "we nearly wore it out, pulling it around town, finding scrap." Due, in part, to the labors of such industrious youngsters, it was commonplace for local scrap heaps to sport curtain rods and plumbing fixtures, bird cages and barbed wire, erector sets and vanity boxes, steam boilers and bed pans, as well as stove pipes and sleds. If something, anything, around the house or farm or business contained metal, it received serious scrutiny. As Red Willow County's women found out, even intimate articles of clothing were of interest to Uncle Sam. The local *McCook Daily Gazette*, citing sources in the garment industry, tactfully informed readers that the steel in corset stays was "very valuable," and urged area women "to remove the metal from worn-out garments and contribute it to the nation's stock-pile." McCook's corsetiers then announced, with apparent patriotism, that they would assist any women who wanted to donate metal pieces from their undergarments to the Red Willow scrap pile.[41]

What made all of these items—from corsets to corn harvesters—become so priceless to the scrappers in greater Nebraska was the campaign's emerging reliance on militarizing language. As the North Platte merchant's ad demonstrated, the campaign was constantly ready to transform everyday metal objects into weapons of war. *Editor & Publisher* later told its readers that in the Nebraska contest "scrap metal was made understandable to the women by translating flat-irons into helmets, [and] steel bedsprings into machine guns; to the farmer by beating his plowshares into howitzers." That linguistic and visual sleight-of-hand had quickly become the everyday vocabulary of the campaign. Courthouse cannons, of course, were easy to depict as munitions, since they were *already* weapons, even if they were crumbling into pieces. But transforming toasters, grain binders, rusty pipes, nails, and radiators into grenades, bombers, bayonets, army jeeps, and the like required a forceful imagination. The most successful scrappers, in short, soon developed the ability to look beyond the rust and must in order to visualize, in a fanciful way, their metallic heaps as violent tools destined for Axis destruction. As scrapper Ruby Schulz remembers, "Every piece of scrap we picked up, we'd say, 'Well, I wonder what this is going to be? Is it going to be a ship, or is this going to be rifle bullets?'" It was little wonder that one elderly Scottsbluff resident was overheard muttering these words as he departed the county scrap pile: "It's like I took a jab myself at that Hitler, Hirohito, and Mussolini. Makes a feller feel right good."[42]

In a roundabout way, then, the developing competition in greater Nebraska embodied the potential for the various scrap teams to become much more than just partisan competitors in a grand county vs. county wrangle. After all, if scrapping meant that one were handling the weapons of war, it followed that the scrappers themselves were functioning as a kind of military unit. The *World-Herald*, not surprisingly, was already pitching this perspective, using a July 27 story to depict "the huge Nebraska Army that is laying siege to the points of resistance along the state's salvage front." To be sure, this proposed sense of a common statewide mission was a bit of an ironic twist, given Nebraska's widely diverse regions, underlying county tensions, and passionately competing scrap teams. However, there were signs that a militarized camaraderie might in fact be underlying the campaign's competitive surface. As Doorly had anticipated, the paradox of simultaneous competition and camaraderie seemed to have a particular appeal for these rural Cornhuskers. Frederick Ware, Doorly's point person for the campaign outside of Omaha, appeared to agree with this assessment, recalling that the drive essentially "built Nebraska spirit."[43]

Still, as the campaign neared the final week, it was increasingly clear that the state's enthusiastic scrapping spirit would soon need to grow even more intense. True, most of the counties by this point had tendered an unofficial report in the competition. One could reportedly "pick out any one of the dots on a Nebraska map" and find that it "represents a community that is being searched as it never was searched before." Yet by July 31, thirteen days into the competition, only Grant and Red Willow Counties had successfully reached Doorly's goal of 100 pounds of scrap per capita, raising the statewide average to a meager 18 pounds.[44] Even worse, a huge percentage of the state's farm and ranch scrap remained uncollected. It was becoming more and more evident that a modest, jingle-jangle effort would not be enough for the drive to succeed. The state's scrap teams, in other words, would need to find a way to conquer Nebraska's great distances and relatively empty spaces in a stirring, come-from-behind finish. The nation, after all, was watching.

5

The Second-Half Comeback

A community like an individual has a work to do.
—Inscription from Aristotle's *Poetics*, Nebraska state capitol

Their hard-working team had failed to make a comeback in the second half. That painful memory was fresh in the minds of many wartime Nebraskans. On January 1, 1941, their beloved Cornhuskers had taken the field in Pasadena, California, to compete in the twenty-seventh annual Rose Bowl in front of 92,000 spectators. It was the team's first bowl game, and the state's passionate fans were optimistic. After all, their team had lost only once during the regular season, in a close game to top-ranked Minnesota. But it was not to be. After a strong start, the Cornhuskers fell behind the Stanford Indians by one point. In the second half, the team staged a spirited goal-line defense, but then decided to punt on first down after regaining possession of the ball. Stanford quickly returned the punt for a touchdown. Before long, Nebraska's humbled team found itself trudging back to the locker room with no points to show for the entire second half.[1]

Some eighteen months later, Governor Dwight Griswold—apparently well aware that Henry Doorly's salvage drive was not on track to meet its ambitious goal of 100 pounds of scrap for every Nebraskan by August 8—had come to believe that the state's scrap drive could not afford a similar letdown. In a statewide radio address, he reminded Nebraskans that "the thing that has made Cornhuskers famous in football circles is the fact they always put up a great fight." The scrap campaign, he suggested, needed a similar effort: "If the people of Nebraska can be considered a great football team, then we must start to win at the beginning of the second half." So far, he said, "the score is against us. Are we going to lie down and quit or are we going to fight back? I appeal to you as a great fighting people—as Cornhusker scrappers—to do your best." There could be no doubt, as the scrappers were aware, that Doorly's drive had generated a lot of enthusiastic noise. The Scrap Mountain in downtown Omaha, as well as many of the county operations in rural areas of the state, were good cases in point. But enthusiasm was not enough, and the governor knew it.[2]

In fact, by this point the desperate need for scrap metal in the war effort was becoming more acute. Steel industry insiders warned that "the scarcity of scrap iron and steel continues to plague the War Production Board for it is one of the most serious factors facing the nation on the production end." In Washington, President Roosevelt did his part to help raise the alarm, using a late July press conference to ask that all Americans turn in "every possible item . . . to local receiving points or junk dealers." Despite the government's efforts, however, the crisis appeared to be spreading to actual production facilities. On July 18, Higgins Industries of New Orleans announced that construction on some 200 Liberty ships had been halted by the U.S. Maritime Commission due to a lack of adequate steel supplies.[3] The *World-Herald*, by now hyperaware of the national scrap situation, printed such alarming details for readers to see even as the statewide campaign inched toward the finish line. The point was clear: it was time for Nebraska's scrappers to challenge themselves and their neighbors even more intensely in hopes of turning the faltering scrap campaign around.

But how in the world could the state possibly elevate its scrap contest total from a mere 18 pounds per person to over 100 pounds in the second half of the campaign? Fortunately, the drive had a few hidden advantages that would help immeasurably. One vital factor in the scrappers' favor was a natural byproduct of Nebraska's great spaces and the time it took to haul, weigh, and report so much scrap metal. As it turned out, the standings reports that garnered so much attention tended to lag significantly behind the actual pace of the campaign, since there was no way for them to reflect scrap material that was awaiting transport, that was still unweighed, or that remained unreported. The 18-pound average published on July 31 thus unavoidably provided information that was at least several days old. By the time that report had appeared in Nebraska's newspapers, the scrappers were already closer to the overall goal than it appeared.[4]

A second hidden advantage for the scrappers' second half involved the timing of the summer harvest. As the campaign's planners had discovered, a good proportion of Nebraska's agricultural workers had had to bypass the start of the contest because they were immersed in the greatest harvest in recent memory.[5] But in many counties with this concern, farmers worked overtime to finish harvesting chores so that they could get down to the business of scrapping later in the drive. This factor—and the growing assistance of townsfolk who came into the countryside after scouring their own homes and businesses—essentially saved the largest, heaviest, and highest quality caches of scrap for the end of the campaign. If the scrappers had actually been a football team, it was almost as if the coaches had waited until after halftime to put in the starters.

Unlike the Cornhuskers' disappointing plight in the Rose Bowl, then, the second half of the scrap contest had the potential for a lot of action. As Doorly's newspaper put it in an August 3 editorial, "All that preliminary work is finished," and so only "one job remains: to get the scrap!" Still, a successful outcome would not be easy. Ray L. McKinney, a local American Legion commander, offered a similar view. As he told readers of the *McCook Daily Gazette*, "Our governor has likened this drive to a football game and every Nebraskan gets the idea!" But he reminded his audience that winning the game by August 8 would require a determined closing effort. "We all know," he concluded, "that if our home boys make any yardage through the line, we here at home will have to do a lot of blocking to help clear the way."[6] McKinney, like many of his fellow scrappers, seemed resolved to make the close of the campaign an aggressive one.

In retrospect, however, this determined spirit and the drive's hidden advantages fail to offer an adequate account of the campaign's striking, come-from-behind finish. A deeper examination of the experience of the scrap crescendo suggests that something more was at work. Intriguingly, while some of the competitive rivalries that had brought the drive through its first half remained, in its culminating days the contest element gradually seemed to diminish in intensity. Instead, the scrappers found themselves immersed in a rhetoric of crisis and coming together in a sense of militarized unity. Each factor helped produce an exuberant and thoughtful celebration of the drive's remarkable comeback miracle.

Cultivating a Crisis

As July turned into August, the *World-Herald*'s scrap managers appeared to be more and more concerned that the drive had reached a plateau that it would not escape. The good news on the first day of the new month was that "one more county, Hooker, climbed into the rarefied atmosphere of the one hundred pound per person class," joining Grant and Red Willow Counties. Unfortunately, it was "the one high note in a scrap symphony that was played largely by the bass section." At 21.46 pounds, the statewide average genuinely appeared to be making little progress. The article noted that with only a week remaining, the scrap total was "a good many cadenzas below the campaign's bare minimum . . . and a whole orchestration under what the state can render." The question, to extend the *World-Herald*'s musical metaphor, was how to increase the volume and tempo of the campaign's tune, ultimately producing a loud "clashing of cymbals."[7]

It soon became obvious that one means of doing so was for Doorly's newspaper and its publishing partners to pressure the scrappers to such a degree that every citizen felt compelled to respond in a dramatic fashion. The scrap campaign needed to establish a *crisis mentality*, one that could help push the effort into its highest levels of intensity and urgency — and hopefully force the statewide scrap average into a much higher range.

It is easy to see why the experience of a crisis might have had a great deal of motivational power. Eugene Hollahan explains that the word *crisis* generally refers to "a state of affairs in which a decisive change for better or worse seems imminent." In crisis situations, he adds, one typically goes through "feelings of insecurity, difficulty, and suspense." The human impulse, of course, is to avoid a crisis until it is inevitable, and then to act decisively and quickly in order to reach a suitable post-crisis resolution. Bishop F. J. McConnell writes that in crises there is almost always "a slow movement toward a critical point, or toward 'the turning of a corner,' and then the process is by leaps and bounds."[8] Arguably, if the scrap campaign were able to foster such a state in Nebraska's scrappers, there would be a good chance that the momentum of the drive could change suddenly and remarkably.

The scrap drive appeared to adopt several means of inducing a crisis mentality in that final week. To begin with, scrap stories routinely started to condemn the drive's apparent lack of progress. Among the first such stories was a front-page *Morning World-Herald* report on July 28, which frankly stated that recent contributions had "proved rather disappointing." The "needles and pins" collected thus far across the state amounted to only 5,000 tons, which was "just about enough to build one cruiser. At that rate it will be pretty slow work constructing a five-ocean navy." Another condemnation, displayed just above the contest standings on August 2, bashed unnamed counties that were allegedly "'waiting for fall' in the scrap drive." For its part, the *Norfolk Daily News* was more succinct, concluding that "the drive has fallen far short of expectations." The *Hooker County Tribune*, after noting that "well over one hundred thousand pounds of scrap have been delivered" in the county, went on to emphasize that "this is not enough — WE MUST HAVE TONS AND TONS OF SCRAP." Bluntest of all, perhaps, was an early August headline that essentially yelled at readers: "Hey, Let's Get Move On — 17,324 Tons Not Enough."[9] With only a week remaining in the drive, Nebraskans were being inundated with surprisingly negative feedback on their progress.

The campaign also ratcheted up the pressure on scrappers by enlisting steel industry officials to offer testimony about the national scrap emergency and the vital contribution Nebraska's scrap metal could play in addressing that emergency. "The heads of the great steel companies in America," explained the *World-Herald*, "sent messages to Nebraska Saturday, appealing to the people to redouble their efforts in the scrap drive." Horace E. Lewis, president of Pittsburgh's Jones & Laughlin Steel Corporation, wrote that "the people of Nebraska have set out to do a good job. Please urge them not to lag in their final efforts, for millions of tons of scrap are urgently needed in the steel mills." R. J. Wysor of Republic Steel had a starker message for the Cornhuskers, warning that without adequate scrap, "We are faced right now with the possibility of shutting down open hearth furnaces in the near future." The "road to victory," summarized Edwin C. Barringer of the Institute of Scrap Iron and Steel, "is paved with scrap. Nebraska can help mightily." With an imposing total of twenty-three such messages directed at Nebraskans from the steel industry, the desperate need for scrap in the war effort could not have been clearer.[10]

An even simpler crisis-inducing tactic emerged in a continual emphasis on the drive's looming deadline. As the campaign's conclusion crept closer, newspapers increasingly adopted an urgent tone to remind scrappers how little time was left for turning in scrap metal. One headline bellowed this compelling message: "Scrap Contest Enters Final Week—Hurry!" Another proclaimed that it was the "'Last Half of Ninth' for Scrap." A *World-Herald* story stressed "the inexorable fact that on the contest calendar there remained only five days—five short days." The *Evening State Journal* chimed in by reminding readers that the "state has 3 more scrap days," with the *Chadron Chronicle* similarly noting that there were "only two more days to get in that scrap metal that is so important." The *Evening World-Herald* then expanded on these warnings, editorializing that there were only "two days left. Today and tomorrow. Let's finish the job in a big way—like real Nebraskans."[11] As if the state's scrappers were not already under significant pressure, such dire messages about the campaign's ticking clock must have seemed ominous indeed.

Finally, scrap officials emphasized and compounded their various crisis messages by intensifying descriptions of the drive at nearly every turn. At times, the fervor of the campaign's ballyhoo was striking. "Comprehensive

Time is slipping by . . . $2,000.00 Scrap Metal & Rubber Contest Closes Aug. 8th!

Rough Outline of What Losing War Would Cost

DON'T LEAVE IT ALL UP TO GEORGE!

13. As the end of the statewide drive neared, the *World-Herald* did what it could to intensify its appeals, as in this detail from a full-page ad featuring a demonic Hitler. Image courtesy of the Douglas County Historical Society, reprinted with permission from the *Omaha World-Herald*.

plans adopted for the windup by practically all counties," noted one report, "promise to produce a rip-snorting, blood-in-the-eye tussle [in] the coming week." Valley County was said to be plotting a "home stretch sprint," Knox County was ready for its own "intensive three-day scrap metal drive," Holt County was "preparing to deliver its knockout punch," and Merrick County was aiming for a "grand finale" that would finish up the campaign with a flourish. On August 2, the *Sunday World-Herald* intensified what was at stake in these climactic efforts by printing a full-page ad that depicted a demonic Adolf Hitler, complete with glaring red eyes (see fig. 13). The dictator's claws held a news clipping that described Americans as potential slaves to the Nazis and "as human targets for Japanese bayonet practice." All were results, it implied, of what might happen if the final scrap drive efforts were to fail. "Time is slipping by," advised the ad. It then added a telling question: "Are you doing everything you can?" Meanwhile, state salvage chair Mark T. Caster offered his own intensifying remarks, pleading for Nebraskans to "devote every spare moment" to gathering scrap in the final days. Failing to do so might actually "cost the life of a soldier, sailor, or marine." From nearly every side, it was obvious that the scrap campaign planners were trying to encourage an intense conclusion to the drive. It was little wonder, as the *Scottsbluff Daily Star-Herald* reported on August 4, that "Nebraskans figuratively gave a hitch to their belts" as they "tore into the job of adding the last tons to the state-wide scrap collection campaign."[12]

But even as the scrap campaign planners worked on numerous fronts to establish a crisis mentality for the drive's concluding segment, they were also wise enough to provide several well-publicized opportunities for scrappers to resolve that crisis by finding and hauling significant amounts of scrap. In Omaha, for example, organizers announced on August 2 that in addition to the regular schedule of daytime neighborhood pickups, residents would be able to take advantage of a twilight pickup during the last four days of the drive. The *World-Herald* called for 300 volunteers to staff the evening trucks and was quick to let readers know that officials were "surprised and disappointed" when only 25 showed up for the first night. That initial glitch, however, set up a resounding success story on August 6. On that night, 225 Union Pacific laborers marched to the staging area "like the Marines . . . galloping to the rescue" (see fig. 14). With the addition of some 50 volunteers from local unions, each truck during the session averaged 6 helpers, allowing crews to load numerous heavy items that had been bypassed in previous pickups. In all, the Thursday evening session collected an impressive 112 tons of scrap, and the twilight pickup on Friday garnered 126 additional tons.[13] It was a clear sign that the drive's crescendo was under way.

Sensibly, the campaign provided children with a fitting resolution to the culminating crisis as well. Eva Grimes, the campaign's state chairwoman, persuaded the state movie theater association to ask every local venue to sponsor a scrap matinee for area youth. The price of admission

14. On August 6, over 200 Union Pacific workers marched as a unit to volunteer for Omaha's twilight pickup, making the evening a tremendous success. Image reprinted with permission from the *Omaha World-Herald*.

for many of the shows was at least five pounds of scrap material, although some venues, like Custer County's Lyric Theatre, confided that they would admit any youngsters who had with them "all the scrap they can carry, even though it weighs less" than the admission weight. The state's theater owners pledged to find their own scrap, too, which would join the children's admission fees in a heap in the middle of the street in front of each theater. Accordingly, on Friday, August 7, tens of thousands of young Nebraskans showed up at movie houses across the state, dragging, hauling, or carrying their scrap for the show. In Omaha alone, some 12,500 youngsters invaded the city's theaters, producing over 75 tons of scrap that, in several cases, caused traffic jams.[14] As with their elders, then, Nebraska's youngest generation appeared to be responding to the campaign's ending crisis with an enthusiastic resolve.

The scrap drive's most climactic opportunity, however, originated in the governor's office. On August 5, Governor Griswold issued a bold executive proclamation, noting that "fine as our effort has been, the results must be much greater if this campaign is to succeed." Published on the front page of newspapers across the state, the proclamation designated Friday, August 7, as Harvest Festival Day for every village, town, and city in the state. The townsfolk, directed the governor, should abandon their usual activities for the day in order to scour "every inch of home, attic, basement, yard, and business place" for additional scrap material. The proclamation also designated the last day of the drive, August 8, as "Farm Scrap Holiday in Nebraska." The governor advised that on that Saturday, every farmer should "turn from his field work and devote himself to collecting and taking to his nearest town, the scrap metal our soldiers must have." Not surprisingly, the official announcement was welcomed with approval by organizers. As the *Evening State Journal* reported, scrap officials "expected a tremendous pickup in collections to result from Governor Griswold's action."[15]

Local scrappers responded to the governor's call for a fitting climax to the drive. The town of Bennington, for instance, decided to shut down entirely on Friday afternoon, sending twelve trucks into the countryside, with fifty eager volunteers in tow. Norfolk's American Legion post used the scrap holiday to dispatch crews to dismantle much of a 110-foot-tall water tower that had perched atop Standpipe Hill since 1888. In Benkelman and Haigler, local scrap officials sounded the town siren at 5:45 a.m. on Friday, summoning the Dundy County scrap commandos to a full day of collection tasks. Plattsmouth, nerve center of the Cass County salvage effort, chose to throw a gigantic "Skrap Karnival" on Saturday, attracting 5,000 people with a colorful parade that included numerous truckloads of fresh scrap (see fig. 15). Farms and ranches in locations scattered across the state spent the weekend hosting swarms of scrapping townspeople. And, back in Omaha, the city's Civilian Defense Council issued a call for 100 women to staff a phone center during the scrap holiday, with the aim of calling every one of Omaha's 74,000 telephone numbers to offer a final scrap reminder. In an amazing display of motivation, nearly 400

15. Numerous climactic events took place across the state in the drive's closing days, including Plattsmouth's Skrap Karnival parade. Image reprinted with permission from the *Omaha World-Herald*.

volunteers showed up, swamping the center.[16] It was more evidence, if any were needed, that the governor's proclamation had been a smashing success.

As the scrap drive came to a close, it was increasingly apparent that the people of Nebraska had responded to the widespread rhetoric of crisis in an unprecedented fashion. Indeed, noted *Editor & Publisher*, "the final two days of the campaign found Nebraska working at fever pitch, with volunteer men and women scouring for scrap throughout the day and far into the night." The *World-Herald*'s unofficial standings reflected this dramatic increase in activity. During the early portion of the contest, the statewide per capita figure had crept upward by only about 3 pounds per day. In August the daily increase jumped to about 4 or 5 pounds. But not until county reports gradually began to emerge from the final scrap barrage did the state's average truly begin to surge. In standings published on August 10, there was a 17-point jump over the previous day's average. On the same day, the number of counties with individual averages over 100 pounds per person leapt from 18 to 28, and the reports were still coming in as the various county chairmen worked furiously to catch up from the late deluge of scrap.[17]

The impressive upswing in results was a bona fide cause for celebration in the *World-Herald*'s scrap headquarters. Even Doorly's various detractors could not deny that the crescendo had been tremendous. At long last, it seemed, the newspaper's desire for a scrap-themed musical performance, clashing cymbals and all, had been granted.[18] Even better, however, was the fact that the state's metaphoric orchestra had done it all with a twist: as it turned out, the tune they were playing was not a moving symphony but a spirited military march.

Out of Many, One Army

One of the many sports figures caught up in the scrap drive's thunderous crescendo had the curious name of Bosco. No one remembered where the name had come from, and Bosco remained silent on the matter. Neither was he listening as the drumbeat of public opinion to draft him forcibly into the war effort grew louder and louder in the scrap campaign's closing days. But when the *World-Herald* proclaimed, on August 6, that the "opportunity is passing swiftly for the removal of a civic eyesore," it was clear that the situation had become serious.

The unfortunate Bosco was, of course, a sculpture, and he was almost universally loathed by the good people of Omaha. He had been placed on his pedestal in Elmwood Park in 1927 as an expression of gratitude to the city from the Omaha Amateur Baseball Association. Unfortunately, once it was put on display, the figure had instantly looked less like a fearsome home run hitter and more like a hapless player who had just struck out in embarrassing fashion. "Bosco the Fly-Swatter," jeered the *World-Herald*'s Frederick Ware. There he "stands . . . mocking every baseballer who ever took a batting stance." Maybe "Bosco should be set forthwith to making cartridge jackets, shell casings, [or] bearings."[19]

Bosco's sudden transformation from civic monument to potential scrap metal early that August was probably not a surprise to the many citizens who had disliked him from the start. The *World-Herald*'s campaign had, after all, trained them to look high and low for any source of scrap metal, and Bosco, frankly, was hard to miss. Yet a surprise did emerge on the last day of the campaign, when the sculpture mysteriously appeared in the midst of a scrap truck load in downtown Omaha. Scrappers unknown, it seemed, had pried him from his pedestal, then forcibly removed his metallic baseball cap and bat. In their place the mirthful contributors had supplied Bosco with a doughboy helmet and an ancient rifle, essentially putting him on guard duty at Scrap Mountain. "It was the last of [the] ninth," exulted the *World-Herald* the following day, but Bosco and his metal outfit were now "in the army for the duration."[20]

The drafting of Bosco was a fitting reminder of how far the scrap campaign had come in only three weeks. From the opening day it had been evident that fanciful appeals could easily transform radiators into rifles and garden hoes into grenades, just as they later transformed Bosco into ball bearings. Yet by the drive's final week, those sorts of appeals had gone a step further. In a process that began to emerge with Mrs. Stewart's "port arms" image on July 20, Nebraskans came to realize that they had themselves somehow enlisted in a unified, statewide army. The internal competition and rivalries were still present, to be sure. But at some point the spirit of the campaign had transformed the scrappers just as surely as Bosco the baseball player had become Bosco the soldier. Here was a second way to account for the scrap campaign's convincing second-half rally. Put most simply, as the drive negotiated its remarkable crescendo, scrappers across the state found themselves working together in a distinct sense of *militarized unity*.[21]

One of the initial stages in this transformation was the outright redefinition of the competition itself. Earlier perspectives on the contest element had returned again and again to emphasize that the state's ninety-three counties were involved in an aggressive horse race. "COUNTY VS. COUNTY," proclaimed a July 23 advertisement for the campaign.

"Which is Nebraska's most patriotic county? Which will organize best and pitch in to collect the greatest number of pounds of scrap per capita? The race is on. The competition is hot." Newspaper reports on the drive naturally reflected this view, such as when Dawes County was said to have had "no mercy for its competitors" as it "jumped into the saddle . . . and rode roughshod into the lead."[22] The numerous counties that had stated, from the start of the drive, that they were out to win the top prize were another indication of the high value many scrappers had initially placed on the cutthroat competition.

In the campaign's final week, however, the nature of the race underwent a startling change. The contest element seemed to lose ground as scrap officials began to stress themes of collaboration and solidarity. On August 3, the *World-Herald* presented an editorial underneath the headline "Down the Stretch." The title alone appeared to suggest that the horse race viewpoint was still central. On the contrary, the editorial staff suggested instead that the state's scrappers should *work together* during the culmination of the drive. In the newspaper's words, "If this campaign is to be pushed through to a smashing success, everyone will have to co-operate." The editorial concluded by crying, "Let's go, Nebraska—down the home stretch!" The newspaper used this stirring appeal not to stress the scrap competition but rather to remind readers that the drive was actually a struggle to make the state "a shining model of what patriotic co-operation among all the people can accomplish."[23]

Scrap officials were walking a fine line here. It would have been folly for them to overtly devalue the competition, since that feature of the drive was in fact a crucial motivating element for many counties and their scrappers. Indeed, the last week of the campaign did feature a few incidents that reflected aggressive competition. In McCook, for instance, the Kiwanis and Rotary Clubs began borrowing cars from the opposing service group and leaving them for scrap at the Red Willow County heap. Another incident took place up in Knox County, when the town of Crofton resolved an impasse with nearby Bloomfield over a sizeable cache located midway between the two areas by preemptively seizing it in a midnight scrapping raid.[24]

But such combative aspects of the drive seemed much less prominent during the campaign's crescendo, as the scrap coverage increasingly stressed that the competition was healthy, not for its own sake but for the sake of the greater cause. An impressed Caster, the state's salvage chair, told the *Evening State Journal* that "people all over the state became so much interested in getting the scrap from homes, shops, and farms that they forgot all petty differences." The state's numerous scrap piles, agreed *Editor & Publisher*, "were not hideous, rusting heaps, but things representing the united effort of a people." Doorly's editorial staff was also impressed with the culminating show of unity, noting that by the drive's end, all of the state's scrappers had "stood together, pushing, shoving, hauling, cheering for America."[25]

The most poignant depiction of this statewide unity appeared in a full-page *World-Herald* advertisement on August 5. The top half of the ad consisted of a detailed drawing by the newspaper's staff cartoonist, Walter LaHue (see fig. 16). The amusing image portrays more than twenty Nebraskans throwing, or preparing to throw, various pieces of scrap material directly at caricatures of Axis leaders Adolf Hitler, Benito Mussolini, and Hideki Tojo. Horseshoes, safes, bedsprings, anvils, tractors, jalopies, stoves, and many more scrap items pummel the besieged enemy figures, who are depicted in humiliating and defeated positions. Mussolini, for example, has both an ice pick and a pitchfork stuck in his hindquarters, and one of his fingers is being crushed in a mousetrap. Even worse, a water trough is about to be thrown at the trio; on its side, "for hosses" is crossed out and replaced with "for jack asses."

Significantly, Nebraskans from every walk of life are included in the cartoon fun, from children to Scouts to rural folks to city dwellers. Several urban buildings, including what might be Omaha's ornate post office, anchor the upper left portion of the image, while a series of farm structures are just as prominent on the upper right. On the lower right, a sign in the shape of Nebraska affirms that this barrage is a *statewide* effort; no region or demographic is excluded. Indeed, there is no sign of backstabbing competition in the cartoon at all. The ballplayers, farmers, housewives, businessmen, and laborers are

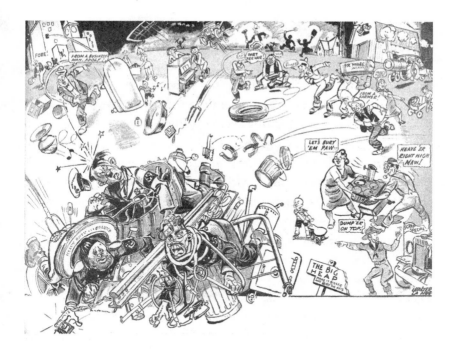

16. In this detail from the *World-Herald*'s full-page scrap ad on August 5, one can see a broad cross-section of cartoon Nebraskans working together to bury the Axis leaders with scrap. Image courtesy of the Douglas County Historical Society, reprinted with permission from the *Omaha World-Herald*.

all focused solely on the collaborative work of burying the Axis with their scrap.

In part, this cartoon was yet another fanciful way of portraying scrap as a weapon of war that would directly impact the Axis powers. Yet it was also, by extension, a means of demonstrating that the Nebraskans in the image were enacting a new role as home front soldiers in the war effort against that enemy. The primary caption on the bottom half of the ad confirmed this notion, intoning that there was "Not a Slacker in the Lot." A *slacker*, for these 1940s citizens, would have meant someone who was avoiding the draft or other service related to the military. But there were, according to the ad, no such slackers in this scrap effort. Instead, scrappers from every part of the state had patriotically become part of a quasi-military unit, their camaraderie deriving from a single-minded effort to "give 'em the works."[26]

Fittingly, the notion that the scrappers had somehow overcome regional differences and competitive animosities to become a militarized force in their own right appeared frequently during the drive's crescendo. "We've got boys in the fighting service," Phelps County officials told local scrappers on August 5, so "let's do a little fighting on our own front." Two days later, the *Omaha Star* wrote that members of the city's black community were "filled with a zeal to do their part in turning back the onrush of Hitler and his fascist hordes." On the same day, the *Benkelman Post and News-Chronicle* marveled at the power of a "civilian population on the march in an uprising against the Axis forces," while Scotts Bluff County likewise exulted that it had "marshaled its reserve troops in the battle to keep the blast furnaces of the nation at white heat against the Axis hordes." The *Beatrice Sun* seemed to agree with these sentiments, pointing out on August 4 that Gage County scrappers had "gathered everything from old keys to old furnaces" as a way to assault not fellow county competitors but "dear Adolf (the !c,?@)." There was indeed tremendous martial power, summarized the *World-Herald*, "when the people move as a mighty army against any obstacle to their purpose." That obstacle, as LaHue's cartoon had demonstrated, was not rival service groups, counties, or even regions. Instead, it was the Axis enemy, and the patriotic duty of these militarized scrappers was to work together so that their accumulated labors would soon be "rattling the walls of Berlin."[27]

The figurative transformation of Cornhusker civilians into soldiers in the war effort was also present in more private contexts, as the *World-Herald*'s J. M. Harding found out on the last day of the campaign. On that day, an Omaha resident called the scrap headquarters downtown and asked for someone to come pick up her son's metal toys. A truck driver eventually arrived at the woman's home, only to find that the toys in question amounted to just a few meager pounds of metal. Instead of being upset, however, the driver ended up taking the tiny load to the Scrap Mountain with great reverence. As he told Harding, the mother had explained that her son had died twenty years earlier, while still an infant. The toys were among the only items belonging to him that she had kept over the years. But now the scrap drive had made her realize that if her son had lived, he would probably be in the army, doing his part to fight the Axis. The mother's emotional conclusion was inevitable: her son's cherished toys would have to do his part now. Those toys, Harding related later, might only "have made a few bullets, but it meant that she gave something that she had prized above anything in the world, and she did that because for three weeks she had been reading these stories and seeing what people were doing." Like her fellow Nebraskans, this grieving woman had come to see her scrap contribution as being primarily military in nature. Her contribution to the cause was a small one, to be sure. But it was heartfelt, and as such it revealed how fervently many citizens had come to believe in the Nebraska Plan and its martial goals.[28]

Thus much as Bosco had found himself transformed during the drive's climax into a militarized unit of scrap, so too did the citizens of Nebraska find themselves transformed during that climax into a militarized scrap unit. This "army of Nebraskans to whom only defeat is impossible," to use the *World-Herald*'s admiring description, had responded to the drive's ending crisis with determination, urgency, and teamwork. As scrapper Ruby Schulz remembered it, "Everybody worked together" as the drive went on. "Nobody worked as just one person," she continued. "We're Americans, and that's what went through our minds: we are Americans." Little wonder, then, that their concluding labors had produced an inspired comeback in the all-important second half. Scrap officials were by this point working overtime to process the overwhelming onslaught of metallic objects, meaning that the official results would take several more days to calculate. Yet the dramatic heaps of scrap material located in countless places across the state seemed to contribute to a general sense that something miraculous had just occurred in this campaign, regardless of the final tally. As Doorly's staffers chose to put it in a rare front-page editorial: "You people of Nebraska . . . have been magnificent."[29]

The Iron-Clad Miracle

The community bonfire that took place in downtown Omaha at 7:45p.m. on the night of August 8, 1942 celebrated three weeks of stress, tenacity, labor, and exhaustion in service to the nation. Doorly's scrap team shared this sentiment, suggesting earlier in the day that it would be a "blaze of jubilation" that would "write finis to a drive such as no other city in this country has ever conducted." Thousands of citizens were present for the occasion, and they listened avidly as George Grimes, one of Doorly's chiefs of scrap, told them that "you and the other people of Nebraska have given the most amazing demonstration of loyalty and patriotic fervor." As if in response to these words, the massive crowd rose to sing the national anthem together while the city fire chief brought the seventy-five-foot bonfire to life. "Too bad that it couldn't be seen in Berlin," commented the next day's report, "for it announced to the world . . . that the people of this area will do whatever must be done to win the war."[30]

Yet celebration and commemoration shared the stage that evening with a more practical purpose: making the scrap pile just a bit higher. The campaign, as officials had continuously reminded the public, ended at midnight, so this was their last chance to bring in any remaining pieces of scrap for the current drive. In fact, the fire itself shared in the last-minute scrapping work. The designated fuel for the bonfire consisted of two dozen old pianos and 100 pinball machines, all previous donations to the drive. Salvage experts had concluded that the most efficient way to obtain the valuable metal in these items was to burn away the wooden shells (which had prompted the idea for a bonfire in the first place). Between the fire's efforts and the untold number of scrappers who continued to dump material right up to the deadline, it was a most productive night for the campaign.[31]

Behind the scenes, Doorly and his staff were already at work on the next stage of the Nebraska Plan. Grimes had alerted the White House to the state's effort a few days earlier in a personal letter to President Roosevelt. Doorly was doing his part by contacting his colleagues in the American Newspaper Publishers Association, encouraging them to duplicate the *World-Herald*'s effort in their own states. To simplify that process for other newspapers, the scrap team went to work composing and producing a fourteen-page booklet that described the campaign and its results in detail. As the booklet suggested, if Nebraska's campaign "could be repeated in 47 other states our nation would present so strong a front to the enemy, such unity in war effort, that the day of victory would be brought much nearer." The booklet went out to the nation's publishers on August 28, likely serving only to increase the widespread word of mouth that Doorly's plan had already generated.[32]

Back in Nebraska, meanwhile, all eyes were watching the unofficial scrap standings as they slowly caught up to the ending deluge of scrap material. The final tabulation of numerous UP and Burlington heaps—added, for the sake of the contest, to the county totals where they were first located—finally pushed the statewide per capita average over the 100 pound mark on August 15. Several days later, it settled at 103.64 pounds; it was, by far, the most impressive scrap effort in the nation to that point in the war. The feat was certified by the contest judges eleven days later, and the winners were duly invited to the state capitol building for a personal congratulations from the governor (see fig. 17).[33]

The official results were no doubt the subject of myriad animated conversations across the state in that final week of August. The county winner, Grant, deserved much adulation, since it had averaged an otherworldly 637.95 pounds for every one of its 1,327 residents. Hooker and Thomas Counties, both located next to Grant in traditional ranching country, were runners-up, with Phelps, Red Willow, Thayer, and Dundy Counties—all averaging over 200 pounds per citizen—following in close sequence. Elsewhere in the standings, Washington County had finally outdistanced Burt County, while Lancaster County had won its showdown with Lincoln County. Perhaps the most exhilarated scrappers of all, though, hailed from Omaha's Douglas County. Although the city's urban numbers diluted its per capita average down to 103 pounds, its overall totals were easily the largest in the state, with 2,700 tons of scrap ready to be sorted and sent into war production. But what made many of these urban scrappers proudest of all was that every part of the diverse

17. On August 28, Governor Griswold (at microphone) awarded a $1,000 war bond to R. R. Bilstein, Grant County salvage chairman. On the right are F. J. Stoughton, from runner-up Hooker County, and Mark T. Caster, state salvage chairman. Image reprinted with permission from the *Omaha World-Herald*.

city had "learned to co-operate as never before" during the campaign. As the *World-Herald* suggested, a bit wistfully, "perhaps it signalized a new era for Omaha."[34]

Of course, much of the state's pride was also directed at the munitions that were soon to be crafted from their hard labor. On August 16, the *Sunday World-Herald* devoted the top half of a page in its main section to an elaborate scrap pictograph as a way of visualizing what Nebraskans had accomplished. Under the bold title "Nebraska's Scrap: Now 134,110,053 Pounds," the image featured an aerial view of a gigantic heap of scrap metal. Several insets emerged from the pile, each one depicting a military use that might result from the state's total. In addition to 200 57-ton tanks, the diagram showed that in three weeks Nebraskans had also produced the equivalent of 1 million steel helmets, 10,000 antiaircraft machine guns, 1,000 three-inch antiaircraft artillery guns, 5 million hand grenades, 2,000 blitz buggies, 1 million three-inch antiaircraft shrapnel shells, and 10,000 500-pound bombs. It was an impressive list, not to mention a suitable means of justifying all of the effort that had gone into the three weeks of the drive.[35]

Yet there was a more important significance here, one that went beyond the logistics of scrap, steel, and munitions in a time of war. As the *World-Herald* had been at pains to point out over the summer, a great many Americans seemed to be apathetic about the war effort. Too frequently, citizens on the home front and soldiers on the battlefront seemed like they were worlds apart. In the wake of the statewide drive and its unforgettable crescendo, however, Doorly and his staff came to believe that there was a possible solution to the home front's malaise. They had demonstrated that committed and intense local leadership could draw on the dormant patriotism of most civilians and draw them into involvement, and it likely did not matter whether the cause was war bond sales, victory gardens, civil defense work, or just about any other activity related to the war effort.

In the case of scrap collection, the state's newspapers had used an all-out editorial and publicity blitz to entice, cajole, and push readers into the contest, and before long the competitive citizens had become intensely conscious of the need for scrap. As Doorly said a few weeks later, "There is another hundred pounds [per capita] in Nebraska that we are going to get before the end of October. We will get that because the people now are more war conscious and scrap conscious . . . than they have ever been before." Along with that growing consciousness, those citizens had developed pride in and taken fierce ownership of the effort. They had, in a word, militarized, and in the process the scrappers had somehow bridged the gap between home front and battlefront and between citizens and soldiers. "The people are awake!" exulted the *World-Herald*.[36] And in the aftermath of the three-week campaign, it seemed that the newspaper had it right. In many respects, that monumental accomplishment was the true miracle of the Nebraska scrap metal drive.

To be sure, such intangible results would have been difficult at best to describe to anyone who had not been there to experience it. Indeed, it was not at all easy to communicate to those from outside the state how tremendous the effort had been. By the end of the drive, most of the metaphors that had been used previously no longer seemed to fit. In transcending the bounds of competition, for instance, the drive no longer seemed as much like a football game, despite the rousing comeback. Neither would describing it as a musical symphony or a martial march really provide a very good characterization of its nature. Clearly, describing the campaign accurately to the rest of the nation would take a bit more thought. Henry Doorly, by this time trying to communicate to the Roosevelt administration and to his fellow publishers what had gone on in Nebraska, finally found himself reaching for another metaphor altogether, one that instantly communicated the drive's heartland roots, intense effort, and sweeping finish. "It was," he said with a mixture of wonderment and pride, "just like a prairie fire and make no mistake about it."[37]

6

The Nebraska Plan Goes National

The Omaha people certainly did an outstanding job. We are considering what we might be able to do.
—Richard W. Slocum to Lessing J. Rosenwald, August 25, 1942

On August 19, 1942, Leonard T. Kittinger sent a surprising memorandum to his boss, A. I. Henderson. As head of the Materials Division Salvage Section, Kittinger was one of the War Production Board's (WPB) central figures on the subject of scrap metal collection. Part of his unit's assignment was to determine how much civilian scrap metal might be available for collection across the country and to plot ways of obtaining it. Since Pearl Harbor, news of ambitious scrapping efforts in various areas of the country had occasionally come across his desk. Most of them, however, had turned out to produce only a modest—and temporary—jump in local scrap totals. And then, out of the blue, had come the news of a truly massive statewide campaign in Nebraska.[1]

This stunning effort, Kittinger's memo informed Henderson, had not been sponsored by salvage officials at all but by a large regional newspaper. "In three weeks," it exclaimed, the *Omaha World-Herald*'s drive had produced "an average per capita of over 101 pounds for every citizen in the State!" The figure was so unprecedented that it might well have been a typo. And yet the midwestern newspaper had the documentation to prove that what had seemed impossible could be done. These were "such outstanding results," Kittinger recommended, that "every effort should be made to have similar programs begun across the country."[2]

The Kittinger memo appears to have been the first time that an official from the Roosevelt administration truly understood the potential implications of Henry Doorly's Nebraska Plan. To be sure, other functionaries within the government had heard about the campaign before this point. One example was the anonymous Office of Price Administration official who had accidently come across Omaha's Scrap Mountain back in late July. Another was Stephen Early, President Roosevelt's press secretary, who had only recently turned down George Grimes's request for a congratulatory note from FDR to the state's scrappers.[3] In neither case did word about Doorly's plan appear to have made it across town to WPB, which was the government organization that was most desperate to do something about the scrap situation.

There was good reason for desperation. Secret war planning now anticipated an invasion of North Africa in late 1942, prompting the military leadership to order, among other equipment, over 12,000 new landing crafts from the Bureau of Ships. But as *Newsweek* intoned, the "steel situation was growing more critical by the hour," and so it was no real surprise when the military was told that faltering scrap supplies were having an impact on the amount of steel that would be readily available for their order. General Lucius D. Clay told the administration that the projected shortfall of steel plate — some 1.5 million tons in all — "would be disastrous to the Army program." WPB chief Donald M. Nelson was well aware of the problem, since he had been warned by his staffers in early July that if the situation remained unchanged, "the armed forces will have to make serious choices about what munitions it needs to prosecute the war." Nelson, in turn, cautioned a national radio audience on August 27 that "there is no possibility of over-emphasizing the importance" of the scrap problem. "This war is being fought with metals," he reminded his listeners. "When we have done everything we can to increase our ability to get the ores out of the ground, we shall still fall short unless we get the scrap metal to the furnaces also." There could be little doubt, as an internal WPB report on the meager scrap supply noted, that "special action of some kind is imperative."[4]

Ironically, when the WPB staffers finally did come across Doorly's plan, the kind of special action that it called for appeared to puzzle them to no end. How was it possible, they must have thought, for a private entity—one that was so far outside of the government's direct influence—to enlist over a million people so energetically in the gritty business of scrap collection? The question was all the more frustrating given the government's own failed efforts to popularize civilian salvage work. Since mid-July, WPB's Conservation Division had even been running a nationwide advertising campaign, pleading for the public to turn in scrap. But even with thousands of official salvage committees in every part of the country, the government's most strenuous efforts were having little or no apparent effect on the vast majority of civilians on the home front.[5]

As Kittinger reviewed the particulars of the Nebraska Plan, he began to suspect that the federal approach's essential problem was its inability to adapt to local and regional contexts. "It seems apparent," he mused to Henderson, "that what the whole thing lacks is local punch, dramatization, and direction which will stir up the public enthusiasm [that is] so essential." Evidently speaking with one official voice from Washington and relying on a confusing scrap bureaucracy was exactly the wrong strategy for getting the public interested in supporting the war effort. This plan that "evolved in Nebraska," Kittinger finally decided, "must be geared to the local situation as it exists today."[6]

To their credit, it did not take the members of WPB's scrap team long to decide that the Nebraska Plan was their best chance to turn the looming scrap disaster around. Kittinger and Henderson consulted with Lessing J. Rosenwald, the director of WPB's Conservation Division, who brought WPB chief Nelson himself into the conversation. They agreed to contact Doorly and ask him to make arrangements for his team to come to Washington. Rosenwald also sought the guidance of Richard W. Slocum, general manager of the *Philadelphia Evening Bulletin*. Slocum was an officer in the American Newspaper Publishers Association and had already been instrumental in showing how a major newspaper could cooperate with the federal government, albeit on a campaign to sell war stamps to children. It was agreed by all concerned that a meeting of publishers from around the country should be held, its agenda to center on one item: the possibility of an emergency national scrap campaign led not by the government but by newspapers. That the meeting was to be held on September 4, just two weeks after Kittinger first recognized the value of Doorly's approach, illustrates how desperate WPB really was to take immediate action.[7]

It so happened that the flurry of activity within WPB in the closing days of August was a precursor to the momentous events that were soon to take place across the vast home front. The stages of the plan were no doubt clear to Kittinger, Henderson, and Rosenwald. First, the meeting in the capital would need to persuade publishers to lend their support to a national scrap effort, and this could well prove to be a challenging task. If the meeting were to be successful, the newspapers would need to work rapidly to prepare a publicity blitz. Those preparations would then usher in a tremendous scrap competition among the states, with local newspapers directing the efforts of millions of formerly oblivious citizens. Finally, by the time snow began to bury much of the nation's potential salvage material, a bountiful scrap harvest would have been gathered. If all went well, they hoped, their plans would help ensure the production of steel at maximum capacity throughout the winter months and well into 1943.

A Capital Meeting

Lessing J. Rosenwald called the all-important meeting to order at 10:15 a.m., Eastern War Time. It was muggy and overcast in Washington DC, as nearly 200 publishers from around the country filed into the auditorium in the sparkling new Social Security Building on Independence Avenue. Their programs revealed that an imposing lineup of speakers would be addressing them. Nelson would be present, of course, as would Elmer Davis, director of the Office of War Information. Lieutenant General Brehon B. Somervell and Vice Admiral Samuel M. Robinson were there to represent the military perspective, while Robert W. Wolcott, president of the Lukens Steel Company, would offer the steel industry's view on the scrap emergency.

In a bit of a contrast, two relative unknowns had joined these captains of government, military, and industry on the stage. The pair turned out to be Henry Doorly and J. M. Harding of the *Omaha World-Herald*.[8]

It would have been clear to everyone present that this was no low-key meeting. Nelson and Davis were all but daily fixtures in the national media, not to mention regular advisors to the White House. Robinson and Somervell were the key military figures in charge of supplying and arming the navy and the army. Their schedules, in the midst of the ongoing buildup of U.S. forces and munitions, had little room for frivolous gatherings. A further sign of the occasion's critical nature was that reporters from several major news outlets were present, ready to tell the world about the events in this room. WPB had even arranged for a stenographic service to transcribe the meeting for the many publishers who had not been able to travel to the capital on such short notice.

The high profile nature of the meeting was essentially a means of reinforcing the urgency of scrap metal collection. As a group, the publishers were aware that the government was going to ask for a significant commitment on their part, and many of them were likely to be uncertain and even wary. Slocum, the publisher from Philadelphia, had communicated as much to WPB's staffers. "To do the job right," he warned, will require "a very substantial amount of newspaper space . . . as well as special editorial treatment." But many of the nation's newspapers were already committing significant resources to the war effort. Slocum's own publication, for example, had loaned some of its key staffers to the government for war projects, was currently donating space for war bond advertising, and had by this point spent $100,000 in the separate war stamps drive. "You may be sure," he had told Rosenwald, "that despite all of the other calls on us we want to lend your very important effort as much assistance as possible." But Slocum's unwritten implication was clear: the government would need to prepare some truly compelling reasons why the newspaper publishers should offer their wholehearted support to yet another campaign.[9]

With only two hours to work with, then, WPB would need to present a concise and persuasive case. As Kittinger's memo had proposed, the central aim of the meeting would "be to have the seriousness of the materials problem stressed and to enlist nation-wide publisher support for this plan." In what appeared to be a well-coordinated agenda, the speakers at the meeting set about doing exactly that. In essence, their remarks focused on detailed answers to two important questions that would have been in the publishers' minds even as the meeting opened: *Why is the scrap situation so urgent? And how do you think we can help?*[10]

Nelson began to address the initial question with the dire comment that "we are not yet doing a very good job of winning the war." Part of the reason, the WPB chief explained, was that the task was so inherently colossal. The U.S. production system was supplementing Britain's output, sending significant amounts of munitions to the Russian ally, supplying materiel to Australia, India, and China, and, of course, trying to keep the domestic economy healthy. "That is only part of the job that we have to do with our left hand," he added, "and with the right hand we have to equip an army . . . of the size that we have never before contemplated." These wartime requirements were dependent on a fully functioning steel industry, which itself was relying on a constant stream of scrap metal. "But today," he intoned, "and I don't want you to feel that I am exaggerating in the slightest, that junk . . . [is] as important as any single problem that we have in the country." In fact, "there are some four million tons of that scrap that we can get out this year," he concluded, "and we need every ounce of it to keep our furnaces going."[11]

General Somervell confirmed Nelson's testimony about the vital nature of the steel industry in prosecuting the war. As he told the publishers, "there is practically no article of Army equipment — and the same is true of the Navy — that doesn't require metal, and the basic metal is steel. If we can lick our steel problem, we have gone a long way towards licking the whole problem." Admiral Robinson was equally emphatic, noting that "it takes 25,000 tons of steel to build an aircraft carrier like the Essex, which we launched a month ago, and 2,000 tons to build one of our larger destroyers." To ignore the scrap supply problem, he said, would be to fail to provide "the Army and Navy with all the strategic materials they need to forge their weapons on an adequate scale and in sufficient time to guarantee our winning of the war."[12]

The heart of the problem, as Wolcott then outlined it, was that steel mills were not receiving sufficient amounts of scrap material to keep their furnaces running without the risk of slowdowns or shutdowns. The steel industry representative's testimony pulled no punches. "Unless a miracle happens," he revealed, "two furnaces in Chicago are going to close down over the weekend. San Francisco is in bad shape. Pittsburgh and Youngstown are in horrible shape." And the outlook for the near future was grim, since the nation's steel mills "only have two weeks scrap supply." The bottom line, he emphasized, was that the steel industry was "going to end up the year of 1942 with having produced 5,000,000 tons less than our capacity. And, gentlemen, to all intents and purposes, this can be laid to the inadequacy of the supply of scrap in the hands of steel mills."[13] Through such somber testimony, it seems quite possible that the urgency of the scrap situation had suddenly become much more apparent to the gathered publishers.

But what could the newspaper industry actually do about the desperate need for scrap metal? Wolcott acknowledged that the challenge lay not only in convincing the public that the need was immediate but also in actually motivating citizens to roll up their sleeves so they would undertake "the dirty job of finding and hauling this scrap." Davis, the OWI chief, pointed out that local newspapers would be "the natural leaders of such an effort," one that would come "up from the grass roots." Admiral Robinson agreed, suggesting that the newspaper industry had tremendous persuasive powers at its disposal. "It takes imagination," he remarked, "to translate an old and rusty crowbar into the casing of a shell for one of our battleship guns." He specified that "you gentlemen must supply that imagination. Through your columns you must bring vividly home to the people the picture of steel as the backbone of our ships and planes and guns and show them how they can help to make that backbone strong."[14]

WPB's view was that the *World-Herald* had already shown how a series of committed local newspapers could create just such a vivid picture of scrap for readers. Nebraska's statewide campaign, confessed Rosenwald, "caused us to do some fresh thinking on the subject of salvage." He introduced Doorly and Harding, who proceeded to outline their experience in the summer drive. The publisher explained how his wife had shamed him into coming up with a plan and how the initial coverage of the effort had expanded from two columns per day up to ten. He described, to general laughter, how the campaign had grown into "what you might call a Billy Sunday revival, combined with a horse race." The final result, he concluded, was not just nearly 70,000 tons of scrap, but a general public whose awareness of the need for scrap was now at an all-time high. Harding, in turn, offered plentiful details on the mechanics of the plan, as well as moving testimony on its emotional impact for both the newspaper staffers and the scrappers themselves. In the end, he said, "This campaign is an editorial proposition, pure and simple. To be a success it has got to be lived and breathed by your editorial department." But despite the difficulties and the time and the expense, he said in his final appeal, "this is something that the newspapers can handle."[15]

Doorly and Harding were the final speakers on the program. Unfortunately, with a scheduled group luncheon at the elegant Raleigh Hotel approaching quickly, there was little time for formal deliberation among the attendees. It seemed to matter little. Walter M. Dear, the president of the American Newspaper Publishers Association, recognized that the publishers had been more than convinced by the panel of speakers. "We accept the challenge," he told Nelson on the publishers' behalf. "So far as the newspapers are concerned we have got the ability and we can produce the scrap." This sentiment was put to a voice vote, and the publishers affirmed unanimously that Dear should immediately appoint a select committee of newspaper representatives in order to begin planning a national version of the Nebraska Plan. The publishers' meeting had been a resounding success, but now the intense preparations for the drive lay ahead.[16]

Preparing for a Scrap

The word about the publishers' meeting and the upcoming scrap campaign soon went out across the nation. "Nelson Appeals to Press to Spur Scrap Collection" was the headline in the *Los Angeles Times*. Robert De Vore's story in the *Washington Post* noted that the newspaper industry had been "called upon . . . for the 'miracle' that will keep the country's steel mills from shutting down for want of scrap." It was "Nebraska to the Rescue," proclaimed *Life* magazine, suggesting that Dear's committee was so motivated to promote Doorly's template that it had "blood in its eye and a plan hot in its hand." Not surprisingly, much of the coverage looked back at Nebraska's original drive and considered whether or not other states would be able to measure up to it. "Can Ohio do as well?" asked the *Toledo Blade*'s Grove Patterson. The *San Antonio Express* expressed a similar sentiment, asking its readers: "May not Texans and others be counted upon to respond as generously?"[17]

Acting quickly, Dear's committee sent a formal challenge to thousands of daily and weekly newspapers on September 11, asking that editorial staffs begin to draw up plans for a local rendition of what was now being called the Newspapers' Scrap Metal Drive. The effort was to last three weeks, ideally beginning on Monday, September 28, and ending on October 17—with an introductory blast of publicity starting a week before the kickoff. Local variations were encouraged, as long as the newspapers supported the effort as much as they feasibly could at the current time. To simplify the planning process, the committee also sent out a campaign manual containing a detailed list of suggestions for initiating the campaign, sample editorials, speech texts for use by local dignitaries, scrap-themed cartoons, and even advertising copy designed for adaptation to regional needs. Perhaps most important, the manual urged that the newspapers foster local scrap contests, much like the earlier experience in Nebraska. Of course, the most prominent competition this time would be the state vs. state race, with the top three contestants to receive from WPB an engraved victory plaque meant for permanent display in their respective state capitols. However, counties from across the nation would compete as well, joining local contests among countless schools and service groups. At the same time, each city and county that reached the goal of 100 pounds of scrap per person would receive a pennant that it could display at the courthouse, post office, or city hall. In many areas, newspapers and civic groups would likely add their own local prizes to boost interest and motivation.[18]

Nebraskans, who were watching these preparations with great interest, received an early taste of the competitive aspect of the upcoming campaign. In mid-September, the *World-Herald* sent a team of reporters to Kansas to offer details on their summer drive to a number of publishing colleagues. Oscar Stauffer, patriarch of the Stauffer newspaper chain, concluded the meeting by challenging the visiting Cornhuskers to a one-on-one scrap contest within the context of the national effort. "We've never sat by in Kansas and let Nebraska beat us in anything," he said, and "we won't let Nebraska beat us in scrap collection." One of the *World-Herald* staffers was quick to retort that for the previous twenty-five years, the Kansas Jayhawks had experienced a prolonged "lack of success in defeating Nebraska's Cornhuskers in football." Clearly a passionate "scrap duel" was brewing. Soon Governor Griswold and Governor Payne Ratner were formally wagering a $25 war bond on the head-to-head "Corn-Hawk" contest, with the winner to auction the bond for charity at halftime of the October 31 Kansas-Nebraska game.[19]

Elsewhere, forty-six other states were making plans, too. Ohio salvage officials began to organize a "junior army" of scrapping schoolchildren, with principals and teachers asked to serve as majors and captains in the effort. In St. Paul, Minnesota, officials ordered 40,000 small flags so that every household contributing scrap to the drive could proudly display the Stars and Stripes on their front lawn. The mayor of nearby Minneapolis offered a challenge to St. Paul's mayor, wagering a barrel of flour against a St. Paul lamb that his city would gather more scrap. In Iowa, Cass County and Montgomery County renewed their traditional rivalry in a head-to-head scrap duel, with the losing side's administrators obligated to sweep the streets of the winner's county seat for all to see. And on September 22, Idaho governor Chase A. Clark followed in Griswold's footsteps by issuing a scrap proclamation that urged citizens to participate in the drive in every way possible, as did Wisconsin governor Julius Heil two days alter.[20]

The typically festive mood of these sorts of preparations emerged in numerous references to the drive in popular culture. Poet Margaret Fishback set the scrap campaign to verse, advising Americans in an issue of *Collier's* magazine to

Save all your metal caps and cans,
Your venerable pots and pans,
Old razor blades and paper clips,
For metal helps build planes and ships.

Dr. Seuss provided a visual example of this cheerful approach in *Junk*, a government booklet distributed to the nation's fourth, fifth, and sixth graders that fall (see fig. 18). The cartoon was a typically fanciful representation of the ultimate objective of the scrap process, vividly showing youngsters how ordinary metal objects could transform into weapons that would batter the Axis enemy (in this case, a crude Japanese caricature). Moreover, the artist portrayed the cartoon's young scrapper as being physically present on the battlefield and even engaging in the attack himself. The fact that the drawing simultaneously managed to communicate that such young scrap soldiers were having fun while engaged in their task likely made it all the more attractive.[21]

Yet such good-natured ballyhoo was usually balanced by more sober commentary, which often relied on both fact and fancy in relating the importance of the campaign. In its hastily distributed publication *Scrap: And How to Collect It . . .* , for example, the American Industries Salvage Committee calculated that "each individual American soldier requires an average of 4,900 pounds of steel—in the form of carried or supporting equipment. In World War I he needed only 90 pounds!" The booklet insisted that homeowners needed to provide that steel immediately: "Those old golf clubs . . . that rusty plow . . . those obsolete castings—you won't save them for tomorrow when you know they could provide tough steel helmets to save young American lives . . . *now!*" The *World-Herald*'s own George Grimes offered similar testimony in a widely republished column, arguing that it was enough to "let a mother know that the old flat iron will make two helmets . . . for she has two sons at the front and they will need those two helmets, or the 30 hand grenades her iron will make." With over 1,800 dailies and 10,000 weeklies already promoting the upcoming drive by mid-September, these no-nonsense sorts of appeals achieved a tremendously wide currency.[22]

Dr. Seuss

18. The national scrap campaign's appeals appeared in many formats, as in this Dr. Seuss cartoon targeting younger Americans. Image courtesy of the National Archives.

As the opening day approached, the sweeping publicity for the campaign had clearly attracted a massive volunteer force of willing scrappers. The *Wall Street Journal* marveled that the campaign's "organization . . . is on an almost epic scale, with a locust-like army to assist citizens and industries to give their all in iron." Educational leaders anticipated that between 20 and 30 million of the country's schoolchildren would participate in the effort, ably led by some 8 million classroom teachers and principals. Thousands of local scrap committees—most of them relatively dormant before the newspapers' call to action—were also springing to life for the effort. Finally, the steel industry itself committed to sending 2,000 representatives door-to-door during the drive, reminding citizens across the country of the vital need for scrap.[23] There was, it seemed, a widespread recognition of the newspapers' challenge to the home front. The scrappers, in short, had been prepared for action; it was time for the race to commence.

State vs. State

Across the country, scrappers set to work promptly on September 28. Washington DC began its effort at 8:00 a.m., with 220 trucks and 37 collection points for eager scrappers to use. Officials in Queens declared it the start of a "salvage month," immediately sending out 700 trucks into borough neighborhoods. In Florida, diving crews used the first day to salvage a submerged pirate ship, sending its moldering cannons back into battle. And before long, over 1 million children, newly sworn-in members of a scrap-themed Junior Texas Rangers Division, began scouring the Lone Star State for metal. Elinor Morgenthau (who happened to be married to the secretary of the Treasury) aptly summed up the campaign's energetic start by explaining to the *Scrapper* that "the treasure we seek isn't bright gold—it's rusty metal to turn into new guns and bombs."[24]

No doubt more than a few of the scrappers were humming Bing Crosby's latest tune as they labored. "Junk Ain't Junk No More ('Cause Junk Will Win the War)" was the official theme song of the national scrap campaign, reminding Americans to give up their "old automobiles, old iron wheels, and the plow that works no more." Crosby joined other celebrities in advancing the drive, including Gene Autrey, Jack Benny, Barbara Britton, Walt Disney, Roy Rogers, and Rita Hayworth, who famously gave up her car's bumpers to the scrap heap (see fig. 19). Even President Roosevelt found himself in an unexpectedly prominent role, with the White House mail room soon becoming deluged with pieces of scrap metal dutifully sent in by the nation's children to their commander-in-chief. FDR let the public know that he was "very grateful," but he advised other patriotic scrappers to send their finds to the local salvage committee instead.[25]

As impressive junk heaps began to rise in all forty-eight states, however, local officials soon discovered that transporting all of that scrap material to central collection points was frequently a problem. Gas rationing, particularly on the East Coast, made it difficult for many communities to move individual and neighborhood piles to more useful locations. To help with what some came to call "scrap indigestion," administration officials decided to ease rationing for any volunteer scrap trucks—freeing up thousands of gallons of fuel for use in the drive. At the same time, the military directed all stateside naval and army installations to offer unused trucks and any personnel who could be spared to nearby scrap collection efforts.[26]

But in spite of the occasional congestion glitch, the scrappers found countless ways and means to haul the astonishing variety of metal treasures that they found. The ingenuity on display in their wild search was probably no surprise to Doorly, whose original plan had valued tricycles as much as tractors. Following this principle, the national drive featured the demise of a Susquehanna River bridge in Maryland and that of a miniature locomotive that had been used for generations by the Cincinnati Zoo. In Manhattan the Second Avenue El, a massive framework of abandoned overhead train tracks, turned almost overnight into 27,000 tons of scrap, while across town Helen Traubel, a Metropolitan Opera soprano portraying the Teutonic Brünnhilde, cheerfully donated the character's spear, shield, and helmet. Further south, schoolchildren in Louisiana excavated the banks of the Red River, ultimately salvaging several thousand tons of metal in the muddy remains of long-abandoned riverboats. Finally, in Illinois, the crime-free town of Old Ripley voted to donate its entire jail complex, worth 12 tons of scrap. The Associated Press praised the energy and drive of these patriotic Americans, writing that "they worked by the millions to root out steel and iron junk. Nothing was too small for them—they turned in keys—nor too big for them—they tore up old locomotives."[27]

By October 12 scrap officials announced that Kansas, Utah, and Oregon were leading in the state competition. In the community contest, two

19. Numerous celebrities participated in the national scrap drive, including Rita Hayworth, here showing that her car's bumpers have joined a scrap heap. Image courtesy of the National Archives.

towns in Massachusetts, Falmouth and nearby Dover, had notable early records, each collecting over 200 pounds per family. Nationwide, drive organizers estimated that the average citizen at the halfway point of the effort had collected 32 pounds, a rate that actually doubled Nebraska's initial pace in the earlier drive. More impressive, perhaps, was that the number of Americans reporting that a volunteer had personally appealed to them for a scrap contribution jumped from 35 to 68 percent between September and October. Best of all, new Gallup polls showed that 94 percent of Americans had heard about the campaign, a figure that was "within 3 per cent of the literate population." As George Gallup himself commented, if this "drive doesn't go hurtling over the top, it won't be because the nation's newspapers have failed to tell the people about it."[28]

To be sure, the tireless scrappers occasionally found themselves mired in public controversy. In Elmira, New York, the Ministerial Association protested against plans for a huge Sunday collection, prompting the local *Star-Gazette* to editorialize that the scrap campaign "is God's work and . . . if Christ were here, He would man one of the trucks." Halfway across the country, Ralph Coghlan, the editor of the *St. Louis Post-Dispatch*'s editorial page, found himself in an even nastier dispute, this one involving Missouri governor Forrest C. Donnell and three antique cannons that were guarding the state capitol building in Jefferson City. When the governor refused to scrap the relics for the national drive, Coghlan suggested in an editorial that some patriotic Missouri scrappers ought to haul them away in a midnight raid. Two citizens tried to do exactly that, but their actions only landed them in jail—and, by order of the governor, Coghlan later joined them behind bars. Meanwhile, a more successful nighttime raid allegedly took place back in New York City. On October 8, Richmond Borough president Joseph A. Palma claimed that "several loaded junk wagons were seen . . . crossing from Staten Island to New Jersey," presumably after their drivers had rifled through the borough's scrap piles. The city's outraged leadership responded by assigning police officers to scrap heap duty as a defense against any further "attempt to hijack or loot the scrap."[29]

Wisely, New Jersey's scrap organizers had no comment on the allegations, perhaps because they were busy organizing the Garden State's

20. Some 15,000 scrap matinees were held across the home front in October 1942, including this one in Port Washington, New York. Image courtesy of the Port Washington Public Library Local History Center (Ernie Simon Collection).

collection efforts. In Newark, for example, 1,176 truckloads of scrap had already been gathered, with five collection points piled high. Elsewhere, Boston's totals exceeded the 1 million pound mark on October 10, with scrap piles growing faster than trucks could haul material away. In Phoenix, organizers sponsored a desert collection that turned up 500 tons of bailing wire, while Chicago's proud organizers claimed that 90 percent of the city's citizens had participated. Back in the Midwest, students at the University of Nebraska collected 150 tons in a four-day sweep of campus leading up to homecoming festivities, which replaced the usual decorations with an intense scrap metal collection. And in venues across the country, scrap matinees began to raise their curtains at over 15,000 theaters, with millions of America's children each bringing at least 5 pounds of scrap material as the price of admission (see fig. 20).[30]

Much like the earlier summer drive, then, the national campaign ulti-mately reached a notable crescendo in what some were calling the "last lap" of the drive. Radio ads and movie newsreels joined the newspapers in raising "public enthusiasm to a fanatical pitch." As Pennsylvania leapt to the top of the national standings, Connecticut officials declared a state emergency; under this authority they approved the extraordinary step of scrapping the *Genius of Connecticut*, a sculpture which had for years adorned the state capitol building's golden dome. In Louisville, Kentucky, over 10,000 volunteers spent an entire day of scrapping, bringing in 1,500 tons. Local officials in Butte, Montana, used an all-out media blitz to declare a weekend "Scrap Raid," with 7,000 schoolchildren enlisted to pile household and business scrap on the curb and adults pitching in both labor and trucks to haul it away (see fig. 21). And businesses across the country began to shut down in a de facto scrap holiday as myriad citizens left their daily routines in order to take to the streets, basements, alleys, and fields of the nation. As the *Christian Science Monitor* remarked, "Perhaps never had the seriousness of the war effort been brought home so clearly to the people everywhere, for in all corners of the country they were responding."[31]

In most states, the drive finally reached its conclusion on Saturday, October 17, and the wait for the official results began. Several commu-nities had already weighed in with impressive local totals. For example, the citizens of Edgewater, New Jersey, had turned in over 2,500 tons to compile a per capita total of 1,300 pounds. But the residents of Somerset, Vermont—population 5—were not impressed. This small town took home the community prize by gathering over 6,000 pounds for each resident. The totals in the county contest were also quite impressive. It turned out that Nevada's Lincoln County joined Iowa's dueling Cass and Montgomery Counties at the top, each area having produced over 400 pounds of scrap per capita. Montgomery was slightly behind Cass, however, and thus members of its executive team were soon spotted in the town of Atlantic, sweeping the streets.[32]

The state vs. state race took a bit longer for officials to assess. Wyoming appeared to have built a commanding lead on the last day, but then fell

21. The "Scrap Raid" in Butte, Montana, mobilized much of the city for an entire weekend of scrapping duty. Image courtesy of the Library of Congress.

back into the pack as other states made their reports. On November 25, three states at last claimed the coveted victory plaques. Finishing in third place, the state of Washington had accumulated a per capita total of 141.5 pounds, while Vermont finished in second place with 155.4 pounds per person. But the overall champion—not to mention the winner of the "Corn-Hawk" scrap duel—turned out to be Kansas, with a per capita total of 158.7 pounds.[33]

In all, the veritable army of scrappers had located and hauled just over 5.3 million tons of scrap for the country's steel mills, leading to an astounding average of 82 pounds for every American on the home front. "This is the stuff of which a people's achievement is made," announced the American Newspaper Publishers Association. "This is what happens in a democracy when the people, informed and led by their newspapers, go into action." The publishers might have been forgiven for their exuberant sense of pride in the accomplishment; after all, during the drive the newspaper industry had donated over 30,000 full pages of space to the campaign.[34] Regardless of which party deserved the credit, however, it seems clear that the states and their citizens had risen to the challenge of the competition, in the process producing a veritable harvest of scrap metal for the war effort. One could argue, in retrospect, that it was a harvest with many admirable features.

Assessing the National Scrap Harvest

WPB officials were visibly pleased with the results of the intense, three-week scrap campaign. Donald Nelson told reporters that "the job that the newspapers have done is absolutely unprecedented in this country. It has been magnificent. The results have surpassed . . . [my] fondest hopes." In terms of sheer numbers, Nelson was absolutely right. He had asked the newspapers to motivate the home front to find 4 million tons of scrap metal, and the public had responded by producing 5.3 million tons. An estimated 1.5 million of them had been brought in by the nation's children. "Even if I do say so," commented Paul Cabot, one of Nelson's deputies, "I think this represents a damn good job."[35]

Of course, the most immediate beneficiary of this accomplishment was the steel industry and its ambitious munitions production. Dramatic headlines told part of the story, as when Pennsylvania's *Gettysburg Times* blared that the "Newspapers' Scrap Drive Saves Mills," or when *American City* magazine proclaimed that "Bethlehem Steel Feels Scrap Transfusion." But a more prolonged look at the industry's rising output revealed that the national drive's overwhelming surge of metal had quickly expanded national scrap metal inventories by 50 percent. In fact, as WPB exulted privately, scrap reserves had reached "an all-time recorded peak with excellent prospects that no furnaces will shut down during the coming winter months for lack of scrap." The bottom line for the steel mills in the wake of the scrap campaign was that production had been able to jump to 100.2 percent of the industry's rated capacity, with little fear of slowing down through the upcoming winter.[36]

The significantly improved steel situation in turn gave the armed forces a stronger foundation for planning and prosecuting the war. Many in the government felt that it had salvaged the war effort itself. Perhaps it was no surprise, then, that even as the scrap campaign entered its final week President Roosevelt was telling the nation in a fireside chat that "we are getting ahead of our enemies in the battle of production." To be sure, there were a number of factors underlying the president's public optimism about munitions factories. Moreover, contrary to what many civilians likely believed, the path from scrap heap object to lethal armament was by no means short or direct. But as the military moved ever closer to its planned invasion of North Africa in early November, the sudden swell in the available supply of scrap metal helped ensure that there would be a steady output of finished, high-quality steel for use in producing the overwhelming number of ships, planes, tanks, and other munitions that the military required to go on the offensive. When he was asked about the actual military usefulness of the campaign's scrap piles, R. A. Lewis, general manager of the Bethlehem Steel Company, put it this way: "Every pound of iron or steel scrap [that was] turned in means just so much more steel for the equipment we must have to win this war." WPB's Rosenwald affirmed the military impact of the drive, telling scrappers that "without your untiring efforts, our supply of this vitally needed war material would now be near the bottom."[37] Put most simply, there was a direct and undeniable connection between the scrap campaign's overwhelming success and the sudden optimism about the military's ability to take the fight to the enemy.

Yet the U.S. home front itself also reaped benefits from the scrap harvest. Perhaps the most tangible benefit was that, much like the Nebraska drive that preceded it, the national campaign managed to produce an ongoing scrap consciousness. "To mistreat a paper clip or to throw away a tomato can," remarked the November issue of the *Rotarian*, "has suddenly become almost treasonable in a land long shamed as wasteful." Given the immense war production feats that the government hoped to achieve in 1943 and beyond, this growing civilian awareness of the importance of scrap metal to the war effort was an invaluable accomplishment. After all, barring a miraculously quick end to the war, the steel industry was eventually going to need even more scrap to complete its all-important task. As

Scholastic reminded its young readers, "From now on, for the duration of the war, salvage will be the continuous duty of every citizen."[38] Thanks to the newspapers' immense scrap campaign, future salvage projects—even those not involving metal—would find that the American public was now hyperconscious of its potential to contribute directly to the war effort.

A final (and related) benefit of the scrap harvest was the increased sense of home front unity it seemed to have created. Back in August, OWI's Elmer Davis had bluntly told the home front that "we could lose this war." One of the reasons, he had argued, was that civilians were too often disengaged from the war effort altogether; in his words, "As a nation we are not yet more than ankle deep in war." In many quarters of the country, agreed the *World-Herald* at about the same time, "there is a nightmarish sense of frustration. What is this that is happening to our country?" Fortunately, the experience of camaraderie that emerged from the Nebraska campaign reappeared on a larger scale in the national drive. Repeated references to the scrappers as commandos, as squads, as battalions, and as a de facto army inevitably signified a militarized sense of duty and unity. The campaign, agreed the publishers' association, was at its most basic "the story of an aroused American public marching as to war." The *Saturday Evening Post* also commented on this sense of patriotic unity, recalling that "from the Pacific Coast to the Atlantic and from Canada to the Gulf, the same things were going on everywhere" in the drive. The essence of the scrap campaign, concluded the magazine, was that the relationship between the government and the people had unexpectedly become reversed. Armed with a newfound sense of unity, it was now "Main Street [that] was out to show Pennsylvania Avenue how to win a war."[39]

Back in Nebraska, these outcomes were naturally of tremendous interest to the *World-Herald* and to citizens across the state. "You can be proud of leading the scrap metal charge," the newspaper had told readers as the national campaign approached, and that pride persisted throughout the fall. In fact, the Cornhusker scrapping team had been in the thick of the national race, finishing in sixth place with a per capita total of 123.1 pounds. It was a total, many Nebraskans would have been quick to add, that completely discounted their contributions in the earlier drive.[40] It was enough, though, to know that the state's experience had turned out to be so influential. The Nebraska Plan may have begun with one man from a sparsely populated state. But it had finished up on the grandest stage imaginable, changing the course of life on the home front and ultimately having an impact on the battlefronts as well. Even the neighboring team of scrapping Kansas Jayhawks, convincing winners of the national contest, would have had trouble disputing that verdict.

Epilogue

Home Front, Battlefront (Revisited)

To American production, without which this war would have been lost.
—Joseph Stalin, offering a toast at a meeting of
   Allied leaders in Tehran (1943)

Henry Doorly had spoken about scrap metal on the radio before, but this was his largest audience yet. It was May 18, 1943, and the Blue Network show "This Nation at War!" was interviewing the publisher because the *World-Herald* had recently won the Pulitzer Prize for public service due to its leadership in the national scrap metal campaign. Doorly explained again, this time for a nationwide audience, how his wife had challenged him to do something about the scrap situation and how the newspaper had then sponsored the effort. The statewide campaign, he now emphasized, was successful not only because it ultimately made it possible to keep "the steel mills going throughout the winter and the spring" but also because "the whole population of Nebraska had only one purpose" during the drive, "and that was collecting and donating scrap." He gracefully concluded that it was "the people of Nebraska . . . who made it possible for us to secure the honor of the Pulitzer Prize."[1]

The publisher's broadcast interview took place less than a year after the Nebraska Plan first began to take shape, and so it is probable that he was still too close to the event to be able to offer a distanced assessment.

Yet although the passage of over seventy years makes it easier to see that the campaign was not without its flaws, it also does not fundamentally challenge his reasons why the campaign was a success. If anything, post-war access to the records of the War Production Board suggests that the Nebraska Plan was even more influential than the publisher could have known at the time.

For this reason, the aim of this book has been to contend that, on one level, Doorly's drive was a success in gathering sufficient amounts of a desperately needed raw material at a critical point. On a second level, this book has argued that the campaign was successful in altering the experience of the war in such a way that civilians were able to see themselves as home front soldiers. The following pages offer a broader context for these twin successes.

Of Hoaxes, Miscalculations, and Critical Timing

The suggestion that the scrap metal campaign was a vital contribution to the war effort is not without some controversy. Some observers were led even during the war years to question the strategic usefulness of civilian scrap collection. Ralph Robey, for example, was not convinced that scrap metal was the steel industry's biggest problem. Even as news of the *World-Herald*'s statewide drive was spreading across the country, the associate editor and columnist for *Newsweek* was insisting that the primary steel bottleneck was "purely a matter of allocation." If the country could just "clean that up," Robey wrote, then "we will no longer have a serious steel problem." While such views were uncommon at first, the questions grew more widespread in the wake of the national drive. When the nation's scrap heaps did not disappear within a few weeks, sporadic rumors begin to emerge that the entire effort had been a government-sponsored boondoggle, with the goal of building up artificial morale on the home front. The scrap industry found itself explaining over and over again that the collected piles could not possibly move all at once, since the huge variety of metals made for a lengthier sorting, disassembling, baling, and loading process—even as scrap yards were continuing to lose workers to the military draft. The most crucial point, of course, was that those piles were now available for industrial processing and not rusting away in fields, basements, or river bottoms. Fortunately, as the winter season came to a close, the scrap metal stockpiles had visibly shrunk; the rumors, however, remained in some quarters.[2]

More recently, as historians have continued to examine and reexamine the World War II home front, questions about the actual usefulness of the scrap metal efforts have persisted. Susan Strasser, for example, suggests that the "scrap drives had more utility as propaganda than as a means of collecting strategic materials, and their importance has been exaggerated in public memory." Similarly, Carl A. Zimring writes that "there is some question as to whether the scrap drives had any more than a symbolic effect upon the collection and use of materials." Finally, Hugh Rockoff presents economic data to support his contention that "the scrap drives did not push collections to unprecedented heights."[3] Although such postwar assessments often blend together the various kinds of home front salvage campaigns, it is important to address them, at least in terms of the need for scrap metal during the war years.

If it were indeed true that the national campaign to collect scrap metal had little or no strategic value to the war program, the effort's very size suggests that it must therefore have been either a gigantic hoax or a colossal miscalculation on the part of WPB. In the case of a hoax, of course, one would not expect to find published governmental statements admitting to the ruse. However, it is likely that evidence of such a plot would have survived within the government's archival records of private meetings and correspondence. A conspiracy theorist thus might look no further than a late 1940 memorandum from William J. Barrett that has been preserved in WPB's official records. The German onslaught in continental Europe and the formal signing of the Axis pact had by this point made the Roosevelt administration acutely concerned about the state of public morale, leading Barrett to observe that many in the government did not think that Americans were truly "aware of the necessity of buckling down to defense." But how could the administration increase this awareness? "My thought," he continued, "is that the scrap and reclamation program is perhaps just one phase in a possible general scheme of awakening and arousing public opinion."[4] At first glance, this memorandum would seem to support charges that the scrap drives were essentially a hoax, intended not for industrial necessity but to bolster morale.

However, other documents from within the Roosevelt administration show that this idea never gained traction. On April 4, 1941, for instance, the Office of Price Management's William Batt noted that Roosevelt himself had requested "the outline of a program for public participation in the defense effort." Batt suggested that war bond sales "should probably come first" in any effort to get Americans more involved, with other options being less palatable. In particular, he noted that "since the actual material advantages to accrue from scrap collection are of doubtful value . . . we ought to do nothing about the program now." At the time of Batt's writing, Gano Dunn's report on national steel needs had not been revised, so there was as yet no obvious need for scrap metal collection. However, such a perceived lack of industrial necessity would have been irrelevant if the government had in fact been planning a hoax. Indeed, as Edward R. Stettinius Jr. of the National Defense Advisory Commission (who was also a former steel industry executive) had told FDR the previous summer, "A public scrap collection program should be properly conceived and timed. At present steel scrap presents no problem," and therefore "at this time a public program for scrap collection is not desirable."[5] The administration, one must conclude, flatly did not view scrap metal campaigns as a tool to build artificial morale, but instead launched them when it believed the industrial need was authentic.

So if the scrap metal effort was not a hoax designed to arouse an apathetic public, is it possible that it was all just a gigantic miscalculation on the part of WPB and therefore unnecessary? Rockoff, in particular, appears to support this view, suggesting that the scrap drives in total produced somewhere between three to eight weeks of additional scrap material that would not otherwise have been available during the course of the war. Similar questions regarding the actual necessity of the scrap effort were prevalent enough on the home front that the military found itself emphasizing to the public that "scrap collecting is no Easter egg hunt, nor is it a boondoggling gesture." Even WPB was forced to acknowledge that "it is a little hard to see just what" scrap collection "has to do with beating Hitler."[6]

As before, a number of primary documents offer a useful perspective on the controversy. In this case, they generally affirm that the 1942 scrap metal efforts were not only necessary but that they sufficiently addressed a fundamental shortage that winter. A few months after the national drive, for example, an unnamed WPB official noted privately that "the number one problem . . . in early 1942 was the pressing need for iron and steel scrap. During the early months of the year, between 40 and 45 steelmaking furnaces were reported down at times for lack of scrap." In the spring of 1943, however, WPB's minutes noted that "the salvage campaign has been sufficiently successful to warrant the belief that there will be no shortage of scrap this year." By the summer of 1944, steelmakers were able to offer a slightly longer-term view, pointing out that "between April 1, 1942, and the close of that year the steel industry's stocks of scrap more than doubled." After that July, "only one steel furnace is known to have suspended operation for lack of scrap—and that one for only a day or so." Lest there be any doubt, the steelmakers' account drew a direct connection between the "acute" scrap situation, the newspapers' national drive, and the moderation of the crisis.[7] From these viewpoints, at least, there appears to have been no miscalculation.

The confusion that could lead one to believe that the scrap efforts were either a hoax or a miscalculation probably lies in the critical timing of the campaign. As the scrap crisis grew more dire late in 1941 and into 1942, government and industry collaborated to focus on several ways to address the problem. Pushing existing blast furnaces to the limit in order to increase pig iron supplies that would be able to replace at least some scrap iron in the steelmaking process was almost as seasonal an option as scrap collection itself, due to the challenge of mining and transporting iron ore during the winter months. Adding additional blast furnace capacity was in the works, but most new facilities would not be coming online until 1943. Importing scrap, whether from other Allied nations (especially those in South America) or from the recovery of battlefield scrap, would not bring in significant levels until after 1942. Every logical measure, in other words, failed to address adequately the immediate crisis of the upcoming winter season, even as the demands for steel kept increasing.[8] The only exception was the possibility of a large national scrap metal drive that fall. By the end of the war, all those other measures had been in operation for some time and so the newspapers' 1942 drive appears to be relatively minor when considered among them. Hence the scrap campaign's significance emerged not only in the amount of scrap that it gathered but in the timing — both of the crisis and of the means of addressing it.

To illustrate the vital nature of the Nebraska Plan's timing, it is worthwhile to consider two scenarios that might have come to pass had the national scrap metal drive never taken place. The first is the more extreme, suggesting that the Allies might actually have lost the war without that emergency supply of scrap material. This possibility is, of course, difficult to grasp when one knows how the conflict eventually turned out. Yet "up to 1942," counters Richard Overy, "the balance favoured the aggressor" in the war, and it "might well have allowed them to win before American economic power could be placed in the scales." Although in retrospect, an "Allied victory might seem somehow inevitable, the conflict was poised on a knife-edge in the middle years of the war."[9]

Indeed, some aspects of the war's middle game could have gone either way. Operation Torch, the tremendous November 1942 invasion of North Africa against entrenched Axis forces, is a case in point. Rick Atkinson criticizes the unpreparedness of the American invading forces in the operation, writing that the incursion "revealed a nation and an army unready to fight and unsure of their martial skills." One of the most crucial concerns in the battle, however, was actually the uncertain supply of landing craft, the machines meant to enable the amphibious invasion in the first place. Although the military had ordered the crafts in midsummer, American manufacturers still had not fully completed work on them. Thus, in an operation that Atkinson describes as no less than "a pivot point in American history," the nation's GIs initiated battle with a precarious supply of equipment.[10]

No one could justifiably ascribe the narrowness of the success in that late 1942 landing to the scrap crisis alone. But with "the margin of victory or defeat often . . . so slender" at that point in the war, the 5 million ton shortfall of finished steel production that seemed likely that winter without the scrap metal drive would surely have endangered the whole of the North African campaign as it unfolded in early 1943 — not to mention the later battles for Sicily and mainland Italy. The American soldiers in those first days of Operation Torch were not yet the battle-tested veterans they would gradually become. Sending them into battle with even less equipment and arms than they ended up with on those beaches would have been an alarming prospect for any war planner. Whether the projected shortfall would have been enough to tip the scales in favor of an Axis victory is impossible to say, but the soldiers are surely fortunate that they did not have to see what the outcome might have been.[11]

The second scenario, in contrast, is probably a more realistic assessment of the war's eventual course in the absence of a major scrap metal drive in the fall of 1942. This scenario envisions not an Allied defeat without the civilian campaign's collected scrap but a *much longer road to victory*. In this perspective, the ultimate outcome of the war would have remained the same with or without the newspapers' scrap drive; the Allies would eventually have defeated the Axis powers. Yet significantly less steel going into the war effort at the critical point when the Allies were shifting to the offensive would have weakened not only U.S. forces but, through lend-lease attrition, British, Soviet, and Chinese forces as well. The cumulative effect on the number of Allied casualties it would take to win the war would have been difficult to bear. Every ton of home front scrap gathered for the drive and melted into munitions that fall, in this view, was a rough measure of GIs who would come home in a transport ship and not in a body bag, with the opposite effect on enemy soldiers.

By and large, the Roosevelt administration appears to have subscribed to this second scenario when it came to the scrap problem. Donald Nelson hinted at it as early as July 1942, suggesting that "the biggest part of the job is still ahead" and that any production slowdowns in the near term could well "mean years more of war and hundreds of thousands more lives." WPB later offered an even more specific claim, arguing that "the length, if not the outcome, of our struggle with the Axis powers hinges, to a very large extent, upon our ability to supply scrap iron and steel in sufficient quantities to keep our steel mills operating at full capacity."[12] To the extent that the newspapers' late 1942 scrap campaign was able to address the unrelenting need for steel throughout that critical winter season and into the first half of 1943, then, the length of the war may well have been reduced and countless Allied lives saved in the process.

While both of these scenarios dramatize the critical need for scrap metal in 1942, it is important to remember that the munitions emerging from those all-important scrap supplies did not win battles by themselves; planning, training, and the raw courage of actual GIs were necessary as well. Yet it was hard for Nelson, in particular, to downplay the value of the military's metal-based arsenal. As he told *Reader's Digest* in late 1943, steel "is the extra heft of material that breaks the enemy's back, pulverizes his resistance, and destroys his ability to strike back." Consequently, "Steel saves lives. It is the weight of metal thrown against the enemy which has kept down our casualties." But just as there was a soldier behind every gun, Nelson was well aware that there was a scrap source behind virtually every steel product. For this reason, he seemed compelled to remind everyone that much of that life-saving battlefield steel had been made possible by the "pins and needles and paper clips" that home front civilians had collected for their country.[13] For the WPB chief, it was a vitally important way in which home front and battlefront had crossed paths during the war effort.

As Doorly spoke to his nationwide audience in that May 1943 interview, his understanding of such issues as the length of the war or calculations of potential casualties would obviously have been limited by his context. He was, after all, still living through the unfolding events of that war. Yet he, too, would have been familiar with Nelson's arguments why scrap was so critical to the military, and it is safe to assume that he did not believe the Nebraska Plan was either a hoax or a miscalculation. Rather, he would have been more inclined toward the view of the Pulitzer Prize committee, which had matter-of-factly described the success of his vision "in supplying our war industries with necessary scrap material."[14] Doorly, the Pulitzer committee, and WPB surely realized that the drive had *not* been an ideal solution. But they also likely understood that it had been the only feasible option at that point in the war. And in the end, it appears reasonable to conclude that the campaign was successful in collecting sufficient amounts of scrap, at just the right time, to keep the steel mills ahead of demand until other industrial measures could come into play.

Citizens, Scrappers, Soldiers

The Nebraska Plan's second success related less to the battlefronts and more to the home front. Specifically, this book has suggested that Doorly's drive played an instrumental role in altering the way that U.S. civilians understood themselves during the war years. From this perspective, the intense effort to gather scrap in the summer and fall of 1942 became exactly the kind of campaign that Barrett's memorandum had proposed back in late 1940: it succeeded in enlisting an uncertain and occasionally listless public into active service on behalf of the war—essentially "awakening and arousing" a legion of home front soldiers, all of them working together on a specific task in a kind of civilian army.[15]

This contention is also not without its share of controversy, most of it of relatively recent vintage. After decades of neglect, the U.S. home front came into its own as a vibrant area of historical inquiry in the 1970s. At first, scholars tended to emphasize that the popular nature of the war had led to widespread unity, cooperation, and esprit des corps among virtually all Americans. Such histories, as Richard Polenberg describes them, portrayed a war that "was fought by a largely united people, whose shared purpose not only led them to make sacrifices for the common good but also enabled them to transcend ethnic divisions and religious differences." It was in many ways the "good war," summarized Studs Terkel. Although the oral historian placed the title of his book in quotation marks to emphasize the irony in that phrase, the description has taken on a life of its own, and popular memories of the war continue to celebrate its overwhelming unity of purpose.[16]

By the 1990s, however, a later generation of scholars had begun producing a series of revisionist histories of the home front. These new works frequently attacked the unquestioned notion that civilians had experienced some sort of communal transcendence during the war. It was "the myth of national unity in World War II," says Michael C. C. Adams, but what it left out was the "selfishness and cupidity" that were also present at home. Steven Casey, examining the public mood in early 1942, similarly avers that instead of widespread unity, the home front frequently was marked by "a vague and inchoate popular mood described variously as apathy or complacency," with "divisionism" and "defeatism" also present in good measure. In these sorts of revisionist analyses, the home front unity so prominent in earlier histories is largely seen as illusory.[17]

Each side in this debate offers an important perspective on the home front experience. Certainly, there was an impulse to craft a "perfecting myth" near the end of the conflict—a relatively sanitized version of the war in which Americans were the heroes who saved the world and not a single word of dissent was uttered from Pearl Harbor until Nagasaki.[18] Such a narrative embroidered some basic aspects of the war to the point that they became an affirming cultural fable. At the same time, however, the earlier historians were right to observe that it was not uncommon for an identifiable sense of community to become visible, at least occasionally, during the war years. Tellingly, much as Barrett had projected back in 1940, it was the various home front campaigns that helped provide the most obvious opportunities for that sense of unity to emerge and thrive.

The scrap metal drive of 1942 was not the earliest of these campaigns; that honor goes to the defense bonds (later, war bonds) effort, inaugurated in the spring of 1941. But the U.S. Treasury's war bond publicity machine did not consistently emphasize descriptions of bond purchasers as home front soldiers until the debut of its First War Loan drive starting in November 1942. This event came *after* Doorly's Nebraska Plan had gradually embraced that appeal in the initial summer campaign and after the same appeal became prevalent in the national scrap drive in September and October. Remarkably, the war bond effort had been floundering until it shifted to a focused drive model (much like Doorly's campaign), whose intense deadlines fostered a militarized approach in which war bond purchasers could seem to become home front soldiers in their own right.[19]

As I have suggested, an important key in these sorts of campaigns was to connect the home front to the battlefront and civilians to soldiers, constructing what Cynthia Lee Henthorn terms the "home front/front line juxtaposition."[20] The scrap metal campaign offered what was probably the most natural way to make this connection because the underlying purpose of scrap collection was to produce more munitions. If those citizens who were gathering the scrap were metaphorically gathering weapons for use in the war, then by extension those same citizens could easily have come to see themselves in the role of home front soldiers. At the same time, collecting scrap was nearly always a group effort, a factor multiplied significantly when Doorly layered in a competitive element so that scrappers became contributing members of a team. From that one innovation, the opportunities for militarized unity were increased and, in many cases, made manifest.

Although the civilians-are-soldiers mentality did spread to other home front campaigns, the scrap metal drives appear to have been among the earliest to adopt it and were likely the most successful at exploiting it. To be sure, the appeal was in some respects an accidental development that emerged almost incidentally during the latter half of Doorly's three-week summer drive. Yet by that campaign's climax, those down-to-earth, hardworking Nebraskans appear to have become used to the idea that they had been militarized. At the least, the intensity of their labors in the final days was more reminiscent of a highly motivated army than of a lackluster and indifferent populace.[21]

A similar phenomenon took place during the national drive as the country's scrappers attacked the Axis powers in their own intense way. Like the Nebraska-based drive before it, the nationwide effort relentlessly militarized its scrappers in what the government's Bureau of Campaigns described as "the biggest community effort ever partaken of by the public." The ultimate results of the drive were "much more far reaching than just scrap collected," although no one could doubt that the country's scrap stockpile had grown tremendously that fall. Rather, the campaign's deepest impact was that "it has served to make the people far more 'war conscious.'"[22] For a home front that had been widely perceived as apathetic and uninvolved in mid-1942, such an accomplishment was indeed a remarkable success.

In the remaining years of the war, the scrappers inevitably took that militarized success into other home front activities, whether it involved purchasing war bonds, participating in civil defense work, planting victory gardens, or any other of dozens of home front activities that were so good at mobilizing civilians for the war program. There were even additional and ongoing opportunities to serve in the scrap metal army. Fortunately, the scrap crisis of 1942 did not recur; the introduction of new blast furnaces and various sources of imported scrap metal gradually ensured a relatively consistent supply for the steel industry. Yet the need for scrap continued to accelerate as the fabled Arsenal of Democracy churned out ever more munitions into 1943. Moreover, WPB believed that only about half of the nation's potentially available farm scrap had been secured in 1942, and it was certain that other scrap caches remained hidden on the home front. For the duration of the war, then, sporadic scrap metal campaigns continued to mobilize scrap soldiers, battalions, and platoons. Most of these late-war scrappers did not know it, of course, but they could have traced their quasi-military lineage back to the innovations of a certain newspaper publisher from Omaha. It was Henry Doorly, after all, whose idea for a "campaign to help make the world a safe place in which to live" had not only helped transform the home front but, ironically, had subtly played a part in salvaging the war effort itself.[23]

Conclusion

As Doorly left the radio station after his Blue Network interview that day in May 1943, it is possible that he was thinking about the twin successes that had emerged from his wife's challenge and from the massive response of his *World-Herald* team. It was a response, he knew, that had reverberated across the country. Just a week earlier, Malcolm Cowley, an editor at the *New Republic*, had emphasized to Doorly in a personal letter that the national scrap metal campaign, as impressive as it turned out to be, would not have been successful without "the example and leadership furnished by the *World-Herald*." Cowley concluded his letter by telling the midwestern publisher that he and his team "should be very proud."[24]

Doorly did indeed have much to be proud of. In constructing a formidable forge on the prairie, he and his army of scrap commandos had been instrumental in prompting home front Americans to understand at an early point that this worldwide conflict was at its most basic a war of steel. The signs of that war of metals, by now, were just about everywhere. At this point, for example, children who had worn out their all-steel Red Flyer wagons while hauling scrap were out of luck; the metal for making new wagons had gone to war. Likewise, anyone playing Monopoly as they listened to Doorly's interview would have discovered that the game now used wooden tokens; the iconic cannon and battleship markers had gone off to become the real thing.[25] Elsewhere, new automobiles were not being manufactured for the duration, significant numbers of courthouse cannons had gone missing, and many municipal sculptures had found themselves drafted into war service. Curiously, this ever-present undercurrent of the need for metal even seemed to be reflected in the names of some of the war's major players, such as Eisenhower ("iron striker") and Stalin ("steel"), not to mention the "pact of steel," as the alliance between Germany and Italy was known.

Perhaps it is not surprising, in the end, that Doorly's Nebraska Plan became one of the most indelible postwar memories of the conflict for many scrappers. The campaign was responsible for bringing the war of steel home to Nebraskans and then to Americans. Their resulting labors turned out to be no hoax, no boondoggle, and no miscalculation. Even Bill Nicholas and his compatriots ended up being a vital part of the effort. In retrospect, it might have been easy to mistake that group of adventurous young Cornhuskers for modern-day Don Quixotes, grappling with windmills while engaged in a fruitless quest. But it is clear looking back that their particular quest had a patriotic and meaningful purpose: they were focused on what they believed was their duty as citizens. Their efforts — alongside those of so many other scrapping civilians during the biggest war in history — deserve to be remembered.

In memoriam
William D. Nicholas, 1925–2013

Appendix

Table I Nebraska County Scrap Results (in pounds per capita)

COUNTY	POPULATION (1940 CENSUS)	SUMMER DRIVE	NATIONAL DRIVE	COMBINED
Adams	24,576	62.46	157.94	220.40
Antelope	13,289	144.17	158.30	302.47
Arthur	1,045	62.42	105.94	168.36
Banner	1,403	21.09	513.30	534.39
Blaine	1,538	270.48	35.86	306.34
Boone	12,127	60.35	125.02	185.37
Box Butte	10,736	26.08	226.60	252.68
Boyd	6,060	119.16	269.04	388.20
Brown	5,962	142.73	76.39	219.12
Buffalo	23,655	100.60	60.03	160.63
Burt	12,546	74.94	101.97	176.91
Butler	13,106	66.60	133.03	199.63
Cass	16,992	172.86	71.85	244.71
Cedar	15,126	41.35	139.55	180.90
Chase	5,310	127.83	278.01	405.84

COUNTY	POPULATION (1940 CENSUS)	SUMMER DRIVE	NATIONAL DRIVE	COMBINED
Cherry	9,637	86.22	121.27	207.49
Cheyenne	9,505	185.94	315.62	501.56
Clay	10,445	62.76	51.99	114.75
Colfax	10,627	151.86	186.74	338.60
Cuming	13,562	30.22	103.74	133.96
Custer	22,591	45.65	102.43	148.08
Dakota	9,836	70.14	129.96	200.10
Dawes	10,128	155.95	154.35	310.30
Dawson	17,890	105.30	239.12	344.42
Deuel	3,580	35.78	405.31	441.09
Dixon	10,413	48.49	145.40	193.89
Dodge	23,799	122.62	128.46	251.08
Douglas	247,562	103.12	49.47	152.59
Dundy	5,122	287.46	162.08	449.54
Fillmore	11,417	24.24	249.51	273.75
Franklin	7,740	92.92	67.93	160.85
Frontier	6,417	137.14	217.03	354.17
Furnas	10,098	97.44	145.43	242.87
Gage	29,588	37.45	88.55	126.00
Garden	4,680	64.64	324.41	389.05
Garfield	3,444	81.86	121.02	202.88
Gosper	3,687	113.02	203.18	316.20
Grant	1,327	637.95	265.26	903.21
Greeley	6,845	67.15	98.76	165.91
Hall	27,523	83.53	115.89	199.42
Hamilton	9,982	50.96	95.24	146.20
Harlan	7,130	131.23	63.35	194.58
Hayes	2,958	83.28	236.89	320.17

COUNTY	POPULATION (1940 CENSUS)	SUMMER DRIVE	NATIONAL DRIVE	COMBINED
Hitchcock	6,404	100.21	113.25	213.46
Holt	16,552	81.37	143.42	224.79
Hooker	1,253	541.45	454.35	995.80
Howard	8,422	99.29	107.72	207.01
Jefferson	15,532	46.90	67.79	114.69
Johnson	8,662	68.21	207.94	276.15
Kearney	6,854	98.43	146.24	244.67
Keith	8,333	33.06	204.47	237.53
Keya Paha	3,235	7.08	113.00	120.08
Kimball	3,913	187.08	271.91	458.99
Knox	16,478	60.73	135.15	195.88
Lancaster	100,585	151.94	135.79	287.73
Lincoln	25,425	88.23	123.40	211.63
Logan	1,742	43.95	271.06	315.01
Loup	1,777	124.35	117.45	241.80
Madison	24,269	161.40	125.54	286.94
McPherson	1,175	65.77	127.38	193.15
Merrick	9,354	65.04	126.45	191.49
Morrill	9,436	128.58	106.61	235.19
Nance	7,653	65.94	169.68	235.62
Nemaha	12,781	65.13	87.81	152.94
Nuckolls	10,446	164.64	150.56	315.20
Otoe	18,994	80.85	189.38	270.23
Pawnee	8,514	53.35	184.22	237.57
Perkins	5,197	131.33	272.39	403.72[1]
Phelps	8,452	426.22	292.31	718.53
Pierce	10,211	53.97	118.31	172.28
Platte	20,191	69.25	163.01	232.26

COUNTY	POPULATION (1940 CENSUS)	SUMMER DRIVE	NATIONAL DRIVE	COMBINED
Polk	8,748	66.79	168.72	235.51
Red Willow	11,951	374.95	106.20	481.15
Richardson	19,178	24.39	53.47	77.86
Rock	3,977	90.73	90.51	181.24
Saline	15,010	49.96	138.49	188.45
Sarpy	10,835	181.14	125.88	307.02
Saunders	17,892	158.02	213.50	371.52
Scotts Bluff	33,917	138.69	71.38	210.07
Seward	14,167	25.18	98.31	123.49
Sheridan	9,869	70.42	226.97	297.39
Sherman	7,764	15.46	146.90	162.36
Sioux	4,001	71.58	147.46	219.04
Stanton	6,887	34.81	153.89	188.70
Thayer	12,262	325.80	51.87	377.67
Thomas	1,553	507.51	110.00	617.51
Thurston	10,243	68.34	123.86	192.20
Valley	8,163	50.00	263.20	313.20
Washington	11,578	118.77	129.61	248.38
Wayne	9,880	113.62	147.39	261.01
Webster	8,071	32.34	96.80	129.14
Wheeler	2,170	54.02	59.28	113.30
York	14,874	72.61	153.42	226.03

Source: "Nebraska Scrap Score in 2 Drives," *Sunday World-Herald*, November 1, 1942.

1 The original table lists Perkins County's total as 503.72 pounds per capita, but that number appears to be a mathematical error based on results from the two drives, which actually add up to 403.72 pounds.

Notes

Introduction: Home Front, Battlefront

1. Interview with Bill Nicholas, Scrap Drive Collection, Douglas County Historical Society, Omaha NE (DCHS).

2. Marr McGaffin, "Somber War Atmosphere Grips Capital," *Sunday World-Herald*, July 12, 1942. On the dramatic Bataan losses, see "Bataan Worst Blow to an American Army," *New York Times*, April 10, 1942.

3. On the number of scrap committees, see "Nelson's Scrap Rally Plea Inspires Action," *Scrapper*, no. 1 [undated]; American Industries Salvage Committee, *Scrap and How to Collect It . . .* , booklet, September 1942, 29, in American Iron and Steel Institute Vertical Files, box 116, folder 9, Hagley Museum and Library, Wilmington DE (Hagley). (The ellipsis in the title of the booklet is original.)

4. Internal government discussion of the scrap problem is available, for example, in Materials Branch, Statistics Division, War Production Board, "Preliminary Report: Availability of Data Relating to Scrap Materials," ts., July 3, 1942, p. 4, in War Production Board Policy Documentation File, RG 179, box 917, folder "Scrap Campaign: January–August 1942," National Archives and Records Administration, College Park MD (NARA); and in "Minutes of the 3rd Meeting of the Steel Plate Committee," ts., July 30, 1942, p. 2, in Combined Production and Resources Board, Records of the Combined Steel Committee, RG 179, box 2, folder "CPRB 2nd SPC Mtg.," NARA. The Rosenwald quotation is from "Non-Stop Campaign for Scrap Started," *New York Times*, July 14, 1942. Nelson put his warning in "An Emergency Statement to the People of the United States," advertisement, *Life*, July 27, 1942, 16 (note that the ad was published in numerous magazines and newspapers).

5. William L. O'Neill, *A Democracy at War: America's Fight at Home and Abroad in World War II* (Cambridge: Harvard University Press, 1998), 135.

6. "The People's Response," *Evening World-Herald*, August 10, 1942. More context on the Nebraska home front is available in Frederick C. Luebke, *Nebraska: An Illustrated History*, 2nd ed. (Lincoln: University of Nebraska Press, 2005), 298–306, and Robert M. Armstrong, "Nebraska and Nebraskans in World War II," *Nebraska History* 24 (1943): 174–80. Numerous other perspectives are evident in a special World War II–themed issue of *Nebraska History*, published as the summer/fall issue in 1995.

7. "Nebraska to the Rescue," *Life*, September 21, 1942, 38; "Liberal News Space Boosts Scrap Drive," *Christian Science Monitor*, December 2, 1942; George Gallup, "94 of 100 Have Read about Metal Drive in Newspapers," *Washington Post*, October 10, 1942; "That Scrap Drive," *Newsweek*, October 26, 1942, 64; American Newspaper Publishers Association, *The Nation's No. 1 Success Story* [December 1942], 14, 13, 16, in Advertising Council Records, 1935–99 and undated, box 36, folder 6, Rare Book, Manuscript, and Special Collections Library, Duke University (Duke).

8. Hollis J. Limprecht, *A Century of Service, 1885–1985: The World-Herald Story* (Omaha: Omaha World-Herald, 1985), 29. For examples of historical accounts that blend the various salvage efforts, see Lisa L. Ossian, *The Forgotten Generation: American Children and World War II* (Columbia: University of Missouri Press, 2011), chap. 3, and Susan Strasser, *Waste and Want: A Social History of Trash* (New York: Henry Holt, 1999), chap. 6. A good primary source that differentiates the various scrap drives is Mildred Adams, "Our Precious Junk," *New York Times Magazine*, May 24, 1942, 14, 28. Note that the *World-Herald* campaign itself initially included rubber as part of the collection effort. The appeals for scrap metal, however, soon eclipsed thoughts of rubber collection for most of the drive.

9. James J. Kimble, "The Militarization of the Prairie: Scrap Drives, Metaphors, and the Omaha *World-Herald*'s 1942 'Nebraska Plan,'" *Great Plains Quarterly* 27 (2007): 84. As Alan L. Gropman argues, "World War II was won in largest part because of superior Allied armaments production," with the United States eventually turning out arms at a rate nearly equal to the combined amount produced by all other combatants. See his *Mobilizing U.S. Industry in World War II* (Washington DC: Institute for National Strategic Studies, 1996), 1–2.

10. A more visually oriented retelling of the scrap drive story is available in *Scrappers: How the Heartland Won World War II*, DVD, directed by James J. Kimble and Thomas R. Rondinella (South Orange NJ: Catfish Studios, 2010). The anecdote about the salvage official certain that the state had already found all it would be able to is from Doorly's testimony, as recorded in "American Newspaper

Publishers Scrap Collection Drive (Transcript of the Proceedings of a Meeting of American Newspaper Publishers, Called by Donald M. Nelson, Chairman of the WPB, in Cooperation with the American Newspaper Publishers Association, on Friday, September 4, 1942, in Washington DC)," ts., pp. 22–23, in War Production Board Policy Documentation File, RG 179, box 917, folder "Scrap Campaign: September 1942," NARA.

11. Quoted in "American Newspaper Publishers Scrap Collection Drive," 17.

12. Russell W. Davenport, "Life's Report: The Nebraska Plan," *Life*, October 5, 1942, 12.

13. "Time Is Slipping By . . . $2,000.00 Scrap Metal and Rubber Contest Closes Aug. 8th!" advertisement, *Sunday World-Herald*, August 2, 1942.

14. George H. Roeder Jr., *The Censored War: American Visual Experience during World War Two* (New Haven CT: Yale University Press, 1993), 59; William L. Bird Jr. and Harry R. Rubenstein, *Design for Victory: World War II Posters on the American Home Front* (New York: Princeton Architectural Press, 1998), 1.

15. James T. Sparrow, *Warfare State: World War II Americans and the Age of Big Government* (New York: Oxford University Press, 2011), 173; James J. Kimble, "The Home as Battlefront: Femininity, Gendered Spheres, and the 1943 Women in National Service Campaign," *Women's Studies in Communication* 34 (2011): 84–103; War Food Administration, *Food Fights for Freedom: Grow More in '44* (Washington DC: War Food Administration, 1944); James J. Kimble, *Mobilizing the Home Front: War Bonds and Domestic Propaganda* (College Station: Texas A&M University Press, 2006), 26–29.

16. On the dearth of war bond sales in the first half of 1942, see Kimble, *Mobilizing the Home Front*, 35. On the hoarding problem that same year, see Adelaide Handy, "Drive on Hoarding Has National Force," *New York Times*, March 22, 1942. Sydney Weinberg discusses the national poll in "What to Tell America: The Writers' Quarrel in the Office of War Information," *Journal of American History* 55 (1968): 78; the quotations are from "Capital Is Wide-Open to Raid, Bolles Warns Smug Citizens," *Washington Post*, February 23, 1942, and James B. Reston, "Washington Paints a Confused War Picture," *New York Times*, February 15, 1942.

17. "Needed: Lots of Scrap," *Evening World-Herald*, June 8, 1942; "Americans Eagerly Enlist in Hunt for Needed Scrap," *Morning World-Herald*, October 1, 1942.

18. Bob Greene, *Once upon a Town: The Miracle of the North Platte Canteen* (New York: William Morrow, 2002).

19. The quotation is from Elinor Morgenthau (who was married to the Treasury secretary), "We Search the Attic and the Basement," *Scrapper*, no. 4 [undated].

To be sure, there was a vast difference between actual combat operations and gathering scrap on the home front. My emphasis here is not only on the ways that those at home could *envision* themselves as fighting in the war but also upon strategic necessity, both of specific battles and of gathering scrap for munitions.

1. The Scrap Deficit, or How Not to Win a War

1. Franklin D. Roosevelt, "'The Will for Peace on the Part of Peace-Loving Nations Must Express Itself to the End That Nations That May Be Tempted to Violate Their Agreements and the Rights of Others Will Desist from Such a Course.' Address at Chicago. October 5, 1937," in *The Public Papers and Addresses of Franklin D. Roosevelt*, 1937 vol., ed. Samuel I. Rosenman (New York: Macmillan, 1941), 407; "U.S. Warned Not to Let Its Scrap Iron Go," *Washington Post*, February 6, 1939 (ellipsis in original newspaper quotation).

2. "Iron Exports Held a Danger to Nation," *New York Times*, February 5, 1939.

3. "U.S. Warned Not to Let Its Scrap Iron Go."

4. "Uncle Sam Sells Steel Scrap as the World Arms," *Business Week*, April 8, 1939, 16.

5. "'The Militarists of Berlin and Tokyo Started This War. But the Massed, Angered Forces of Common Humanity Will Finish It'—Address to the Congress on the State of the Union. January 6, 1942," in *The Public Papers and Addresses of Franklin D. Roosevelt*, 1942 vol., ed. Samuel I. Rosenman (New York: Harper and Brothers, 1950), 37; Michael Kirwan to Roosevelt, January 8, 1942, in FDR Official File, box 2, folder "Jan–June 1942," Franklin D. Roosevelt Presidential Library and Museum, Hyde Park NY (FDR Library).

6. *Scrap Happy Daffy*, DVD, directed by Frank Tashlin, on *Looney Tunes: Golden Collection, Vol. 5* (1943; Warner Bros., 1996).

7. *Steel and America*, VHS, directed by Les Clark (Washington DC: American Iron and Steel Institute, 1965). The production was made with the help of Walt Disney. Note that one important postwar innovation involved oxygen converters, which produced steel at a much faster rate than open-hearth furnaces. The relationships among iron ore, pig iron, and scrap, however, remained essentially the same.

8. War Production Board, "Synopsis of Story on Making STEEL," ts., [Sept. 1942], in American Iron and Steel Institute Vertical Files, box 117, folder "Scrap: Campaign Material," Hagley.

9. *Steel and America*; R. Douglas Hurt, *American Farm Tools: From Hand-Power to Steam-Power* (Manhattan KS: Sunflower University Press, 1982), 115; Jack Gutstadt, *Scrap Iron and Steel: An Outline of the Many Ramifications and Developments of a Major Industry, Together with Statistics, Formulas, and Other Similar Data* (Chicago, 1939), 7.

10. R. F. Fowler, "Substitution of Scrap for Pig-Iron in the Manufacture of Steel," *Quarterly Journal of Economics* 52 (1937): 129–54; Edwin C. Barringer, *The Story of Scrap* (Washington DC: Institute of Scrap Iron and Steel, 1947), 2, 60.

11. Barringer, *The Story of Scrap*, 11; Gutstadt, *Scrap Iron and Steel*, 7. The source for the figure is American Iron and Steel Institute, "To Make 1 Ton of Ingot Steel," *Steel Facts*, December 1960, 6, in American Iron and Steel Institute Vertical Files, box 106, Hagley.

12. Scrap Iron and Steel Inc., *Scrap Is Fighting Metal: Vital for Victory* (Washington DC: Scrap Iron and Steel Inc., 1943), 11; Gutstadt, *Scrap Iron and Steel*, 6.

13. Barringer, *The Story of Scrap*, 2, 6–7.

14. Barringer, *The Story of Scrap*, 7.

15. *Steel and America;* Joel 3:10 (New International Version). In two other places (Isaiah 2:4 and Micah 4:3), the Old Testament describes the reverse process of turning swords into plowshares.

16. American Iron and Steel Institute, *Steel's War Record* (New York: American Iron and Steel Institute, 1944), i; U.S. Steel Corporation, *Steel in the War* (New York: U.S. Steel Corporation, 1946), 9. Churchill is quoted in Martin Gilbert, *The Churchill War Papers*, vol. 3, *The Ever-Widening War, 1941* (London: Heinemann, 2000), 141.

17. American Iron and Steel Institute, *Steel's War Record*, 14, 6.

18. "Collection of Scrap Metals Enforced by Death Penalty," *Science News Letter*, July 13, 1940, 22–23.

19. "Scientists to Inaugurate Sessions Today," *Washington Post*, May 10, 1940; Franklin D. Roosevelt, "Radio Address before the Eighth Pan American Scientific Congress. Washington, D.C. May 10, 1940," in *The Public Papers and Addresses of Franklin D. Roosevelt*, 1940 vol., ed. Samuel I. Rosenman (New York: Macmillan, 1941), 187.

20. The administration's concerns over the growing global crisis are discussed in Richard W. Steele, "Preparing the Public for War: Efforts to Establish a National Propaganda Agency, 1940–1941," *American Historical Review* 75 (1970): 1640–53, and Kimble, *Mobilizing the Home Front*, 19–21. Konoe is quoted in Herbert P. Bix, *Hirohito and the Making of Modern Japan* (New York: HarperCollins, 2000), 383.

21. Wayne Cole, *America First: The Battle against Intervention, 1940–1941* (New York: Octagon Books, 1971), 30.

22. Franklin D. Roosevelt, "Export of War Materials and Strategic Raw Products Prohibited Except by License. Proclamation No. 2413. July 2, 1940," in *Public Papers*, 1940 vol., ed. Samuel I. Rosenman (New York: Macmillan, 1941), 277–81. McNutt is quoted in Frank L. Kluckhohn, "Roosevelt Moves: Bars

Export of Metal to All Except Britain and New World Nations," *New York Times*, September 27, 1940. Smith's previous concerns, from early 1939, could not have foreseen that the United States would export 2 million tons of scrap to Japan throughout that year and then 963,000 tons in 1940 (before the scrap export embargo). These figures were reported in Irving Perlmeter, "Scrap Steel Rummage Urged to Avert Threatened Shortage," *Washington Post*, January 15, 1942.

23. W. R. Slaughter, "Steel and the War Department (A Narrative of Events Affecting the Supply of Steel)," ts., October 21, 1941, 3, in Harry L. Hopkins Papers, box 323, folder "Book 7: Production: Steel," FDR Library.

24. "Gano Dunn Sifts Conflicting Data for Roosevelt," *Wall Street Journal*, January 10, 1941; J. A. Krug, "Production: Wartime Achievements and the Reconversion Outlook (A Report to the War Production Board)," ts., October 9, 1945, 45, in War Production Board Policy Documentation File, RG 179, box 921, folder "Production-Wartime," NARA; "Good Humor Man," *Time*, March 10, 1941, 77–78.

25. Slaughter, "Steel and the War Department," 9.

26. American Iron and Steel Institute, *Steel's War Record*, 4. Dunn is quoted in "Roosevelt Studying Question of Further Cut in Civilian Supply or More Expansion," *Wall Street Journal,* May 29, 1941. The original Dunn reports are available in FDR Official File, box 2, FDR Library, while the government's official narrative of these events is summarized in Civilian Production Administration, *Industrial Mobilization for War: History of the War Production Board and Predecessor Agencies, 1940–1945*, vol. 1, *Program and Administration* (Washington DC: GPO, 1947), 137–38.

27. Frederic Chapin Lane, *Ships for Victory: A History of Shipbuilding under the U.S. Maritime Commission in World War II* (Baltimore: Johns Hopkins University Press, 2001), 314; Keith E. Eiler, *Mobilizing America: Robert P. Patterson and the War Effort, 1940–1945* (Ithaca NY: Cornell University Press, 1997), 185; H. L. Vickery to Harry Hopkins, July 3, 1941, in Harry L. Hopkins Papers, box 323, folder "Book 7: Production: Steel," FDR Library; Krug, *Production*, 45. A more detailed discussion of the priorities system is available in Eiler, *Mobilizing America,* particularly on 183.

28. American Iron and Steel Institute, *Steel's War Record*, 4; Krug, *Production*, 45; William A. Hauck, *A Report of Steel Division, War Production Board, on Steel Expansion for War* (Cleveland: Penton, 1945), 16, 30.

29. "Scrap Shortage: A Problem in Steel Operations," *Scientific American*, December 1941, 321. The Sheffield conclusion is in Herbert R. Aronoff to Stephen Early, September 13, 1941, in FDR Official File, box 2, folder "July–Dec 1941," FDR

Library; American Iron and Steel Institute, *Steel's War Record*, 11; Krug, *Production*, 45; "Steel Priorities—A Portent," *Business Week*, August 16, 1941, 13.

30. "Scrap Ban Backed by Steel Trade: Embargo Held Aid to U.S. Market," *New York Times*, September 27, 1940.

31. Anonymous biography of Donald M. Nelson, ts., January 20, 1942, in Donald M. Nelson Papers, box 1, folder 7, Huntington Library, San Marino CA (Huntington); War Production Board Minutes, Meeting I, ts., January 20, 1942, 1–2, in Records of the War Production Board, General Records, Minutes of Meetings, Nos. 1–100, January 1942–October 1945, RG 179, box 1, volume 1, NARA.

32. War Production Board Minutes, Meeting I, 1–2; Perlmeter, "Scrap Steel Rummage"; "Steel Needs Widen for War Purposes," *New York Times*, January 12, 1942.

33. Kirwan to Roosevelt; War Production Board Minutes, Meeting I, 2.

34. "Salvage for Victory," *National Waste Review*, January 1942, 14; W. C. Bryant, "Foundries and Smelters Need a Lot: Junkyards Will Be Combed for It," *Wall Street Journal*, January 15, 1942. By late summer, the number of local salvage committees was over 13,000, according to "Nelson's Scrap Rally." Faddis's radio address is quoted from his text, as published in "Scrap and Waste Materials," *Vital Speeches of the Day*, May 15, 1942, 473.

35. A good example of the local complaints about WPB's salvage bureaucracy, and the difficulty of communicating within it, is in Robert T. Fisher to Reese Taylor, August 8, 1942, in War Production Board Policy Documentation File, RG 179, box 917, folder "Scrap Campaign: January–August 1942," NARA. In a later review of WPB's early attempts to gather scrap, Harold Fleming wrote that "many of the thousands of committees formed to get in the scrap . . . were little more than skeleton organizations without much life." See his "Scrap Pours In as Salvage Campaign Scours the Nation," *Christian Science Monitor*, November 18, 1942. Hugh Rockoff discusses the failed aluminum drive in "Keep on Scrapping: The Salvage Drives of World War II," working paper (National Bureau of Economic Research, 2007), http://www.nber.org/papers/w13418 (accessed February 3, 2013).

36. "Scrap-Happy," *Business Week*, February 28, 1942, 14; American Iron and Steel Institute, *Steel's War Record*, 11–12. The Republic Steel material information was reported by C. M. White, the corporation's vice president, who was discussing the previous spring's scrap situation in "Lack of Scrap Keeps Steel Furnaces Idle," *Scrapper*, no. 7 [undated].

37. "Gallup Poll on Salvage Collections," *National Waste Review*, April 1942, 11; "Lee Accuses 2 of Discouraging State Scrap Collection Drives," *Washington Post*, May 6, 1942; "Defends 'Scrap' Figures," *New York Times*, June 27, 1942.

38. "Scrap Steel Piles Draw WPB Threat," *New York Times*, June 5, 1942; Krug, *Production*, 47. The problem with iron ore transportation in the winter was pointed out in "United States Faced by Steel Shortage," *American Observer*, September 28, 1942, 8, while Robert W. Wolcott, president of the Lukens Steel Company, discussed the expected additional 1943 blast furnaces in "American Newspaper Publishers Scrap Collection Drive," 19; George S. Pettee to R. Keith Kane, July 23, 1942, in Records of the Office of Government Reports, U.S. Information Service, RG 44, box 1849, folder "Sources Div: Shipping, Steel, and Information Policy," NARA.

39. "Steel Production at New High Mark," *New York Times*, May 4, 1942; WPB's estimate is in Frank I. Weller, "Metals for War Is Next on List of Salvage Drives," *Washington Post*, June 28, 1942; Roosevelt to John J. Cochran, June 1, 1942, in FDR Official File, box 2, FDR Library. Roosevelt went on to describe plans for additional blast furnace (pig iron) capacity in the works, but it is not clear if he knew that the furnaces would not be online until 1943.

40. House Committee on the Merchant Marine and Fisheries, *Shortage of Steel in Shipbuilding: Hearings on H. R. 281*, 77th Cong., 2nd sess., 1942, 36; "Report of the Chairman, War Production Board, to the Special Committee Investigating the National Defense Program," ts., June 22, 1942, 17, in Donald M. Nelson Papers, box 12, folder 7, Huntington.

41. *War Facts: A Handbook for Speakers on War Production* (Washington DC: Office for Emergency Management, 1942), 3; Donald H. Wallace, "Relation of Wartime Price Administration to the Scrap Metal Industry," *National Waste Review*, March 1942, 18, 19.

42. On the pressure to go on the offensive in 1942, see Richard W. Steele, *The First Offensive 1942: Roosevelt, Marshall, and the Making of American Strategy* (Bloomington: Indiana University Press, 1973), 172, 180–81; Quentin Reynolds, "We Will Make It," *Collier's*, July 11, 1942, 99.

2. Henry Doorly and the Nebraska Plan

1. "Notes on Mrs. Henry Doorly," ts., December 13, 1962, *Omaha World-Herald* File, DCHS.

2. The account of the Doorlys' exchange is drawn from "American Newspaper Publishers," 21, from "*World-Herald* Wins Pulitzer Prize Award; Chance Talk Started Scrap Campaign," *Morning World-Herald*, May 4, 1943, and from "Nebraska Miracle Reverberates in Washington," *Newsweek*, September 21, 1942. A detailed report on the failed rubber campaign is in W. H. Lawrence, "Rubber Collection Extended 10 Days," *New York Times*, June 30, 1942.

3. "Lease-Lend Steel Taking First Place," *New York Times,* June 29, 1942.

4. Limprecht, *Century of Service,* 25. There are some indications that the administration suspected Doorly of holding isolationist views even after Pearl Harbor. An internal government report in April 1942 listed Omaha as one of fourteen cities that continued to be centers of isolationist activity, with the anonymous author blaming "the publishers and editors of a small number of metropolitan newspapers" for being at the heart of the problem. See "Isolationist Aims, Arguments and Organizations," ts., April 7, 1942, 2, in Records of the Office of Government Reports, U.S. Information Service, RG 44, box 1842, folder "Spec. Services: Isolationist Aims," NARA.

5. "World-Herald Wins."

6. Limprecht, *Century of Service,* 25; "To Arouse the People," *Time,* September 14, 1942, 81.

7. Limprecht, *Century of Service,* 25; "Henry Doorly, 81, Omaha Publisher," *New York Times,* June 27, 1961. The circulation figures are from clippings in the Henry Doorly Scrapbook, pp. 2 and 8, Nebraska State Historical Society (NSHS). Hitchcock's years in DC were unusual because he served two terms as a representative and two as a senator.

8. Limprecht, *Century of Service,* 24; "To Arouse the People"; "Doorly Pushes Scrap Drive," *Greater Nebraskan,* July 1942. The anecdote on Doorly's loans is in "An Independent Steps Aside," *Time,* September 5, 1955, 78. Doorly could occasionally take on a less formal guise, as with the select few he allowed to call him Harry. See, for example, Doorly to Malcolm Cowley, May 13, 1943, in Records of the Office of Government Reports, U.S. Information Service, RG 44, box 1845, folder "Media, Dec. 15–42," NARA.

9. Frederick Ware, "It Seems Like Yesterday," undated ts., pp. 2–3, in Henry Doorly Scrapbook, NSHS. Another example of creativity, this time on the part of one of Doorly's trusted staffers, was the 1926 coverage of the capture of the Omaha sniper, when the newspaper tied up phone lines so that its rivals could not get in to interview witnesses. See Limprecht, *Century of Service,* 27.

10. Ware, "It Seems Like Yesterday," 3. Other examples of Doorly's causes over the years are described in the numerous tributes received by the *World-Herald* upon his death: "Henry Doorly Death Called Loss to U.S.," *Evening World-Herald,* June 27, 1961.

11. "An Independent Steps Aside"; "Fury in Omaha," *Business Week,* August 26, 1944, 42, 44. Yeager is quoted in "Henry Doorly Death."

12. The employee figures are from a clipping in the Rotogravure section of the *Sunday World-Herald,* October 20, 1940, in Henry Doorly Scrapbook, NSHS.

The newspaper's reach was so great within the state that by 1955, estimates were that it reached 60 percent of the state's population, according to "An Independent Steps Aside." The ending quotation is from "*World-Herald* Wins Pulitzer."

13. George T. Eager, "Scrap: Scoop for the American Press," *Saturday Evening Post*, December 12, 1942, 116.

14. "Whirled by Belt; Dies," *Waverly Democrat*, May 22, 1942; "Over 400,000 Pounds of Scrap Is Shipped," *Waverly Democrat*, May 10, 1942; "Salvage Drive Gets Praise," *Waverly Democrat*, May 22, 1942. More details on Bremer County's scrap efforts (both before and after the *World-Herald* campaign) are available in Terrence J. Lindell, "'Bomb 'em with Junk': The 1942 Scrap Metal Campaign in Bremer County, Iowa" (paper presented at the Missouri Valley History Conference, Omaha, March 2010). For a more personal view of Iowa's scrapping efforts, see Carroll Engelhardt, *The Farm at Holstein Dip: An Iowa Boyhood* (Iowa City: University of Iowa Press, 2012), 102–103.

15. U.S. Department of Agriculture, "War Board Activities," summary no. 6, ts., January 12, 1942, 3, in Records of the Office of the Secretary of Agriculture, Records of the War Food Administration, Records of the War Boards, 1941–1944, RG 16, box 1, folder "War Board Activities #6," NARA; "Birmingham Collects Scrap Metals in Whirlwind Campaign," *American City*, March 1942, 93.

16. Strasser, *Waste and Want*, 247; "Harvesting Scrap," *Business Week*, February 21, 1942, 28; "Farms Proving Big Source of Scrap Metal in International Harvester's Salvage Drive," *Wall Street Journal*, March 7, 1942; Raymond Moley, "The Return of the Prodigal," *Newsweek*, June 8, 1942, 72; "Contact!" *Scrapper*, no. 2 [undated].

17. Lukens Steel Company, *Salvage* (Coatesville PA: Lukens Steel Company, [1942]), 5, 7, 9, item 002–0201–12, Imprints Division, Hagley.

18. "Coatesville, Pa.," *Scrapper*, no. 1 [undated]; "Coatesville Cleanup Produces 680,761 Pounds," *Scrapper*, no. 1; "Coatesville's Part in Equipping an Army," *American City*, August 1942, 40.

19. "Break Farm Bottleneck on Scrap Metal," *Omaha World-Herald*, undated clipping in folder "Scrap Metal Drive General File," DCHS; Carlyle Hodgkin, "Scrap Drive Yields Tons of Old Iron," *Omaha World-Herald*, April 29, 1942. The estimated total returns were reported in "Troops Open Scrap Drive," undated clipping in folder "Scrap Metal Drive General File," DCHS.

20. "American Newspaper Publishers," 21. Doorly initially toyed with the idea of leaving the advertising department out of the project altogether, as he was accepting no paid advertising involving the campaign. However, he did need his in-house artists to work on the newspaper's own ads for the drive. J. M. Harding,

who would manage the drive with Grimes, was on vacation when Doorly first came up with the plan, according to "Chance Talk Started."

21. "American Newspaper Publishers," 23; "Chance Talk Started."
22. "American Newspaper Publishers," 23–24, 22.
23. "Doorly Urges State Lead in Salvage Drive," *Sunday World-Herald*, July 12, 1942.
24. Davenport, "Life's Report," 20; "American Newspaper Publishers," 23.
25. O'Neill, *Democracy at War*, 135; *Nebraska "Scrap" Plan*, 1. The ending quotation is in "Doorly Urges." Each county was required to name a charity that would actually receive any prize money. Doorly later related that an additional $2,000 in prize money was awarded by other individuals and businesses for the contest ("American Newspaper Publishers," 22). Throughout the drive (and in the national drive that it inspired), citizens could donate their scrap metal directly to a community pile or to a collection truck for free. Alternatively, if they were willing and able to haul the scrap themselves, they could sell it to a scrap dealer, who would pay for it through the usual channels. Sellers would then turn in a receipt to the drive organizers to ensure that the appropriate amount was added to the team, community, county, or state's scrap total. The funding for the salvage yard purchases ultimately trickled down from the steel mills' government contracts, a monetary incentive system that was little different than the peacetime version albeit one that was moving much more quickly and with greater urgency.
26. "Doorly Urges"; "America's War Plants MUST Have Scrap," advertisement, *Sunday World-Herald*, July 12, 1942.
27. "World-Herald Offers $2,000 to Spur Drive," *Sunday World-Herald*, July 12, 1942.
28. Household scrap tended to be lighter than farm scrap and was often mixed in with other metals. As a result, it required more sorting in scrap yards and also had to be crushed into compact bales so that it did not simply combust in open-hearth furnaces. However, the scrap deficit motivated steel mills to resort to scrap grades that would not have been preferred in the normal order of business. More discussion is available in "Get in the Scrap!" *Business Week*, October 3, 1942, 19–20, 22, 24. Doorly's inclusion of rubber stipulated that 1 pound of rubber would count as the equivalent of 5 pounds of scrap metal. As the drive went on, however, the campaign's references to rubber became secondary to the search for metals. The official contest rules were published in the campaign's first full-page ad, "America's War Plants MUST Have Scrap."
29. Edward T. Folliard, "Aluminum Pots Dot Landscape Weeks after Drive for Metal," *Washington Post*, October 8, 1941. The government blamed the aluminum drive's

problems on poor publicity and fifth column rumors that the drive was just for morale, not for production purposes; see Civilian Production Administration, Bureau of Demobilization, "Aluminum Policies of the War Production Board and Predecessor Agencies, May 1940 to November 1945" (Historical Reports on War Administration: War Production Board, Special Study no. 22), ts., [1945], in RG 179, War Production Board Historical Reports, Special Studies 19–22, box 3, folder 22, NARA. The World War I revelations initially emerged in George Creel, *How We Advertised America: The First Telling of the Amazing Story of the Committee on Public Information That Carried the Gospel of Americanism to Every Corner of the Globe* (New York: Harper and Brothers, 1920).

30. "Doorly Urges"; "America's War Plants MUST Have Scrap."

31. Anne Marie Todd, "Conservation as Wartime Necessity: The Militarization of Consumer Waste in WWII Domestic Propaganda" (paper presented at the National Communication Association convention, New Orleans, November 2011).

3. Summertime Scrapping in the City

1. On the smell of the Omaha stockyards representing money, see Alice Schroeder, *The Snowball: Warren Buffett and the Business of Life* (New York: Bantam Books, 2008), 43, and Michael Rips, *Face of a Naked Lady: An Omaha Family Mystery* (New York: Houghton Mifflin Harcourt, 2005), 48. For background on the stockyards itself, detailed sources are available in Lawrence H. Larsen and others, *Upstream Metropolis: An Urban Biography of Omaha and Council Bluffs* (Lincoln: University of Nebraska Press, 2007), 109–18, and in Nellie Snyder Yost, *The Call of the Range: The Story of the Nebraska Stock Growers Association* (Denver: Sage Books, 1966), 294–314.

2. Rudyard Kipling, *From Sea to Sea: Letters of Travel*, vol. 2 (New York: Doubleday and McClure, 1899), 136; Carl Jonas, *Riley McCullough* (Boston: Little, Brown, 1954), 187. Jonas was an Omaha-based novelist who disguised his native town using the fictional label "Gateway City."

3. The reference to "oldsters" is from 74-year-old Peter Christensen, interviewed in Omaha on the eve of the war by the Federal Writers' Project, as cited in Larsen and others, *Upstream Metropolis*, 278. Doorly's address is quoted from "Doorly Urges."

4. More contrasts among Omaha's various social groupings in this general period are available in Carl Abbott, *How Cities Won the West: Four Centuries of Urban Change in Western North America* (Albuquerque: University of New Mexico Press, 2008), 52–53, and George R. Leighton, *Five Cities: The Story of Their Youth and Old Age* (New York: Arno Press, 1974), 140–46. An extremely thoughtful analysis of the city's immigrant melting pot up through 1920 is available in

Howard P. Chudacoff's "A New Look at Ethnic Neighborhoods: Residential Dispersion and the Concept of Visibility in a Medium-Sized City," *Journal of American History* 60 (1973): 76–93. Useful glimpses into Omaha's African American culture in the 1940s are available in Dennis N. Mihelich, "World War II and the Transformation of the Omaha Urban League," *Nebraska History* 60 (1979): 401–23, and in Writers' Program (Nebraska), *The Negroes of Nebraska* (Lincoln NE: Woodruff Printing, 1940). The city's Italian-born population on the eve of war receives a detailed treatment in Writers' Program (Nebraska), *The Italians of Omaha* (Omaha: Independent Printing, 1941).

5. For a fuller discussion of Omaha's prewar ethnicities and conflicts, see Clare V. McKanna Jr., "Seeds of Destruction: Homicide, Race, and Justice in Omaha, 1880–1920," *Journal of American Ethnic History* 14 (1994): 65–90. Larsen and others have similarly informative material in *Upstream Metropolis*, chap. 7; the "cauldron" quotation is from their p. 234. R. Douglas Hurt, in *The Great Plains during World War II* (Lincoln: University of Nebraska Press, 2008), 392–93, notes that race relations in the Midwest were often strained through much of the war. G. E. Condra and G. A. Loveland discuss the 1913 tornado in "The Iowa-Nebraska Tornadoes of Easter Sunday, 1913," *Bulletin of the American Geographical Society* 46 (1914): 100–107. Alice Scourby examines the 1909 Greek Town incident in *The Greek Americans* (Boston: Twayne, 1984), 33–34. Orville D. Menard covers the 1919 events in his "Tom Dennison, the *Omaha Bee*, and the 1919 Omaha Race Riot," *Nebraska History* 68 (1987): 152–65, as does Leighton, *Five Cities*, 212–17. Prostitution and other vices in prewar Omaha appear throughout Rips, *Face of a Naked Lady*; see also Dorothy Devereux Dustin, *Omaha and Douglas County: A Panoramic History* (Woodland Hills ca: Windsor Publications, 1980), 93–96, 100–103.

6. The circulation figures are from the *World-Herald*'s editorial page throughout July 1942.

7. Davenport, "Life's Report," 14. The original account (and Dodendorf's quotation) was in "Plea for Scrap by Henry Doorly Gets Fast Result," *Sunday World-Herald*, July 12, 1942.

8. "Nebraska Is Challenged to Lead All Other States' Metal, Rubber Salvage"; "World-Herald Offers $2,000 to Spur Drive"; "Gov. Griswold Commends Scrap Contest"; all these stories, as well as the seven photographs, are in the *Sunday World-Herald*, July 12, 1942. The full-page advertisement in the same issue was "America's War Plants MUST Have Scrap."

9. "What You Can Do," *Morning World-Herald*, July 13, 1942; the radio show is discussed in "Trucks Start City Canvass This Morning," *Morning World-Herald*, July 20, 1942.

10. Bill Boni, "That Scrap Will Help Your Uncle Samuel—Look Down This List to See Just Where," *Morning World-Herald*, July 14, 1942.

11. "Maudie Says: Working over This Hot Stove Is Just Dandy," *Omaha World-Herald*, July 13, 1942.

12. As Doorly commented later, "Mr. Jeffers' response was so marvelous that it nearly knocked me out of my chair. . . . Since Saturday morning I've received a constant barrage of telegrams from him." This account is in Lawrence Youngman, "Speakers Tell Urgent Need of Materials," *Morning World-Herald*, July 14, 1942.

13. Ray Mackland, "Battling Bill Jeffers," *Life*, February 22, 1943, 88–90, 92, 94–96, 99. The locomotive quotation is on pp. 89–90. This profile goes on to describe how Jeffers—appointed "rubber czar" by the Roosevelt administration later in 1942—was unfazed by aggressive congressional questioning about the rubber crisis and, indeed, made several senators shrink back in their chairs with his combative nature during hearings. Another useful profile of Jeffers is in J. R. Johnson's *Representative Nebraskans* (Lincoln NE: Johnsen, 1954), 105–109. A less charitable view of his personality is in Maury Klein's *Union Pacific: The Rebirth, 1894–1969* (New York: Doubleday, 1990), esp. 386 and 418–20.

14. As quoted in Maxine Block, "Jeffers, William M.," in *Current Biography: Who's News and Why* (New York: H. W. Wilson, 1942), 414.

15. "U.P. Piles Up Scrap Salvage," *Omaha World-Herald*, July 30, 1942; V. A. Bradshaw, "Salvage Rally," letter to editor, *Evening World-Herald*, July 18, 1942.

16. Doorly's account of Jeffers's suggestions is in Youngman, "Speakers Tell Urgent Need."

17. "Union Pacific Plans Rally for Program," *Sunday World-Herald*, July 12, 1942; "Keep 'Old Glory' Flying," advertisement, *Morning World-Herald*, July 13, 1942; "Big Junk Pile to Be Built in Front of City Auditorium," *Morning World-Herald*, July 13, 1942. The full-page ad was prepared by the Union Pacific, but the newspaper, in accordance with Doorly's policy of accepting no advertisements for the drive, refused payment.

18. "Nebraska State Salvage Drive Hailed as Model for Nation," *Union Pacific Bulletin*, August 1942; Youngman, "Speakers Tell Urgent Need." While the rally did seem to foster a strong spirit of unity among its various attendees—as accounts from the time suggest—it bears mentioning that the culture of the 1940s Midwest still supported social segregation, meaning that African Americans at the rally most likely participated from the balconies. Still, it is clear that much of Omaha's black community was heavily invested in the scrap drive and found reasons to contribute as much scrap as possible. See, for example, "*Omaha Star* Scrap Iron Rally Nets 19,000 Pounds," *Omaha Star*, July 31, 1942.

19. Youngman, "Speakers Tell Urgent Need."

20. "Old Guns, Swords, Tricycles, Beer Tray—Sentimental Scrap Metal to Avenge Bataan," *Evening World-Herald*, July 14, 1942. The anecdote about the tools is from Youngman, "Speakers Tell Urgent Need."

21. The quotations and the number of trucks are in "Old Guns, Swords," while the total number of tons appeared a day later in "Party Lines Dropped for Salvage Push," *Morning World-Herald*, July 15, 1942.

22. "Here Are 2 Men Who Now Know About Scrap Drive," *Omaha World-Herald*, July 16, 1942.

23. The musical extravaganza rally is described in "Scrap Admission at Show Tonight," *Omaha World-Herald*, undated clipping in folder "Scrap Metal Drive 1942 July 1 to 20," DCHS.

24. "Let's Go, Nebraska . . . Let's Top the Nation!" advertisement, *Sunday World-Herald*, July 19, 1942. Emphases as in original, ellipsis in original text.

25. "Let's Go, Nebraska . . . Let's Top the Nation!"

26. "American Newspaper Publishers," 21.

27. Lawrence Youngman to Dr. and Mrs. C. L. Youngman, July 19, 1942, in vertical file, Scrap Drive Collection, DCHS. More details on Youngman's subsequent reporting from the battlefronts are available in Douglas R. Hartman's "Lawrence W. Youngman: War Correspondent for the *Omaha World-Herald*," *Nebraska History* 76 (1995): 100–105.

28. Harding and Grimes's roles are described in "Nebraska Scrap Drive Success Is Lesson in Press Leadership," *Editor and Publisher*, August 29, 1942, 4. The description of Harding's "hardheaded" nature is in Davenport, "Life's Report," 14. The quotation from Harding is from "American Newspaper Publishers Scrap Collection Drive," 24.

29. Ernest Jones, "Reporter Finds Scrap; Safes, Tractor; Asks Readers' Help," *Evening World-Herald*, July 17, 1942.

30. Ernest Jones, "City Scrapping Spirit Fine; More Old Safes Are Donated," *Omaha World-Herald*, July 18, 1942. The tip on one bridge paid off when a resident agreed to donate a trestle that had been washed into a drainage creek on her farm just to the west of the city. The local Fort Crook motor school volunteered to salvage the bridge, ultimately adding 10 tons to the scrap drive. Ernest Jones, "A Bridge Given for Scrap; Now to Move It!" undated clipping, and "Army Offers to Get Scrap," undated clipping, both in folder "Scrap Metal Drive 1942 July 20 to 24," DCHS.

31. Bill Billotte, "'Housewives Go to War,' Forget Wash Day for Bigger Job of Aiding Omaha's Scrap Collection," *Morning World-Herald*, July 21, 1942; "Journey of a Scrap Truck . . . at Unloading Point It Dumped 3,040 Pounds," *Evening*

World-Herald, July 20, 1942, ellipsis in original headline. The newspaper's description was in the caption of a photograph accompanying Billotte's "'Housewives Go to War.'"

32. Billotte, "'Housewives Go to War.'"

33. "NEBRASKA'S WOMEN Have Gone to War!" advertisement, *Sunday World-Herald*, July 26, 1942.

34. Kimble, "Militarization of the Prairie," 90–91.

35. "American Newspaper Publishers Scrap Collection Drive," 24. Harding, who was speaking at a meeting of publishers interested in the Nebraska Plan, was also referring to the effort that other newspapers would need to produce to be successful in the national effort.

36. "'Let's Have It!' Cry Abbott, Costello in Drive for Scrap," *Evening World-Herald*, July 31, 1942.

37. "'One of Most Inspiring Sights I've Seen,' Says OPA Official of Huge Scrap Pile Here," *Evening World-Herald*, July 28, 1942. The official was unnamed in the account.

38. "Set Record for Scrap Collection," *Omaha World-Herald*, July 29, 1942.

39. Bill Billotte, "Railbirds Watch Scrap Pile Grow, Nod Their Approval," undated clipping, in folder "Scrap Metal Drive 1942 July 20 to 24," DCHS; Davenport, "Life's Report," 12.

40. The Institute of Scrap Iron and Steel sent Clarence C. Cohen, of Kansas City, "to see firsthand how a state stages a 'real' scrap campaign." He was duly impressed, telling the *World-Herald* that "it's amazing what the public can do when it is provided the proper organization." "It's Amazing! Says Expert of Nebraska's Scrap Drive," *Evening World-Herald*, July 29, 1942.

41. Stories on Brewer included "Just One Small Woman, but She's Netted 20 Tons Scrap," *Omaha World-Herald*, July 28, 1942, and "1914 Model Car Goes to Scrap Heap," *Omaha World-Herald*, July 23, 1942. Those on Wellshear included Bill Billotte, "On Vacation, Obtains Truck, Helps in Scrap Collection," *Omaha World-Herald*, July 22, 1942, and "'It's Little Enough to Do,' Says Drive Patriot No. 1," *Evening World-Herald*, July 23, 1942. The newspaper told a similar story about Mrs. T. G. Pettegrew, the salvage chair for nearby Carter Lake, Iowa, who had personally located over 62 tons of scrap metal in the first six months of the year: "Little Woman Sweeps Hard, Collects 62 Tons of Scrap," *Sunday World-Herald*, July 12, 1942.

42. For example, the Nebraska Power company put together a prize package totaling $500, exclusively aimed at internal Omaha scrap competitions. This announcement appeared with several others in "Airmen Will Join Search for Salvage," *Omaha World-Herald*, July 15, 1942. There was an additional monetary motivation

for many service groups: since the contest allowed scrappers to donate their materials directly to the city or, alternately, to sell them to a local scrap dealer for cash (within a federally set ceiling rate), many service groups elected to take the cash payment so that they could raise funds and simultaneously benefit the scrap drive's total.

43. J. M. Harding offered a detailed picture of this organizational scheme in "American Newspaper Publishers Scrap Collection Drive," 28.

44. Abbott's *How Cities Won the West*, 52–53, notes that as late as 1920, 49 percent of Omaha residents had been born abroad. On the subject of campaign effectiveness, numerous disciplines have examined the difficulty of attitudinal and behavioral change. For a recent example in the field of persuasion theory, consider the discussion in Daniel J. O'Keefe, *Persuasion Theory and Research*, 2nd ed. (Thousand Oaks CA: Sage Publications, 2002), esp. 1–28.

45. The number of columns was reported by Doorly himself in "American Newspaper Publishers Scrap Collection Drive," 22. According to "Nebraska Scrap Drive Success Is Lesson," the total scrap content amounted to 7,500 inches of stories and photographs — not counting eight full-page ads and one quarter-page ad for the drive, each prepared and paid for by the newspaper itself.

46. "Get Scrap-Happy Today, Ball Fans, and Boost Drive," *Omaha World-Herald*, undated clipping, in folder "Scrap Metal Drive 1942 July 1 to 20," DCHS; "State Softballers Drum Up Tilts to Boost Scrap Drive," *Morning World-Herald*, July 23, 1942; "Storz Team to Pay Scrap for Own Play," *Morning World-Herald*, July 23, 1942; "Golfers Join Drive on All City Courses," *Sunday World-Herald*, July 19, 1942; "Net Pros Aid Drive for Scrap," *Morning World-Herald*, July 15, 1942; "Scrap Shoots Are Planned," *Sunday World-Herald*, July 19, 1942.

47. "Put the Boss to Work — He'll Dig Out the Scrap," *Omaha World-Herald*, undated clipping, in folder "Scrap Metal Drive 1942 July," DCHS; the "commandos unit" phrase appears in "Daily Pickup Downtown, on South Side," *Omaha World-Herald*, July 27, 1942.

48. "Benson Scouts After $25 Prize," undated clipping in folder "Scrap Metal Drive 1942 July 21 to 31," DCHS; interview with Melba Glock, Scrap Drive Collection, DCHS; "All Omaha to Mobilize in Campaign," *Morning World-Herald*, July 16, 1942; "On Vacation, Obtains Truck"; "They Use Magnets to Find Scrap," *Morning World-Herald*, July 25, 1942.

49. "Scrap Pile Boosted by 1,171 Tons," *Omaha World-Herald*, undated clipping, in folder "Scrap Metal Drive 1942 July 1 to 20," DCHS; "Must Work Together, Get Scrap, Say Foreign-Born," *Sunday World-Herald*, July 19, 1942.

50. No doubt many 1942 steel yard and scrap yard heaps exceeded Omaha's pile in size and volume. Among municipalities at this point in the war, however, there

had been as yet no scrap campaign that could rival the volume produced by the *World-Herald*'s drive, making it highly unlikely that any other city in the United States had gathered this much scrap metal in one location. In fact, by October 1942 the magazine *American City* had profiled numerous municipal scrap efforts for the war effort, but its story on the Omaha-based effort was so admiring that it inspired laudatory comments for Nebraska from the British Ministry in charge of scrap metal: "Nebraska Cities' Part in State-wide Scrap Drive," *American City*, October 1942, 46–47, and "How Britain Drives for Scrap Metal," *American City*, March 1943, 39. Although there had been occasional scrap metal collection efforts during World War I, the rate of steel production at that point in time was much lower than in World War II, meaning that there were no comparable campaigns that could have produced massive scrap piles to rival those in the latter conflict. Most likely, however, the Scrap Mountain's unofficial title was short-lived, given the tremendous collection efforts across the country during the national drive in late 1942.

51. Davenport, in "Life's Report," writes that forty pianos were donated in all (they were eventually burned at the end of the drive, which was the easiest way to obtain their metal pieces). The anecdote about the nighttime singing is from an untitled and undated clipping fragment in folder "Scrap Metal Drive 1942 July," DCHS.

4. Mobilizing Greater Nebraska

1. There is a debate about the true source of the name *Nebraska*, with the Omaha tribe's name *Ni brhaska ke* being another candidate (in addition to the Otoe name). Both mean "flat water," an apparent reference to the shallow Platte River, which runs through the area from west to east. See further discussion in Lilian L. Fitzpatrick, *Nebraska Place-Names*, new ed. (Lincoln: University of Nebraska Press, 1960), 171. Ralph C. Morris, "The Notion of a Great American Desert East of the Rockies," *Mississippi Valley Historical Review* 13 (1926): 191–94; the quotation is on 193. Townsend's phrase is in his story "Bullwhack Joe," *Out West*, July 1904, 256. A longer list of early descriptions of Nebraska is in Yost, *Call of the Range*, 17–19.

2. On the slow pace of the pioneers, Greg MacGregor, *Overland: The California Emigrant Trail of 1841–1870* (Albuquerque: University of New Mexico Press, 1996), 6. Hurt's *Great Plains*, 124–30, discusses gas rationing and speed limits in the Midwest, while *Nebraska: A Guide to the Cornhusker State*, by the Federal Writers' Project (New York: Viking Press, 1939), 98, examines the condition of the state's roads on the eve of the war. Donald J. Heimburger and John Kelly

scrutinize the overcrowded domestic train situation in *Trains to Victory: America's Railroads in World War II* (Forest Park IL: Heimburger House, 2009).

3. Federal Writers' Project, *Nebraska*, 3; "A New Link," *New York Times*, August 31, 1860. Nebraska's total territory encompasses 76,484 square miles, meaning that Douglas County takes up less than half of 1 percent of the state's area while (in the 1940 census) hosting 20 percent of the population.

4. For background on the backstabbing debates over the location of the state capital, see A. G. Warner, "Sketches from Territorial History," *Transactions and Reports of the Nebraska State Historical Society* 2 (1887): 18–63, and C. H. Gere, "The Capital Question in Nebraska and the Location of the Seat of Government at Lincoln," *Transactions and Reports of the Nebraska State Historical Society* 2 (1887): 63–80. Myers points out (in "Grain Belt's Golden," 76) that Omaha's business community attempted to address city-rural tensions by founding Ak-Sar-Ben (the state's name spelled backwards), an organization that encouraged rural Nebraskans to participate in its festivities. The "pariah" quotation is from Robert Burlingame, "Nebraska on the Make," *Vanity Fair*, November 1932, 29. Even though many Nebraskans today do not think of the Lincoln metropolitan area as being in the outstate category, in the 1940s the capital city (population around 80,000) was a much better fit for the label.

5. "The Voice of Patriotism," *Columbus Daily Telegram*, July 13, 1942. Despite the editorial's tense undertone, Doorly proudly reprinted it in full: "Scrap Collection Plea Voice of Patriotism," *Morning World-Herald*, July 15, 1942.

6. *Nebraska "Scrap" Plan*, 2.

7. The distinction between ranches and farms is a rough oversimplification, as there is some overlap between the two in many places within Nebraska. A more detailed discussion of the distinction is available in Bradley H. Baltensperger, *Nebraska: A Geography* (Boulder: Westview Press, 1985), 137–41. The description of the Sandhills region is in Yost, *Call of the Range*, 170.

8. Brian J. L. Berry, *Geography of Market Centers and Retail Distribution* (Englewood Cliffs NJ: Prentice-Hall, 1967), 20. A useful discussion of central places in midwestern states is in John C. Hudson, "The Plains Country Town," in *The Great Plains: Environment and Culture*, ed. Brian W. Blouet and Frederick C. Luebke (Lincoln: University of Nebraska Press, 1979), 99–118.

9. *Polk's Lincoln City Directory* (Omaha: R. L. Polk, 1942), 793, 794, 798. The Athens quotation is from Raymond A. McConnell Jr., *75 Years in the Prairie Capital* (Lincoln NE: Miller and Paine, 1955), 129. Since the initial scrap drive took place over the summer (not to mention after many young men had already left for military training), the level of student participation in Lincoln was apparently

negligible, although it would swell in the national drive, after classes were again in session.

10. Burlingame, "Nebraska on the Make," 29.

11. Interview with James W. Hewitt, Scrap Drive Collection, DCHS.

12. Jon Farrar, "Counties by the Numbers," *Nebraskaland*, July 1994, 49; Robert Nelson, "Home Plates," *Omaha World-Herald*, August 6, 1996. Several of Nebraska's neighboring states used a similar county-numbering system in 1942. Wyoming still uses it today, while all but three of Nebraska's counties also continue to use it.

13. In the words of "To Arouse the People," 81, Doorly's paper "blankets the State." In John Gunther's *Inside U.S.A.* (New York: Harper and Brothers, 1947), 237, he notes that the *World-Herald* was so popular in the region that it was widely available in nearby North Dakota and South Dakota. The "dramatize" quotation is from "*World-Herald* Offers," while the "circus" phrase is from Davenport, "Life's Report," 20.

14. The Burlington had lines and employees in seventy-two of Nebraska's ninety-three counties during the war, as discussed in *Nebraska "Scrap" Plan*, 2. In total, the railroad had nearly 2,800 miles of track within the state. The best general historical source on the Burlington is Richard C. Overton's *Burlington Route: A History of the Burlington Lines* (New York: Alfred A. Knopf, 1965). Details on the Burlington railroad in Nebraska history are available in Thomas M. Davis, "Building the Burlington through Nebraska: A Summary View," *Nebraska History* 30 (1949): 317–47; Thomas M. Davis, "Lines West! The Story of George W. Holdrege," *Nebraska History* 31 (1950): 107–25; and Richard D. Loosbrock, "Living with the Octopus: Life, Work, and Community in a Western Railroad Town" (PhD diss., University of New Mexico, 2005).

15. According to Gunther, *Inside U.S.A.*, 253, the rivalry between the UP and the Burlington in Nebraska dated back to the late nineteenth century, when "the UP was always supposed to elect one senator, the Burlington the other." George R. Leighton, in his "Omaha, Nebraska: The Glory Is Departed—Part I," *Harper's Magazine*, July 1938, 124, agrees that "either as enemies or allies they divided the government of the State between them." The taunting exchange between the railroad officials appears in "Rails Prepare for Extensive Part in Drive," *Sunday World-Herald*, July 19, 1942. Harding's account of the Burlington meeting, including Flynn's exclamations, is in "American Newspaper Publishers," 26. The *Nebraska "Scrap" Plan* booklet, 2, suggests (probably erroneously) that the visiting executive was not Flynn but the Burlington president, Ralph Budd. The statewide tour was reported in "County Praised for Organizing Salvage Drives," *Scottsbluff Daily Star-Herald*, July 23, 1942. Additional Burlington rallies took

place in Alliance, McCook, Scottsbluff, and Wymore, while the UP followed up its Omaha rally with events in Elm Creek, Fremont, Kearney, Overton, and Shelton.

16. Gunther, *Inside U.S.A.*, 250; Russell W. Davenport, "Republican Renascence," *Life*, September 6, 1943, 110.

17. "Gov. Griswold Commends"; the governor's rural letter was printed verbatim in numerous outstate newspapers, including "Scrappers in Nebraska Get Busy, Plea of Gov. Griswold," *Dakota County Star*, July 23, 1942; "Scrappers in Nebraska Get Busy, Plea of Griswold," *Thomas County Herald-Clipper*, July 22, 1942; and "Scrappers in Neb. Get Busy: Plea of Gov. Griswold," *Elmwood Leader-Echo*, July 23, 1942.

18. *Nebraska "Scrap" Plan*, 1.

19. "DUNDY COUNTY GLADLY ACCEPTS THE CHALLENGE," advertisement, *Benkelman Post and News-Chronicle*, July 17, 1942.

20. "Huge Salvage Drive Is 'Ready to Roll': County to Join Effort," *Blair Pilot-Tribune*, July 16, 1942; "Burlington's Rally Spurs Scrap Drive," *Evening World-Herald*, July 18, 1942.

21. For a discussion of various hardships in the life of rural Nebraskans in the generations before World War II, see Deborah Fink, *Agrarian Women: Wives and Mothers in Rural Nebraska, 1880–1940* (Chapel Hill: University of North Carolina Press, 1992), esp. 30–36. A poignant focus on the hardships in Depression-era Cheyenne County is available in O. K. Armstrong, "No Spongers in Sidney," *Rotarian*, July 1940, 24–27.

22. "Salvage, Defense Chairmen in Need of Nebraskans' Help," *Sunday World-Herald*, July 12, 1942; "Nebraska Scrap Drive Success Is Lesson," 3.

23. "Plan 'All Out' Effort; Seek Women's Aid," *Morning World-Herald*, July 16, 1942; "Women Get Scrap Orders," *Morning World-Herald*, July 21, 1942. Note that, except in quoted material, I have modernized the use of *chairman* and *chairmen* when used to refer to women (using *chairwoman* and *chairwomen*, respectively). While almost all of the county chairmen were indeed men, at least one—Loup County's Mrs. Floy Fletcher—was not. The full list of county chairmen is in "Salvage, Defense Chairmen," while a partial list of county chairwomen is in "Women Enthusiastic over Scrap Drive," *Evening World-Herald*, July 20, 1942.

24. K. A. Gammill, "Box Butte Scrap Hopes Are High," *Morning World-Herald*, July 24, 1942; "Big Scrap Salvage Is Expected," *Sidney Telegraph*, July 17, 1942; Reed O'Hanlon Jr., "Scrap Hunters Will 'Dig Needles from Haystacks,'" *Evening World-Herald*, July 18, 1942; Carlyle Hodgkin, "RFD," *Morning World-Herald*, July 30, 1942; "This County in Scrap Iron Metal Drive," *Chadron Chronicle*, July 23, 1942; "State Scrap Piles Are Growing," *Morning World-Herald*, July 30, 1942.

25. The initial quotations are from Lettie Morrow, "Scotts Bluff Drafts Men, Women, Children," *Morning World-Herald*, July 24, 1942, while Scotts Bluff County's detailed plans are in "Procedure Outlined for Scrap Campaign," *Scottsbluff Daily Star-Herald*, July 21, 1942, and "Scrap Campaign Hits High Gear in Scotts Bluff," *Scottsbluff Daily Star-Herald*, July 26, 1942. Davenport, "Life's Report," 21. By the end of the drive, Holdrege's Non-Profit Junk Co. was still in debt to the bank, motivating citizens to sort the scrap pile into grades so that it was worth more to scrap dealers.

26. "Let's Go, Nebraska," capitalization as in original.

27. "Hooker County Declares War!" *Hooker County Tribune*, July 23, 1942, capitalization as in original; "Let's Go, Cheyenne County!" advertisement, *Sidney Telegraph*, July 23, 1942; "Huge County Drive for Scrap Metal Now On in Full Swing," *Frontier*, July 23, 1942; "Let's Go McCook," *McCook Daily Gazette*, July 20, 1942; "Get in the Scrap," *Grant County Tribune*, July 22, 1942; and "Get in the Scrap," *Thomas County Herald-Clipper*, July 22, 1942.

28. "*It's not* JUNK," advertisement, *North Platte Daily Telegraph*, July 29, 1942; emphases and capitalization as in original (the original ad's ellipses were in the form of patriotic stars). Some of the elements in this ad were adapted from WPB's national advertising campaign, which had begun earlier in the month.

29. "Salvage Campaign Again Underway," *Dakota County Star*, July 23, 1942; "Women Enthusiastic."

30. "87 Counties Competing in Scrap Contest," *Evening World-Herald*, July 21, 1942; "The Billboard Music Popularity Chart," *Billboard*, July 4, 1942, 22; "Mr. and Mrs. Nebraska Farmer," advertisement, *Evening World-Herald*, July 30, 1942.

31. The quotation from the governor's radio address is in "Trucks Start"; "Slap Jap with Scrap: Drive Opening Today: Every Nebraskan Has Sleeves Rolled Up for Gigantic Task," *McCook Daily Gazette*, July 20, 1942.

32. "Heavy Farm Collection Is Vital Factor," *Morning World-Herald*, July 22, 1942. The standings themselves were first reported in "Salvage Contest Standings," *Morning World-Herald*, July 22, 1942.

33. "County Lags as Salvage Drive Opens: 'Busy,' is Plea of Many," *Blair Pilot-Tribune*, July 23, 1942. The cartoon strip is in "P-T Cartoonist Ray Gillett Views the Scrap Drive," *Blair Pilot-Tribune*, July 30, 1942.

34. The estimate of average farm scrap holdings is cited in Carlyle Hodgkin, "RFD," *Morning World-Herald*, July 14, 1942. General discussions of the relevant revolutions in agricultural mechanization are available in Wayne D. Rasmussen, "The Impact of Technological Change on American Agriculture, 1862–1962," *Journal of Economic History* 22 (1962): 578–91, and in Hurt, *American Farm Tools*. Martin

R. Cooper, Glen T. Barton, and Albert P. Brodell note in their *Progress of Farm Mechanization* (Washington DC: U.S. Department of Agriculture, 1947), 36, that the number of tractors in the United States doubled between 1930 and 1940, and that the Midwest was among the areas quickest to mechanize its agriculture. The Lincoln newspaper's scrap estimate is in "Scrap Metal Drive Begins," *Evening State Journal*, July 18, 1942.

35. "Small Grain Harvest Good," *Morning World-Herald*, July 15, 1942. Doorly himself later acknowledged that "we put on this campaign at a rather inopportune time for Nebraska because it was harvest time," as quoted in "American Newspaper Publishers Scrap Collection Drive," 23. For a vivid description of the haying process, including memories of the various mechanical changes that have affected haying over the years, see Earl H. Monahan, *Sandhill Horizons: A Story of the Monahan Ranch and Other History of the Area* (Alliance NE: Rader's Place, 1987), 184–92.

36. "Veteran to Scrap Pile," *Morning World-Herald*, July 21, 1942; "Seek 'Mine' of Scrap," *Morning World-Herald*, July 22, 1942; "20 Carloads Shipped by Burlington," *Morning World-Herald*, July 21, 1942; "U.N. Campus Gleans Scrap," *Omaha World-Herald*, July 20, 1942; "Nice List of Prizes Is Offered for the Biggest Iron Piles," *Valentine Republican*, July 31, 1942; "Scrap Iron Metal Drive Going Good," *Chadron Chronicle*, July 30, 1942. The Neligh sidewalks are visible in a photograph accompanying the story "Dawes County Takes Lead in Scrap Drive; Omaha's Pickup Nears Million Mark," *Morning World-Herald*, July 23, 1942.

37. "Dawes County Takes Lead"; "Dundy Holding Third in State Salvage Drive," *Benkelman Post and News-Chronicle*, July 24, 1942; "Salvage Contest Standings," *Morning World-Herald*, July 25, 1942; "Salvage Contest Standings," *Morning World-Herald*, July 29, 1942; "Hooker Gets 26.45 to Top Scrap Drive," *Norfolk Daily News*, July 25, 1942; "Grant County," *Evening World-Herald*, August 1, 1942.

38. "Old Guns, Swords"; "Ak-Sar-Ben Enlists 4-H Clubs in Drive; Counties Rallying," *Morning World-Herald*, July 17, 1942; "State Children Are Organized for Roundup of More Salvage," *Evening World-Herald*, July 30, 1942. On the cartoon inspirations, see Bruce Smith, *The History of Little Orphan Annie* (New York: Ballantine Books, 1982), 48–51, and "Junior Commandos," *Nebraska History* 72 (1991): 185. The Holdrege group is described in "Scrap Snoopers Will Join in Salvage Drive," *Holdrege Daily Citizen*, July 23, 1942.

39. The *World-Herald* related a story in which an old Nebraska City steam tractor, on its way to an Otoe County heap, blew its flue, keeping it out of the pile for an extra day: "Final Toot Nearly Doom of Tractor Scrap Pile Bound," *Evening*

World-Herald, August 1, 1942. Scrapper Dick Kleiber, who was six years old at the time, talks about donating his tricycle to the Adams County drive in the Scrap Drive Collection, DCHS. The scofflaw scrap is described in "Nebraska Cities' Part," 46.

40. David Remnick, *Life Stories: Profiles from the* New Yorker (New York: Random House, 2001), 337; interview with Geo. Strassler, Scrap Drive Collection, DCHS.

41. Interview with John P. Shaw, Scrap Drive Collection, DCHS; "Ah! Even Corsets to Be Sacrificed for American War Effort," *McCook Daily Gazette*, July 30, 1942.

42. "Nebraska Scrap Drive Success Is Lesson," 4; interview with Ruby Schulz, Scrap Drive Collection, DCHS; "Scotts Bluff Is Far in Rear on Metals Drive," *Scottsbluff Daily Star-Herald*, July 25, 1942.

43. Ralph Mears, "Fresh Volunteers Massed on State's Salvage Front," *Morning World-Herald*, July 27, 1942; Ware, "It Seems Like Yesterday," 4.

44. "Hamlet or City, All Swing into Nebraska Scrap Drive," *Morning World-Herald*, July 25, 1942; "Salvage Contest Standings," *Morning World-Herald*, July 31, 1942.

5. The Second-Half Comeback

1. The buildup to (and the outcome of) the 1941 Rose Bowl appears in Mike Babcock's *Go Big Red: The Ultimate Fan's Guide to Nebraska Cornhusker Football* (New York: St. Martin's Press, 1998), 168–72. A contemporary report is available in "Rose, Sugar, Cotton . . . ," *Time*, January 13, 1941, 40.

2. "Scrap Drive Plea Issued by Griswold; Likens State to Grid Team, Urges Victory 'In the Second Half,'" *Evening World-Herald*, July 24, 1942.

3. "Scrap Iron," *National Waste Review*, August 1942, 24; "Join in Scrap Hunt, Roosevelt Urges," *New York Times*, July 29, 1942; "U.S. Shuts Down Higgins Ship Plant," *Evening World-Herald*, July 18, 1942.

4. The newspaper acknowledged the multilayered scrap process in "A Challenge," *Evening World-Herald*, August 6, 1942.

5. Carlyle Hodgkin, "Nebraska Is Beautiful as Crops Thrive," *Evening World-Herald*, August 3, 1942.

6. "Down the Stretch," *Evening World-Herald*, August 3, 1942; Ray L. McKinney, letter to the editor, *McCook Daily Gazette*, July 30, 1942.

7. "Hooker Gets Second Spot in Campaign," *Evening World-Herald*, August 1, 1942.

8. Eugene Hollahan, *Crisis-Consciousness and the Novel* (London: Associated University Presses, 1992), 7; F. J. McConnell, "The Significance of Conversion in the Thinking of Today," *Constructive Quarterly* 1 (1913): 137.

9. "Red Willow County Clings to First Place," *Morning World-Herald*, July 28, 1942; "Salvage Contest Standings," *Sunday World-Herald*, August 2, 1942; "State

Scrap Drive below Expectation," *Norfolk Daily News*, July 28, 1942; "Business Men in Mullen Going Hard for Scrap," *Hooker County Tribune*, July 30, 1942; "Hey, Let's Get Move On—17,324 Tons Not Enough," *Sunday World-Herald*, August 2, 1942.

10. "Metal Chiefs Urge State On for Last Lap," *Sunday World-Herald*, August 2, 1942.

11. "Scrap Contest Enters Final Week—Hurry!" *Morning World-Herald*, August 3, 1942; "'Last Half of Ninth' for Scrap," *Evening World-Herald*, August 8, 1942; "State Drive Is Third of Way to Goal," *Morning World-Herald*, August 4, 1942; "Halfway to Goal, State Has 3 More Scrap Days," *Evening State Journal*, August 6, 1942; "Scrap Metal Collectors Mighty Busy Past Ten Days—842,000 Pounds," *Chadron Chronicle*, August 6, 1942; "Today and Tomorrow," *Evening World-Herald*, August 7, 1942.

12. "Hey, Let's Get Move On"; Syl Furtak, "Valley County Plans Home Stretch Spring," *Morning World-Herald*, August 1, 1942; Bill Billotte, "Indian Tactics Spur Knox' Scrap Drive," *Evening World-Herald*, August 7, 1942; J. B. O'Sullivan, "Holt County Set for K. O. Punch," *Morning World-Herald*, August 1, 1942; "Merrick County," *Morning World-Herald*, August 4, 1942; "Time Is Slipping By"; "Caster Says Hurry Scrap," *Evening World-Herald*, August 4, 1942; "County Is Twelfth as Tempo Quickens in Scrap Campaign," *Scottsbluff Daily Star-Herald*, August 4, 1942.

13. "Scrap Equal to 140 Tanks," *Sunday World-Herald*, August 2, 1942; "'Get Out Every Bit of Scrap,'" *Evening World-Herald*, August 6, 1942; "Hail Success of Twilight Scrap Pickup," *Evening World-Herald*, August 7, 1942. The load, volunteer, and truck details are in "'Last Half of Ninth.'"

14. "Theater Men Join in State Scrap Drive," *Sunday World-Herald*, July 19, 1942; "Special Scrap Iron Show Saturday at the Lyric Theatre," *Custer County Chief*, August 6, 1942; "Theaters to Add Own Scrap to Pile," *Evening World-Herald*, August 4, 1942; "Children Bring 75 Tons of Scrap to Omaha Theaters," *Evening World-Herald*, August 7, 1942.

15. The proclamation appeared in numerous Nebraska newspapers, often on the front page. The *Evening State Journal*'s comment is in "Halfway to Goal," next to which it published the governor's proclamation in full.

16. "Douglas Towns Vie in Final Scrap Cleanup," *Evening World-Herald*, August 8, 1942; "Scrap Standpipe," *Morning World-Herald*, August 6, 1942; "County Mobilizing for Scrap Harvest on Friday," *Benkelman Post and News-Chronicle*, August 7, 1942; "Scrap Festival Commandos Raid Dundy," *Evening World-Herald*, August 7, 1942; "'Skrap' King in Festival at Plattsmouth," *Sunday World-Herald*, August 9, 1942. The farm scrap gathered on the governor's holiday is discussed

in *Nebraska "Scrap" Plan*, 4. The Omaha call center anecdote was discussed in some detail in a 1943 radio address by James M. Landis, head of the national Office of Civilian Defense: "Speech on WEAF (New York)," ts., June 6, 1943, p. 4, in Records of the Office of Civilian Defense, Office of Civilian Defense Natl. Hdqtrs., Wash., D.C., Public Counsel Division, May 1941–June 1944, Speeches, RG 171, box 63, NARA.

17. "Nebraska Scrap Drive Success Is Lesson," 4. The standings were published each day during this period in both the morning and evening editions of the *World-Herald*, as well as in the Sunday edition.

18. "Hooker Gets Second Spot in Campaign."

19. Frederick Ware, "Bosco Should Be Drafted!" *Evening World-Herald*, August 6, 1942.

20. "It Was Last of Ninth but Bosco Scored — as Salvage," *Sunday World-Herald*, August 9, 1942. Years later, Omaha resident Bill Kizer admitted that he and a number of his Omaha Central High School friends had been the anonymous scrappers who removed Bosco from his pedestal. Interview with Bill Kizer, Scrap Drive Collection, DCHS.

21. The Mrs. Stewart image is discussed in chapter 3 (see fig. 6). I have drawn the phrase "militarized unity" from my earlier article, "The Militarization of the Prairie," 89.

22. "Scrap Is Needed for Victory," advertisement, *Evening World-Herald*, July 23, 1942; "Dawes County Takes Lead."

23. "Down the Stretch."

24. "Red Willow Clubs Find Unique Way of 'Giving Scrap,'" *Sunday World-Herald*, August 2, 1942; Billotte, "Indian Tactics."

25. "State Collects 54,000 Tons of Scrap in Drive," *Evening State Journal*, August 10, 1942; "Nebraska Scrap Drive Success Is Lesson," 4; "The People's Response." In another sign of statewide cooperation, scrap-themed softball tours took place toward the end of the drive, such as the doubleheader at which two Grand Island teams hosted a pair of Omaha area teams. The price of admission for the day, of course, was five pounds of metal or one pound of rubber. See the full-page ad for the event in the *Grand Island Daily Independent*, August 1, 1942.

26. "Not a Slacker in the Lot," advertisement, *Evening World-Herald*, August 5, 1942. Since the war years, *slacker* has broadened its meaning beyond a militarized context. A good illustration of the way the war generation would have understood the word is in "No. 1 World War Slacker, after 19 Years in Exile, Decides to Return Home," *Life*, April 24, 1939, 27.

27. "Don't Lag on the Home Stretch," *Holdrege Daily Citizen*, August 5, 1942; "Men, Women, and Children Make Their Contribution," *Omaha Star*, August

7, 1942; "County Mobilizing"; Douglas H. Stanton, "Scotts Bluff Stays 9th With 94 Pounds for Each Person," *Scottsbluff Daily Star-Herald*, August 7, 1942; "'Junk Hitler' Scrap Slogan, *Beatrice Daily Sun*, August 4, 1942; "The People Are Awake!" *Evening World-Herald*, August 6, 1942; "Scrap Drive Up to 38.04 Per Capita," *Evening World-Herald*, August 5, 1942.

28. Harding related the grieving woman's story in "American Newspaper Publishers," 29.

29. Ralph Mears, "Scrap Drive Passes 100 Pound Goal," *Evening World-Herald*, August 15, 1942; interview with Ruby Schulz, Scrap Drive Collection, DCHS; "You Have Done a Swell Job," *Sunday World-Herald*, August 9, 1942.

30. "Omaha Prepares Rousing Windup for Scrap Drive," *Morning World-Herald*, August 8, 1942; "Scrap Bonfire Drive Climax," *Sunday World-Herald*, August 9, 1942.

31. The pianos are mentioned in "Gala Fete for Scrap Windup," *Evening World-Herald*, August 7, 1942, while the pinball machines appear in "'Last Half of Ninth.'" A description of last-minute donations at the bonfire is in "Scrap Bonfire Drive Climax." One amusing aspect of the night was the rueful experience of James Farhat, who had donated one of the pianos; only later did he remember that he had previously hidden $20 in cash inside it. The money was never found and presumably burned in the fire. Farhat subsequently told reporters that it was "still the best twenty I ever spent." His anecdote appeared in "Piano Bonfire Was Fed by $20 in Hidden Bills," *Evening World-Herald*, August 10, 1942.

32. George Grimes to Franklin D. Roosevelt, August 2, 1942, in FDR Official File, box 2, folder "July-Dec 1942," FDR Library. Grimes's letter requested that the president send a word of congratulations to be read aloud at scrap celebrations on the last night of the drive. He was turned down, and he then fired off an angry telegram to the White House staff, exclaiming that "the president is missing a bet." The telegram (George Grimes to Stephen Early, August 7, 1942) is in the same folder as above. Doorly's effort is noted in "Newspapers Requested to Lead Scrap Drives," *Hartford Courant*, August 10, 1942. The newspaper's booklet is *Nebraska "Scrap" Plan*, and the quotation is on p. 1.

33. Mears, "Scrap Drive Passes 100"; "Top Scrap Award to Grant," *Evening World-Herald*, August 26, 1942. See the appendix for a table showing the per capita scrap totals of every Nebraska county in both the summer drive and the follow-up national drive.

34. "Top Scrap Award to Grant"; "Omaha Scrap Pile Sold for $25,000; Proceeds to Charity," *Evening World-Herald*, August 19, 1942. The ending quotations are from "Scrap Bonfire Drive Climax."

35. "Nebraska's Scrap: Now 134,110,053 Pounds," *Sunday World-Herald*, August 16, 1942.
36. "American Newspaper Publishers," 23; "The People Are Awake."
37. "American Newspaper Publishers," 23.

6. The Nebraska Plan Goes National

1. L. T. Kittinger to A. I. Henderson, August 19, 1942, in War Production Board Policy Documentation File, 175, RG 179, box 916, folder 2, NARA. One of WPB's studies that attempted to ascertain how much scrap was available was conducted by the ad agency Young and Rubicam even as Doorly's campaign reached a crescendo. The report concluded that each household in the country held an average of 229 pounds of salvageable scrap metal. Young and Rubicam, "A Study of Salvageable Goods Available in American Domiciles," ts., August 1942, in War Production Board Policy Documentation File, RG 179, box 917, NARA.
2. Kittinger to Henderson, 1. Kittinger apparently was reading a report of Nebraska's total that was preliminary, since the state's official average ended up at 103.64 pounds.
3. "'One of Most Inspiring Sights'"; Grimes to Early, telegram, August 7, 1942.
4. Discussion of the proposed invasion of North Africa (and the problem that steel shortages had on landing craft production) appears in Civilian Production Administration, Bureau of Demobilization, "Landing Craft and the War Production Board, April 1942 to May 1944," ts. (Historical Reports on War Administration: War Production Board, Special Study no. 11), in RG 179, War Production Board Historical Reports, Special Studies 4–11, box 1, folder 11, NARA; "Pants Minus Seats: Steel Crisis Faces Nation with Armament Slowdown," *Newsweek*, August 3, 1942, 49. The projection of a 1.5 million shortfall in steel plate production, as well as Clay's reaction, was noted in "Minutes of the 3rd Meeting." The warning to Nelson is in Stacy May and Robert R. Nathan to Donald M. Nelson, July 6, 1942, p. 1, in Combined Production and Resources Board, Records of the Combined Steel Committee, RG 179, box 2, folder "Steel Plate Requirements and Supply, WPB," NARA, while Nelson's radio quotation is from "Talk by Donald Nelson," Mutual Network radio broadcast, ts., August 27, 1942, p. 2, in Donald M. Nelson Papers, box 16, folder 6, Huntington. The conclusion from the WPB report is in Materials Branch, Statistics Division, WPB, "Preliminary Report: Availability of Data Relating to Scrap Materials," ts., July 3, 1942, p. 4, in War Production Board Policy Documentation File, RG 179, box 917, folder "Scrap Campaign: January–August 1942," NARA.
5. Examples of the government's summer ad campaign are preserved in the booklet *Samples of Salvage Campaign Advertising*, 1942, in War Production Board Policy

Documentation File, RG 179, box 916, folder 1, NARA. On the thousands of local scrap committees, see "Nelson's Scrap Rally." A description of the breadth of the WPB summer campaign is in "Mines above the Ground," *Nation's Business*, August 1942, 58.

6. Kittinger to Henderson, 1.

7. Richard W. Slocum to Lessing J. Rosenwald, August 25, 1942, in War Production Board Policy Documentation File, RG 179, box 917, folder "Scrap Campaign: September 1942," NARA; L. T. Kittinger to John R. Newton, September 4, 1942, in War Production Board Policy Documentation File, RG 179, box 917, folder "Scrap Campaign: September," NARA.

8. "American Newspaper Publishers," 1. The transcript suggests that 150 publishers were present, but various media stories on the meeting reported anywhere from 140 to 200. Nelson's schedule for the day before the meeting indicates that he met with Doorly and Harding in the afternoon to help prepare for the presentation to the publishers. See "Thursday, September 3, 1942," ts., in Donald M. Nelson Papers, box 17, folder 8, Huntington.

9. Slocum to Rosenwald, 1, 2.

10. Kittinger to Henderson, 2.

11. "American Newspaper Publishers," 2, 3, 5, 7.

12. "American Newspaper Publishers," 10, 13, 12.

13. "American Newspaper Publishers," 20, 19.

14. "American Newspaper Publishers," 20, 18, 13.

15. "American Newspaper Publishers," 1, 22, 24, 29.

16. "American Newspaper Publishers," 32, 34.

17. "Nelson Appeals to Press to Spur Scrap Collection," *Los Angeles Times*, September 5, 1942; Robert De Vore, "Shortage of Scrap Perils War Output," *Washington Post*, September 5, 1942; "Nebraska to the Rescue," 38; Grove Patterson, "The Way of the World," *Toledo Blade*, September 5, 1942. The *Express* editorial was reprinted as "Nebraska Plan Will Bring in the Scrap," *Sunday World-Herald*, September 13, 1942.

18. American Newspaper Publishers Association, "A Challenge to Newspapers," September 11, 1942, in War Production Board Policy Documentation File, RG 179, box 917, folder "Scrap Campaign: September 1942," NARA; *Newspapers' United Metal Scrap Drive: Manual of Suggestions*, September 14, 1942, in War Production Board Policy Documentation File, RG 179, box 917, folder "Scrap Campaign: September 1942," NARA.

19. "A Challenge to Nebraska! Kansans Ask Scrap Duel, 3 Weeks Starting Sept. 28," *Morning World-Herald*, September 18, 1942; "'Corn-Hawk' Scrap Contest Ready to Go," undated clipping in folder "Scrap Drive, U.S., Sept. 1–28," DCHS.

20. "Children's Army to Go Out after Scrap," *Portsmouth (OH) Times*, September 12, 1942; "When Scrap's Taken, 40,000 Flags to Fly," *Christian Science Monitor*, September 25, 1942; "County Scrap Losers Must Sweep Street," *Scrapper*, no. 3 [undated]; "Region Will Go 'All-Out' Friday in Scrap Drive," *Lewiston (ID) Morning Tribune*, September 22, 1942; "Scrap Proclamation Issued by Governor," *Milwaukee Sentinel*, September 24, 1942. The Minnesota wager was reported in Eager, "Scrap: Scoop for the American Press."

21. Margaret Fishback, "Scraps for the Scrap," *Collier's*, September 19, 1942, 38; War Savings Staff, U.S. Treasury Department, *Junk* (Washington DC, 1942), back cover, in General Records of the Department of the Treasury, Records of the Savings Bond Division (Including Records of Its Predecessor, the War Finance Division), Education Section, Historical and Promotional Records, 1941–1960, RG 56, box 3, folder "Junk," NARA.

22. American Industries Salvage Committee, *Scrap: And How to Collect It . . .* The ellipses and the emphasis are original. Grimes's article appeared widely in the press, as in "Hard Work, and Lots of It, Needed in Scrap Salvage Drive," *Meriden (CT) Record*, September 22, 1942. The number of cooperating newspapers as of September 10 was noted in Eager, "Scrap: Scoop for the American Press."

23. "Steel Scrap Drive: Collectors by the Million Will Succeed This Time; A Race with Winter," *Wall Street Journal*, September 18, 1942. The wave of youth participating in the drive was discussed in further detail in "Our Junior Army," *Parents' Magazine*, October 1942, 40, and in "30,000,000 Soldiers for Our New Third Front," *Saturday Evening Post*, September 26, 1942.

24. "Trucks Ready to Roll, Pick Up Scrap Today," *Washington Post*, September 27, 1942; "Women to 'Guard' Salvage Trucks," *New York Times*, September 28, 1942; "On the Scrap Front," *St. Petersburg Times*, September 29, 1942. The Texas effort was reported in "Children Find Thousands of Tons of Scrap," *Christian Science Monitor*, October 5, 1942, and Morgenthau's quotation is in "We Search the Attic."

25. Bing Crosby, "Junk Ain't Junk No More ('Cause Junk Will Win the War)," lyrics and tune by Austen Croom-Johnson and Allan Kent (New York: Bregman, Vocco and Conn, 1942), 3. Hayworth's photograph is in Photographs of Notable Personalities, compiled 1942–1945, Records of the Office of War Information, 1926–1951, RG 208, 208-PU-91B-5, NARA, as well as in *Scrapper*, no. 8 [undated]. FDR's close encounters with scrap at the White House are described in the summary "Letters to the President," October 21, 1942, in OF 4606, box 1, folder "Scrap Materials 1937–Oct 1942," FDR Library, and his reaction in "President 'Grateful' for Gifts of Scrap," *New York Times*, October 25, 1942.

26. The quoted phrase is from "Kansas Leads among States; Rhode Island in Fifth Place," *Christian Science Monitor*, October 21, 1942, while WPB's fuel rationing decision was reported in "Up to People, W.P.B. Says," *Los Angeles Times*, September 22, 1942. Discussion on the military's decision to lend trucks is in James Forrestal to Donald Nelson, October 2, 1942, in War Production Board Policy Documentation File, RG 179, box 917, folder "Scrap Campaign: October–December 1942," NARA.

27. The bridge and locomotive reports, as well as the ending quotation, are in an AP story that was published as "Americans Eagerly Enlist"; "2d Ave. 'El' Now Just 27,100 Tons of Scrap: Razing of 54th St. Pillar Ends an Eyesore," *New York Times*, October 1, 1942; "Bruennhilde's Spear Now Menaces Hitler," *New York Times*, October 12, 1942; "Nation Swings into Last Lap of Scrap Drive," *Christian Science Monitor*, October 13, 1942; "Crimeless Town Scraps Hoosegow," *Scrapper*, no. 4 [undated].

28. "Nation in Final Week of Newspapers' 21-Day Metal Scrap Campaign," *Wall Street Journal*, October 12, 1942. The town figures and the national average were reported in "Tarleton St. 'Rangers' Pile the Scrap High," *Christian Science Monitor*, October 9, 1942, while the personal appeal figures are from Hadley Cantril, ed., *Public Opinion: 1935–1946* (Princeton NJ: Princeton University Press, 1951), 445. Eager, "Scrap: Scoop for the American Press"; George Gallup, "Effective Aid of Newspapers in Scrap Drive Shown in Poll," *New York Times*, October 10, 1942.

29. American Newspaper Publishers Association, *The Nation's No. 1 Success*, 16 (ellipsis as in original); the Missouri incident was summarized in "Prankster vs. Governor," *Time*, December 21, 1942, 23, while New Jersey's raid is described in "Brooklyn Heaps Scrap Metal High for Drive Today," *New York Times*, October 8, 1942.

30. "Newark Wins Praise for Scrap Salvage," *New York Times*, October 1, 1942; "Bay State Collection Aided by Church and Colleges," *Christian Science Monitor*, October 10, 1942; Eager, "Scrap: Scoop for the American Press"; "Billikens Rally to Save Scrap Metal," *Chicago Defender*, October 10, 1942. Robert Schlater, student editor of the *Daily Nebraskan*, related the university's contributions in an undated letter to FDR, in OF 4606, box 1, folder "Scrap Materials 1937–Oct 1942," FDR Library, while the homecoming information is from R. McLaran Sawyer, *Centennial History of the University of Nebraska*, vol. 2 (Lincoln NE: Centennial Press, 1973), 143. "Movies Schedule Scrap Matinees: Thousands Are Booked for October," *Scrapper*, no. 7 [undated].

31. The opening and closing quotations, as well as the reports from Louisville and of businesses closing are in "Nation Swings"; "Scrap Roundup," *Business Week*,

October 24, 1942, 19; "Pennsylvania Leads States in Scrap Drive," *New York Times*, October 17, 1942; "Connecticut 'Genius' Statue for Scrap," *Christian Science Monitor*, October 8, 1942. Details on Butte's drive are available in "Scrap Raid Information," advertisement, *Montana Standard*, October 8, 1942; "Butte Nation's Scrap Capital Today," *Montana Standard*, October 11, 1942; "Butte Scrap Drive Goes Over Top," *Montana Standard*, October 12, 1942.

32. "Vermont Town of 5 Gives 40,430 Pounds of Scrap," *New York Times*, October 20, 1942; American Newspaper Publishers Association, *The Nation's No. 1 Success*, 16; "They Can Scrap and They Can Sweep," *Scrapper*, no. 11 [undated].

33. "U.S. Scrap Metal Drive May Net 6 Million Tons, Early Returns Indicate," *Wall Street Journal*, October 20, 1942; "Newspaper Scrap Drive, Still on Informally, Nets 6,000,000 Tons, 81.9 Pounds a Person," *New York Times*, November 25, 1942.

34. "U.S. Scrap Metal Drive May Net"; American Newspaper Publishers Association, *The Nation's No. 1 Success*, 18. Later reports suggested that the overall total may have been over 6 million tons, but it was hard to assess precisely because several states ran campaigns with slightly different time frames.

35. "Nelson Praises U.S. Newspapers for Role in Salvage Campaign," *Washington Post*, October 17, 1942; Paul Cabot to H. W. Dodge, November 12, 1942, in War Production Board Policy Documentation File, RG 179, box 917, folder "Scrap Campaign: October–December 1942," NARA. The children's estimate is from Robert Wm. Kirk, "Getting in the Scrap: The Mobilization of American Children in World War II," *Journal of Popular Culture* 29 (1995): 229.

36. "Newspapers' Scrap Drive Saves Mills," *Gettysburg* (PA) *Times*, October 21, 1942; "Bethlehem Steel Feels Scrap Transfusion," *American City*, November 1942, 7; "Iron and Steel Scrap," ts., January 7, 1943, in War Production Board Policy Documentation File, RG 179, box 916, folder 1, NARA. The 100.2 percent figure is from "The Outlook: 'We'll Win' —and Here's How," *Business Week*, October 17, 1942, 13. Nelson was quick to credit the scrap drive for the positive impact on the steel mills, writing in late October that "the fine results achieved nationally have helped to raise American steel production to 100% of capacity." See Nelson to W. F. Prisk, October 31, 1942, in Donald M. Nelson Papers, box 15, Huntington.

37. Franklin D. Roosevelt, "The President Reports on the Home Front. Fireside Chat. October 12, 1942," in Samuel I. Rosenman, ed., *The Public Papers and Addresses of Franklin D. Roosevelt*, 1942 vol. (New York: Harper and Brothers, 1950), 420. WPB claimed that it took only two weeks for a metal donation to make its way to a shipbuilding site, but that was most likely a best-case scenario. See "Two Weeks from Junk to Ships for Victory!" *Scrapper*, no. 4 [undated].

The Lewis quotation is in "Bethlehem Steel," 7, and Rosenwald is quoted in "To Salvage Workers of America!" *Scrapper*, no. 15 [undated].

38. "Getting in the Scrap," *Rotarian*, November 1942, 11; "What You Can Do for Your Country: Get in the Scrap!" *Scholastic*, September 28, 1942, 13. In a sign that WPB was aware that more scrap would ultimately be needed, it followed up the newspaper campaign with an effort to work with the nation's industrial plants and farming communities in gathering still more scrap metal.

39. "'We Could Lose This War' — A Communique from the OWI," *Newsweek*, August 17, 1942, 30; "The People Are Awake!"; American Newspaper Publishers Association, *The Nation's No. 1 Success*, 5; Eager, "Scrap: Scoop for the American Press."

40. "Nebraska Out in Front," *Evening World-Herald*, September 5, 1942; "Nebraska Scrap Average is 226.74 Pounds; Thought U.S. Top; Far Past WPB Goal," *Sunday World-Herald*, November 1, 1942.

Epilogue: Home Front, Battlefront (Revisited)

1. "This Nation at War!" Blue Network radio transcript #45, ts., May 18, 1943, p. 7, in Records of the National Association of Manufacturers, series I, box 160, Hagley.

2. Ralph Robey, "The Good and the Bad in the Steel Situation," *Newsweek*, August 17, 1942, 56. Public dissent about the persistent scrap piles is discussed in "Scrap Roundup," 19, 22. WPB was aware of the negative perception and was relieved when it became obvious that the piles were shrinking a few months after the national drive, as mentioned in L. S. Thompson Jr. to A. C. C. Hill Jr., March 22, 1943, in War Production Board Policy Documentation File, RG 179, box 916, folder 1, NARA.

3. Strasser, *Waste and Want*, 262; Carl A. Zimring, *Cash for Your Trash: Scrap Recycling in America* (New Brunswick NJ: Rutgers University Press, 2005), 94; Rockoff, "Keep on Scrapping," 39–40.

4. William J. Barrett to William Finger, December 20, 1940, in War Production Board Policy Documentation File, RG 179, box 917, folder "Scrap Campaign, 1940–1941," NARA.

5. W. L. Batt to A. I. Henderson, April 4, 1941, and E. R. Stettinius Jr. to Franklin D. Roosevelt, June 26, 1940, both in War Production Board Policy Documentation File, RG 179, box 917, folder "Scrap Campaign, 1940–1941," NARA. In his memo, Stettinius recognized the potential rallying power of a national scrap effort, but his emphasis was on industrial need, and so he rejected that line of thinking.

6. Rockoff, "Keep on Scrapping," 23; DeVore, "Shortage of Scrap Perils"; *Behind the Winning Punch!* film, directed by American Industries Salvage Committee (Washington DC: War Production Board, undated). Although Rockoff's insightful

analysis generally questions the military value of the scrap metal collected in patriotic drives during World War II, it does suggest that timing might have been a critical factor in its value (23–24); the account that follows agrees with his perspective in arguing that the fall 1942 drive was valuable primarily because of its overall timing in the war operation.

7. "Iron and Steel Scrap," ts., January 7, 1943, in War Production Board Policy Documentation File, RG 179, box 916, folder 1, NARA; War Production Board Minutes, Meeting LVII, ts., May 11, 1943, p. 226, in Records of the War Production Board, General Records, Minutes of Meetings, Nos. 1–100, January 1942–October 1945, RG 179, box 1, volume 1, NARA; American Iron and Steel Institute, *Steel's War Record*, 11, 12.

8. On the all-out blast furnace effort, Krug, *Production*, 47; the expansion plans are discussed in Hauck, *Report of Steel Division*, 20. Zimring, *Cash for Your Trash*, 97, discusses both scrap importation and efforts to return battlefield scrap (which became much more successful after the Allies began to advance on the war fronts). WPB also created two subsidiary groups, War Materials, Inc., and the Steel Recovery Corp. Both were aimed at special scrapping projects for which red tape presented a logistical obstacle, such as "abandoned railroads, unused streetcar tracks, bridges, mines, buildings, oil wells, sunken vessels, lumbering equipment, etc." Both projects began around the same time as the national drive and appear to have brought in substantial scrap material over the course of the war. The quotation and additional discussion is in Donald M. Nelson's postwar memoir, *Arsenal of Democracy: The Story of American War Production* (New York: Harcourt, Brace, 1946), 352.

9. Richard Overy, *Why the Allies Won* (New York: W. W. Norton, 1995), 4, 325. These scenarios bring my analysis into the realm of counterfactual history, which is becoming a vibrant strand of historical inquiry. The genre maintains that its scope does not allow for "flights of fancy," a standard that I believe this discussion upholds. See Harold Deutsch, introduction to *If the Allies Had Fallen: Sixty Alternate Scenarios of World War II*, ed. Dennis Showalter and Harold Deutsch (London: Frontline Books, 2010), xiii.

10. Both of Atkinson's quotations are from *An Army at Dawn: The War in North Africa, 1942–1943* (New York: Henry Holt, 2003), 3. On the landing craft issue, see Civilian Production Administration, Bureau of Demobilization, *Landing Craft and the War Production Board*, 6–7, 11.

11. The quotation is from Overy, *Why the Allies Won*, 320. The landing craft issue did in fact continue to plague the Allies throughout much of 1943, as discussed by Norman Friedman, *U.S. Amphibious Ships and Craft: An Illustrated Design History* (Annapolis MD: Naval Institute Press, 2002), 220–21.

12. Nelson was quoted in "Production Progress," *Newsweek*, August 3, 1942, 48; "War Production Board Appeals for More Farm Scrap," *National Waste Review*, December 1942, 11. This appeal acknowledged the fall campaign's contributions, then argued that even more scrap, especially that from industrial and farm sources, would continue to be in high demand as the Allied war machine accelerated into 1943.

13. Donald M. Nelson, "The High Cost of Victory," *Reader's Digest*, December 1943, 31 (this article was not a republication, but an original contribution to the issue). The ending quotation is from Nelson, "What Do You Want Most?" *Washington Star*, magazine section, October 3, 1943.

14. S. J. Monchak, "*Omaha World-Herald* Campaign Wins Pulitzer Medal for 1942," *Editor and Publisher*, May 8, 1943, 5.

15. Barrett to Finger.

16. Richard Polenberg, "The Good War? A Reappraisal of How World War II Affected American Society," *Virginia Magazine of History and Biography* 100 (1992): 296; Studs Terkel, *"The Good War": An Oral History of World War Two* (New York: New Press, 1984).

17. Michael C. C. Adams, *The Best War Ever: America and World War II* (Baltimore: Johns Hopkins University Press, 1994), 148, 8; Steven Casey, *Cautious Crusade: Franklin D. Roosevelt, American Public Opinion, and the War against Nazi Germany* (New York: Oxford University Press, 2001), 52, 53. A good summary of scholarship on the home front is available in Allan M. Winkler, "World War II Homefront: A Historiography," *OAH Magazine of History*, Spring 2002.

18. I use the phrase "perfecting myth" here in the sense that it is a normal human impulse to attempt to put a positive spin on recent events, such as a social movement that has dissolved. The phrase (and more discussion) is in Charles J. Stewart, Craig Allen Smith, and Robert E. Denton Jr., *Persuasion and Social Movements*, 5th ed. (Long Grove IL: Waveland Press, 2007), 104.

19. Kimble, *Mobilizing the Home Front*, 47–48, 39.

20. Cynthia Lee Henthorn, *From Submarines to Suburbs: Selling a Better America, 1939–1959* (Athens: Ohio University Press, 2006), 58.

21. The idea that civilians could be home front soldiers eventually developed a less attractive side. By 1944, war weariness had set in across much of the home front, with predictable results for war bond sales, civilian defense activities, and measures of public morale. At this point the civilians-are-soldiers mentality was firmly entrenched, which allowed the government to exploit it as a means of prodding the public into continued action. It became commonplace, for instance, for the once-laudatory references to civilians as dutiful and irreplaceable soldiers in

the war effort to become taunts which accused citizens of being derelict in their militarized duty. For examples, see Kimble, *Mobilizing the Home Front*, 75–84.

22. Bureau of Campaigns, "Report on the Activities of the Bureau of Campaigns, and the Status of Current Information Campaigns Now Being Conducted," ts., November 10, 1942, in Records of the Office of Government Reports, U.S. Information Service, RG 44, box 1835, folder "Bureau of Campaigns," NARA.

23. On the estimates of remaining scrap on the home front, see R. K. White to All Salvage Managers, Salvage Chairmen, and Executive Secretaries, November 24, 1942, p. 1, in Records of the Office of the Secretary of Agriculture, Records of the War Food Administration, Records of the War Boards, 1941–1944, RG 16, box 2, folder "Scrapper," NARA. The ending quotation is from Jones, "Reporter Finds."

24. Malcolm Cowley to Harry Doorly [*sic*], May 10, 1943, in Records of the Office of Government Reports, U.S. Information Service, RG 44, box 1845, folder "Media, Dec. 15–42," NARA.

25. Radio Flyer, "Radio Flyer in the Forties," http://www.radioflyerlink.com/apps/history/heritage1940.asp (accessed February 3, 2013); Philip Orbanes, *Monopoly: The World's Most Famous Game, and How It Got That Way* (Cambridge MA: Da Capo Press, 2006), 93–94. The government was so confident that the steel industry would keep its momentum going throughout 1943 that officials authorized the elimination of copper pennies (copper was another desperately needed metal in the war effort) in favor of a zinc-coated steel version of the coin. Even as WPB announced that the nation's copper pennies were going to war, however, it reminded the home front not to forget to keep up the search for additional sources of steel scrap. The copper coin returned in 1944. See "Copper Penny Off to War; to Be Replaced by Steel Coin," *Wall Street Journal*, December 12, 1942.

Bibliography

Archival Collections

Douglas County Historical Society, Omaha NE
    Omaha World-Herald Galleys Collection
    Omaha World-Herald Clippings File
    Scrap Drive Collection
Franklin D. Roosevelt Presidential Library, Hyde Park NY
    FDR Official File
    Harry L. Hopkins Papers
Hagley Museum and Library, Wilmington DE
    American Iron and Steel Institute Vertical Files
    Imprints Division
    National Association of Manufacturers Records
The Huntington Library, San Marino CA
    Donald M. Nelson Papers
Library of Congress, Washington DC
    Farm Security Administration—Office of War Information Photograph Collection
National Archives and Records Administration, College Park MD
    Department of the Treasury Records
    Office of Civilian Defense Records
    Office of Government Reports Records
    Office of War Information Records
    War Food Administration Records
    War Production Board Records
Nebraska State Historical Society, Lincoln NE
    Henry Doorly Scrapbook

Microfilm Newspaper Collection

Rare Book, Manuscript, and Special Collections Library, Duke University, Durham NC

Advertising Council Records

Published Sources

"30,000,000 Soldiers for Our New Third Front." *Saturday Evening Post*, September 26, 1942.

Abbott, Carl. *How Cities Won the West: Four Centuries of Urban Change in Western North America*. Albuquerque: University of New Mexico Press, 2008.

Adams, Michael C. C. *The Best War Ever: America and World War II*. Baltimore: Johns Hopkins University Press, 1994.

Adams, Mildred. "Our Precious Junk." *New York Times Magazine*, May 24, 1942.

American Iron and Steel Institute. *Steel's War Record*. New York: American Iron and Steel Institute, 1944.

Armstrong, O. K. "No Spongers in Sidney." *Rotarian*, July 1940.

Armstrong, Robert M. "Nebraska and Nebraskans in World War II." *Nebraska History* 24 (1943): 174–80.

Atkinson, Rick. *An Army at Dawn: The War in North Africa, 1942–1943*. New York: Henry Holt, 2003.

Babcock, Mike. *Go Big Red: The Ultimate Fan's Guide to Nebraska Cornhusker Football*. New York: St. Martin's Press, 1998.

Baltensperger, Bradley H. *Nebraska: A Geography*. Boulder: Westview Press, 1985.

Barringer, Edwin C. *The Story of Scrap*. Washington DC: Institute of Scrap Iron & Steel, 1947.

Behind the Winning Punch! Film. Directed by American Industries Salvage Committee. Washington DC: War Production Board, undated.

Berry, Brian J. L. *Geography of Market Centers and Retail Distribution*. Englewood Cliffs NJ: Prentice-Hall, 1967.

"Bethlehem Steel Feels Scrap Transfusion." *American City*, November 1942.

"The Billboard Music Popularity Chart." *Billboard*, July 4, 1942.

Bird, William L., Jr., and Harry R. Rubenstein. *Design for Victory: World War II Posters on the American Home Front*. New York: Princeton Architectural Press, 1998.

"Birmingham Collects Scrap Metals in Whirlwind Campaign." *American City*, March 1942.

Bix, Herbert P. *Hirohito and the Making of Modern Japan*. New York: HarperCollins, 2000.

Block, Maxine. "Jeffers, William M." In *Current Biography: Who's News and Why*. New York: H. W. Wilson, 1942.

Burlingame, Robert. "Nebraska on the Make." *Vanity Fair*, November 1932.

Cantril, Hadley, ed. *Public Opinion: 1935-1946*. Princeton NJ: Princeton University Press, 1951.

Casey, Steven. *Cautious Crusade: Franklin D. Roosevelt, American Public Opinion, and the War against Nazi Germany*. New York: Oxford University Press, 2001.

Chudacoff, Howard P. "A New Look at Ethnic Neighborhoods: Residential Dispersion and the Concept of Visibility in a Medium-Sized City." *Journal of American History* 60 (1973): 76–93.

Civilian Production Administration. *Industrial Mobilization for War: History of the War Production Board and Predecessor Agencies, 1940-1945*. Vol. 1, *Program and Administration*. Washington DC: GPO, 1947.

"Coatesville's Part in Equipping an Army." *American City*, August 1942.

Cole, Wayne. *America First: The Battle against Intervention, 1940-1941*. New York: Octagon Books, 1971.

"Collection of Scrap Metals Enforced by Death Penalty." *Science News Letter*, July 13, 1940.

Condra, G. E., and G. A. Loveland. "The Iowa-Nebraska Tornadoes of Easter Sunday, 1913." *Bulletin of the American Geographical Society* 46 (1914): 100–107.

Cooper, Martin R., Glen T. Barton, and Albert P. Brodell, *Progress of Farm Mechanization*. Washington DC: U.S. Department of Agriculture, 1947.

Creel, George. *How We Advertised America: The First Telling of the Amazing Story of the Committee on Public Information That Carried the Gospel of Americanism to Every Corner of the Globe*. New York: Harper & Brothers, 1920.

Crosby, Bing. *Junk Ain't Junk No More ('Cause Junk Will Win the War)*. Lyrics and tune by Austen Croom-Johnson and Allan Kent. New York: Bregman, Vocco and Conn, 1942.

Davenport, Russell W. "Life's Report: The Nebraska Plan." *Life*, October 5, 1942.

——. "Republican Renascence." *Life*, September 6, 1943.

Davis, Thomas M. "Building the Burlington through Nebraska: A Summary View." *Nebraska History* 30 (1949): 317–47.

——. "Lines West! The Story of George W. Holdrege." *Nebraska History* 31 (1950): 107–25.

Deutsch, Harold. Introduction to *If the Allies Had Fallen: Sixty Alternate Scenarios of World War II*, ed. Dennis Showalter and Harold Deutsch, xiii–xv. London: Frontline Books, 2010.

Dustin, Dorothy Devereux. *Omaha & Douglas County: A Panoramic History*. Woodland Hills CA: Windsor Publications, 1980.

Eager, George T. "Scrap: Scoop for the American Press." *Saturday Evening Post*, December 12, 1942.

Eiler, Keith E. *Mobilizing America: Robert P. Patterson and the War Effort, 1940–1945*. Ithaca NY: Cornell University Press, 1997.

"An Emergency Statement to the People of the United States." Advertisement. *Life*, July 27, 1942.

Engelhardt, Carroll. *The Farm at Holstein Dip: An Iowa Boyhood*. Iowa City: University of Iowa Press, 2012.

Faddis, Charles I. "Scrap and Waste Materials." *Vital Speeches of the Day*, May 15, 1942, 472–74.

Farrar, Jon. "Counties by the Numbers." *Nebraskaland*, July 1994.

Federal Writers' Project. *Nebraska: A Guide to the Cornhusker State*. New York: Viking Press, 1939.

Fink, Deborah. *Agrarian Women: Wives and Mothers in Rural Nebraska, 1880–1940*. Chapel Hill: University of North Carolina Press, 1992.

Fishback, Margaret. "Scraps for the Scrap." *Collier's*, September 19, 1942.

Fitzpatrick, Lilian L. *Nebraska Place-Names*. New ed. Lincoln: University of Nebraska Press, 1960.

Fowler, R. F. "Substitution of Scrap for Pig-Iron in the Manufacture of Steel." *Quarterly Journal of Economics* 52 (1937): 129–54.

Friedman, Norman. *U.S. Amphibious Ships and Craft: An Illustrated Design History*. Annapolis MD: Naval Institute Press, 2002.

"Fury in Omaha." *Business Week*, August 26, 1944.

"Gallup Poll on Salvage Collections." *National Waste Review*, April 1942.

Gere, C. H. "The Capital Question in Nebraska and the Location of the Seat of Government at Lincoln." *Transactions and Reports of the Nebraska State Historical Society* 2 (1887): 63–80.

"Get in the Scrap!" *Business Week*, October 3, 1942.

"Getting in the Scrap." *Rotarian*, November 1942.

Gilbert, Martin. *The Churchill War Papers*, vol. 3, *The Ever-Widening War, 1941*. London: Heinemann, 2000.

"Good Humor Man." *Time*, March 10, 1941.

Greene, Bob. *Once upon a Town: The Miracle of the North Platte Canteen*. New York: William Morrow, 2002.

Gropman, Alan L. *Mobilizing U.S. Industry in World War II*. Washington DC: Institute for National Strategic Studies, 1996.

Gunther, John. *Inside U.S.A.* New York: Harper & Brothers, 1947.

Gutstadt, Jack. *Scrap Iron and Steel: An Outline of the Many Ramifications and Developments of a Major Industry, Together with Statistics, Formulas, and Other Similar Data*. Chicago, 1939.

Hartman, Douglas R. "Lawrence W. Youngman: War Correspondent for the *Omaha World-Herald.*" *Nebraska History* 76 (1995): 100–105.

"Harvesting Scrap." *Business Week*, February 21, 1942.

Hauck, William A. *A Report of Steel Division, War Production Board, on Steel Expansion for War.* Cleveland: Penton, 1945.

Heimburger, Donald J., and John Kelly. *Trains to Victory: America's Railroads in World War II.* Forest Park IL: Heimburger House, 2009.

Henthorn, Cynthia Lee. *From Submarines to Suburbs: Selling a Better America, 1939–1959.* Athens: Ohio University Press, 2006.

Hollahan, Eugene. *Crisis-Consciousness and the Novel.* London: Associated University Presses, 1992.

"How Britain Drives for Scrap Metal." *American City*, March 1943.

Hudson, John C. "The Plains Country Town." In *The Great Plains: Environment and Culture*, ed. Brian W. Blouet and Frederick C. Luebke, 99–118. Lincoln: University of Nebraska Press, 1979.

Hurt, R. Douglas. *American Farm Tools: From Hand-Power to Steam-Power.* Manhattan KS: Sunflower University Press, 1982.

———. *The Great Plains during World War II.* Lincoln: University of Nebraska Press, 2008.

"An Independent Steps Aside." *Time*, September 5, 1955.

Johnson, J. R. *Representative Nebraskans.* Lincoln NE: Johnsen, 1954.

Jonas, Carl. *Riley McCullough.* Boston: Little, Brown, 1954.

"Junior Commandos." *Nebraska History* 72 (1991): 185.

Kimble, James J. "The Home as Battlefront: Femininity, Gendered Spheres, and the 1943 Women in National Service Campaign." *Women's Studies in Communication* 34 (2011): 84–103.

———. "The Militarization of the Prairie: Scrap Drives, Metaphors, and the Omaha *World-Herald*'s 1942 'Nebraska Plan.'" *Great Plains Quarterly* 27 (2007): 83–99.

———. *Mobilizing the Home Front: War Bonds and Domestic Propaganda.* College Station: Texas A&M University Press, 2006.

Kipling, Rudyard. *From Sea to Sea: Letters of Travel.* Vol. 2. New York: Doubleday & McClure, 1899.

Kirk, Robert Wm. "Getting in the Scrap: The Mobilization of American Children in World War II." *Journal of Popular Culture* 29 (1995): 223–33.

Klein, Maury. *Union Pacific: The Rebirth, 1894–1969.* New York: Doubleday, 1990.

Lane, Frederic Chapin. *Ships for Victory: A History of Shipbuilding under the U.S. Maritime Commission in World War II.* Baltimore: Johns Hopkins University Press, 2001.

Larsen, Lawrence H., Barbara J. Cottrell, Harl A. Dalstrom, and Kay Calame Dalstrom. *Upstream Metropolis: An Urban Biography of Omaha and Council Bluffs*. Lincoln: University of Nebraska Press, 2007.

Leighton, George R. *Five Cities: The Story of Their Youth and Old Age*. New York: Arno Press, 1974.

—————. "Omaha, Nebraska: The Glory Is Departed — Part I." *Harper's Magazine*, July 1938.

Limprecht, Hollis J. *A Century of Service, 1885–1985: The World-Herald Story*. Omaha: Omaha World-Herald, 1985.

Loosbrock, Richard D. "Living with the Octopus: Life, Work, and Community in a Western Railroad Town." PhD diss., University of New Mexico, 2005.

Luebke, Frederick C. *Nebraska: An Illustrated History*. 2nd ed. Lincoln: University of Nebraska Press, 2005.

Macdonnell, A. G. *A Visit to America*. London: Macmillan, 1935.

MacGregor, Greg. *Overland: The California Emigrant Trail of 1841–1870*. Albuquerque: University of New Mexico Press, 1996.

Mackland, Ray. "Battling Bill Jeffers." *Life*, February 22, 1943.

McConnell, F. J. "The Significance of Conversion in the Thinking of Today." *Constructive Quarterly* 1 (1913): 126–42.

McConnell, Raymond A., Jr. *75 Years in the Prairie Capital*. Lincoln NE: Miller & Paine, 1955.

McKanna, Clare V., Jr. "Seeds of Destruction: Homicide, Race, and Justice in Omaha, 1880–1920." *Journal of American Ethnic History* 14 (1994): 65–90.

Menard, Orville D. "Tom Dennison, the *Omaha Bee*, and the 1919 Omaha Race Riot." *Nebraska History* 68 (1987): 152–65.

Mihelich, Dennis N. "World War II and the Transformation of the Omaha Urban League." *Nebraska History* 60 (1979): 401–23.

"Mines above the Ground." *Nation's Business*, August 1942.

Moley, Raymond. "The Return of the Prodigal." *Newsweek*, June 8, 1942.

Monahan, Earl H. *Sandhill Horizons: A Story of the Monahan Ranch and Other History of the Area*. Alliance NE: Rader's Place, 1987.

Monchak, S. J. "*Omaha World-Herald* Campaign Wins Pulitzer Medal for 1942." *Editor & Publisher*, May 8, 1943.

Morris, Ralph C. "The Notion of a Great American Desert East of the Rockies." *Mississippi Valley Historical Review* 13 (1926): 190–200.

Myers, Debs. "The Grain Belt's Golden Buckle." *Holiday*, October 1952.

"Nebraska Cities' Part in State-wide Scrap Drive." *American City*, October 1942.

"Nebraska Miracle Reverberates in Washington." *Newsweek*, September 21, 1942.

"Nebraska Scrap Drive Success Is Lesson in Press Leadership." *Editor & Publisher*, August 29, 1942.

"Nebraska to the Rescue." *Life*, September 21, 1942.

Nelson, Donald M. *Arsenal of Democracy: The Story of American War Production*. New York: Harcourt, Brace, 1946.

———. "The High Cost of Victory." *Reader's Digest*, December 1943.

"No. 1 World War Slacker, after 19 Years in Exile, Decides to Return Home." *Life*, April 24, 1939.

O'Keefe, Daniel J. *Persuasion Theory & Research*. 2nd ed. Thousand Oaks CA: Sage Publications, 2002.

O'Neill, William L. *A Democracy at War: America's Fight at Home and Abroad in World War II*. Cambridge MA: Harvard University Press, 1998.

Orbanes, Philip. *Monopoly: The World's Most Famous Game, and How It Got That Way*. Cambridge MA: Da Capo Press, 2006.

Ossian, Lisa L. *The Forgotten Generation: American Children and World War II*. Columbia: University of Missouri Press, 2011.

"Our Junior Army." *Parents' Magazine*, October 1942.

"The Outlook: 'We'll Win'—and Here's How." *Business Week*, October 17, 1942.

Overton, Richard C. *Burlington Route: A History of the Burlington Lines*. New York: Alfred A. Knopf, 1965.

Overy, Richard. *Why the Allies Won*. New York: W. W. Norton, 1995.

"Pants minus Seats: Steel Crisis Faces Nation with Armament Slowdown." *Newsweek*, August 3, 1942.

Polenberg, Richard. "The Good War? A Reappraisal of How World War II Affected American Society." *Virginia Magazine of History and Biography* 100 (1992): 295–322.

Polk's Lincoln City Directory. Omaha: R. L. Polk, 1942.

"Prankster vs. Governor." *Time*, December 21, 1942.

"Production Progress." *Newsweek*, August 3, 1942.

Rasmussen, Wayne D. "The Impact of Technological Change on American Agriculture, 1862–1962." *Journal of Economic History* 22 (1962): 578–91.

Remnick, David. *Life Stories: Profiles from the* New Yorker. New York: Random House, 2001.

Reynolds, Quentin. "We Will Make It." *Collier's*, July 11, 1942.

Rips, Michael. *Face of a Naked Lady: An Omaha Family Mystery*. New York: Houghton Mifflin Harcourt, 2005.

Robey, Ralph. "The Good and the Bad in the Steel Situation." *Newsweek*, August 17, 1942.

Rockoff, Hugh. "Keep on Scrapping: The Salvage Drives of World War II." Working paper, National Bureau of Economic Research, 2007.

Roeder, George H., Jr. *The Censored War: American Visual Experience during World War Two*. New Haven CT: Yale University Press, 1993.

Roosevelt, Franklin D. "Export of War Materials and Strategic Raw Products Prohibited Except by License. Proclamation No. 2413. July 2, 1940." In *The Public Papers and Addresses of Franklin D. Roosevelt*, 1940 vol., ed. Samuel I. Rosenman, 277–81. New York: Macmillan, 1941.

———. "'The Militarists of Berlin and Tokyo Started This War. But the Massed, Angered Forces of Common Humanity Will Finish It'—Address to the Congress on the State of the Union. January 6, 1942." In *The Public Papers and Addresses of Franklin D. Roosevelt*, 1942 vol., ed. Samuel I. Rosenman, 32–42. New York: Harper & Brothers, 1950.

———. "The President Reports on the Home Front. Fireside Chat. October 12, 1942." In *The Public Papers and Addresses of Franklin D. Roosevelt*, 1942 vol., ed. Samuel I. Rosenman, 416–26. New York: Harper & Brothers, 1950.

———. "Radio Address before the Eighth Pan American Scientific Congress. Washington DC, May 10, 1940." In *The Public Papers and Addresses of Franklin D. Roosevelt*, 1940 vol., ed. Samuel I. Rosenman, 184–87. New York: Macmillan, 1941.

———. "'The Will for Peace on the Part of Peace-Loving Nations Must Express Itself to the End That Nations That May Be Tempted to Violate Their Agreements and the Rights of Others Will Desist from Such a Course.' Address at Chicago. October 5, 1937." In *The Public Papers and Addresses of Franklin D. Roosevelt*, 1937 vol., ed. Samuel I. Rosenman, 406–11. New York: Macmillan, 1941.

"Rose, Sugar, Cotton . . ." *Time*, January 13, 1941.

"Salvage for Victory." *National Waste Review*, January 1942.

Sawyer, R. McLaran. *Centennial History of the University of Nebraska*. Vol. 2. Lincoln NE: Centennial Press, 1973.

Schroeder, Alice. *The Snowball: Warren Buffett and the Business of Life*. New York: Bantam Books, 2008.

Scourby, Alice. *The Greek Americans*. Boston: Twayne, 1984.

"Scrap-Happy." *Business Week*, February 28, 1942.

Scrap Happy Daffy, DVD. Directed by Frank Tashlin. On *Looney Tunes: Golden Collection, Vol. 5*., 1943; Warner Bros., 1996.

"Scrap Iron." *National Waste Review*, August 1942.

Scrap Iron & Steel Inc. *Scrap Is Fighting Metal: Vital for Victory*. Washington DC: Scrap Iron & Steel, 1943.

"Scrap Roundup." *Business Week*, October 24, 1942.

"Scrap Shortage: A Problem in Steel Operations." *Scientific American*, December 1941.

Scrappers: How the Heartland Won World War II. DVD. Directed by James J. Kimble and Thomas R. Rondinella. South Orange NJ: Catfish Studios, 2010.

Smith, Bruce. *The History of Little Orphan Annie.* New York: Ballantine Books, 1982.

Sparrow, James T. *Warfare State: World War II Americans and the Age of Big Government.* New York: Oxford University Press, 2011.

Steel and America. VHS. Directed by Les Clark. Washington DC: American Iron and Steel Institute, 1965.

"Steel Priorities—A Portent." *Business Week*, August 16, 1941.

Steele, Richard W. *The First Offensive 1942: Roosevelt, Marshall, and the Making of American Strategy.* Bloomington: Indiana University Press, 1973.

———. "Preparing the Public for War: Efforts to Establish a National Propaganda Agency, 1940–1941." *American Historical Review* 75 (1970): 1640–53.

Stewart, Charles J., Craig Allen Smith, and Robert E. Denton, Jr. *Persuasion and Social Movements.* 5th ed. Long Grove IL: Waveland Press, 2007.

Strasser, Susan. *Waste and Want: A Social History of Trash.* New York: Henry Holt, 1999.

Terkel, Studs. *"The Good War": An Oral History of World War Two.* New York: New Press, 1984.

"That Scrap Drive." *Newsweek*, October 26, 1942.

"To Arouse the People." *Time*, September 14, 1942.

Townsend, R. B. "Bullwhack Joe." *Out West*, July 1904, 249–61.

"Uncle Sam Sells Steel Scrap as the World Arms." *Business Week*, April 8, 1939.

"United States Faced by Steel Shortage." *American Observer*, September 28, 1942.

U.S. Congress. House of Representatives. Committee on the Merchant Marine and Fisheries. *Shortage of Steel in Shipbuilding: Hearings on H. R. 281.* 77th Cong., 2nd sess., June 25, 1942.

U.S. Steel Corporation. *Steel in the War.* New York: U.S. Steel Corporation, 1946.

Wallace, Donald H. "Relation of Wartime Price Administration to the Scrap Metal Industry." *National Waste Review*, March 1942.

War Facts: A Handbook for Speakers on War Production. Washington DC: Office for Emergency Management, 1942.

War Food Administration. *Food Fights for Freedom: Grow More in '44.* Washington DC: War Food Administration, 1944.

Warner, A. G. "Sketches from Territorial History." *Transactions and Reports of the Nebraska State Historical Society* 2 (1887): 18–63.

"War Production Board Appeals for More Farm Scrap." *National Waste Review*, December 1942.

"'We Could Lose This War'—A Communique from the OWI." *Newsweek*, August 17, 1942.

Weinberg, Sydney. "What to Tell America: The Writers' Quarrel in the Office of War Information." *Journal of American History* 55 (1968): 73–89.

"What You Can Do for Your Country: Get in the Scrap!" *Scholastic*, September 28, 1942.

Winkler, Allan M. "World War II Homefront: A Historiography." *OAH Magazine of History*, Spring 2002.

Writers' Program (Nebraska). *The Italians of Omaha*. Omaha: Independent Printing, 1941.

————. *The Negroes of Nebraska*. Lincoln NE: Woodruff Printing, 1940.

Yost, Nellie Snyder. *The Call of the Range: The Story of the Nebraska Stock Growers Association*. Denver: Sage Books, 1966.

Zimring, Carl A. *Cash for Your Trash: Scrap Recycling in America*. New Brunswick NJ: Rutgers University Press, 2005.

Index

Page numbers in italics indicate illustrations.

Bradshaw, V. A., 58
Brewer, Mrs. C. T., 70
bridges as scrap, 64, 136, 177n30
Bureau of Campaigns, 156
Burk, Robert, 64–65
Burlingame, Robert, 81, 181n4
Burlington Railroad, 83–84, 94, 95,
    119, 182nn14–15
Burt County, 86, 92, 94, 119, 159
business contributions. *See* Nebraska
    Plan, business contributions to
Business Week, 25
Butler, Dan, 60
Butte MT, 140, *141*

Cabot, Paul C., 6, 28–29, 142
Cagney, James, 4
Camp Fire Girls, 71, 74, 88
Carson, Johnny, 96
Casey, Steven, 155
Cass County IA, 132, 140
Cass County NE, 94, 109, 159
Caster, Mark T., 45, 60, 107, 114, *120*
Chadron Chronicle, 105
chairmen and chairwomen of sal-
    vage. *See* salvage chairmen and
    chairwomen
Chase County, 88, 160
Cherry County, 94, 160
Cheyenne County, 88, 90, 94, 160
Chicago, Burlington & Quincy Rail-
    road. *See* Burlington Railroad
children: and national scrap campaign,
    7, 132, 134–35, 136, 139, 140, 142;
    and Nebraska Plan, 48, 52, 74, 95–
    98, 107–8
Christian Science Monitor, 140
Churchill, Winston, 19
Clark, Chase A., 132

Clay, Lucius D., 124
Coatesville PA campaign, 41–42
Coghlan, Ralph, 138
collection of scrap metal. *See* scrap
    metal collection
Collier's, 30, 132–33
Columbus Telegram, 79
committees, local scrap, 27, 135
competition: national scrap campaign,
    131–32; in Nebraska Plan, 3–4, 46–
    47, 70, 72–75, 79–85, 99, 112–14
competition and *camaraderie*. *See*
    Nebraska Plan, competition and
    camaraderie theme of
Connecticut, 140
Coons, Maude, 56
Costello, Lou, 67
county competition of Nebraska Plan,
    79–85
county mobilization of Nebraska Plan,
    85–91
Cowley, Malcolm, 157
crisis strategy. *See* Nebraska
    Plan, crisis strategy of
critical timing of scrap campaigns. *See*
    timing
Crosby, Bing, 135
Cuming County campaign, 42–43, *43*,
    95, 160
curbside collections: national scrap
    campaign, 135–36, 138–40; in
    Nebraska Plan, 70–71, *72*, 107–8,
    108

Daffy Duck, 15
Daily Telegraph (North Platte), 90,
    184n28
Davis, Elmer, 126–27, 129, 144
Dawes County, 88, 94, 113, 160

slacker, term of, 115–16, 188n26

Slocum, Richard W., 123, 125–26, 127

Smith, Emory E., 12–15, 20, 25, 31

Somervell, Brehon B., 126–27, 128

sports community contributions to
  Nebraska Plan, 72–73, 188n25

Stalin, Joseph, 146

Stanley, Richard, 75

Stanton County, 96, 162

Star (Omaha). See *Omaha Star*

Star-Gazette (Elmira NY), 138

Stauffer, Oscar, 132

steel: bottleneck of 1940–41, 22–25,
  147; life cycles of, 18–20; manufacturing process and history of,
  15–20, *17*, 157, 166n7

Steel and America (film), 15–16, 19,
  166n7

steel industry, 2; appeals to Nebraskans, 104–5; expansion, 22, 24–25;
  national scrap campaign of, 135,
  142, 143, 150; and scrap deficit,
  29–31, 101, 128–29

Stettinius, Edward R., Jr., 149, 195n5

Stewart, Mrs. J. J., 65–66, *66*

St. Louis Post-Dispatch, 138

stockyards of Omaha, 51–52

Story, L. A., *75*

Stoughton, F. J., *120*

Strasser, Susan, 148

Strassler, Geo., 97

Supply, Priorities, and Allocations
  Board (SPAB), 24

Susquehanna River bridge, 136

Sweeney, Patty, 91

Terkel, Studs, 154

Texas, 135

Thayer County, 94, 119, 162

theater campaigns, 107–8, 139, *139*

"This Nation at War!," 146

Thomas County, 119, 162

Time magazine, 22–23, 38

timing: national scrap campaign, 150–
  53, 195–96n6, 196n8; Nebraska
  Plan, 93, 98, 102, 185n35

Todd, Anne Marie, 49

Tojo, Hideki, 114, *115*

Toledo (Ohio) Blade, 131

Townsend, R. B., 77–78

tractors and *tricycles* theme. *See*
  Nebraska Plan, tractors and tricycles theme of

Traubel, Helen, 136

Tripartite Pact (Axis nations), 21

Tukey, Allen A., 73

Union Pacific Railroad: scrap rally,
  57–62, *59*, *61*, 176nn17–18; support for Nebraska Plan, 83–84, 107,
  108, 182n15

unity of scrappers, 103, 112–17, 121,
  144, 154–57, 197n21

University of Nebraska, 81, 94,
  139. *See also* football, Nebraska
  Cornhuskers

U.S. Department of Agriculture
  (USDA), 40, 42

Utah, 136

Vanity Fair magazine, 79

variety of scrap materials collected,
  96–98, *97*, 136

Vermont, 140, 141

Vickery, Howard L., 24

Wallace, Donald H., 30

Wall Street Journal, 23, 134

war bonds, 8–9, 46, 88, 149, 155

CPSIA information can be obtained
at www.ICGtesting.com
Printed in the USA
LVHW090259240821
695923LV00011B/949